Handbook for Canadian Consultants

TURNING YOUR EXPERTISE INTO A SUCCESSFUL SMALL BUSINESS

Donald M. Wood, CMC

McGraw-Hill Ryerson

Toronto • Montréal • New York • Burr Ridge • Bangkok • Bogotá • Caracas
Lisbon • London • Madrid • Mexico City • Milan • New Delhi • Seoul
Singapore • Sydney • Taipei

McGraw-Hill
Ryerson Limited

A Subsidiary of The McGraw·Hill Companies

Copyright © 1999 Donald M. Wood

Care has been taken to trace ownership of copyright material contained in this text; however, the publisher will welcome any information that enables them to rectify any reference or credit for subsequent editions.

The material in this publication is provided for information purposes only. Laws, regulations and procedures are constantly changing, and the examples given are intended to be general guidelines only. This book is sold with the understanding that neither the authors nor the publisher is engaged in rendering professional advice. It is recommended that legal, accounting, tax, and other advice or assistance be obtained before acting on any information contained in this book. Personal services of a competent professional should be sought.

ISBN: 0-07-560101-X

1 2 3 4 5 6 7 8 9 0 TRI 99
Printed and bound in Canada.

Canadian Cataloguing in Publication Data

Wood, Donald M.
    Handbook for Canadian consultants: turning your expertise into a
    successful small business

Includes index.

ISBN 0-07-560101-X

1. Consultants. 2. New business enterprises. I. Title.

HD69.C6W667 1999   001'.068   C99-930665-0

Publisher: **Joan Homewood**
Editorial Co-ordinator: **Catherine Leek**
Production Co-ordinator: **Susanne Penny**
Editor: **Focus Strategic Communications (Ron and Adriana Edwards)**
Electronic Page Composition: **Kim Monteforte/Heidy Lawrance Associates**
Cover Design: **Zab Design**

Table of Contents

Preface

Throughout my career as a management consultant it has been common for friends, former clients and managers looking to change careers to ask me "How does one get into consulting?" I have advised them the best I could, always stressing to them the need to examine their commitment and preparedness for a consultant's life.

During the past five years, the frequency of being asked how to be a consultant has increased dramatically. Many colleagues report this as well. Not only have these queries come from managers interested in becoming management consultants, but from scientists, doctors, other medical practitioners, academics, and all nature of early retirees. I have also been asked on several occasions to conduct workshops on consulting, both at home and abroad, and I began to formalize my thoughts on the process and practice of consulting. Friends and colleagues urged me to commit my thoughts and experiences to paper, so I began to consider writing this book.

I was careful not to underestimate the work involved in writing a book such as this, to say nothing about the diversion of efforts from my consulting work, so I approached the commitment with some caution. I toured the large bookstores and libraries in Canada and the US to see what books I could find which I could recommend, rather than beginning my own. I asked colleagues who were teaching consulting-related courses or supervising student consulting services at University business schools what they were using as texts. In addition, as a member of council of the Institute of Certified Management Consultants of Ontario, I observed the growing demand on the Institute to expand its training capabilities, both for its own certification examination process and for the consulting community at large. Most of the books I found on consulting were either old, or incomplete. They often focussed on specific kinds of consulting or specific parts of the process, such as selling professional services, marketing or project management, but few answered the basic questions I continued to be asked, "How does one become a consultant?" and, "How does one become more effective in consulting?"

Times have changed dramatically since many of these books were published, and I felt a new book was needed. It is important that people who wish to explore consulting be able to find the information they need to make such a choice wisely, and with the full knowledge of what consulting is like and what it takes to succeed. This book tries to satisfy that need by describing the disciplines experienced consultants use, and some of the methods I have found useful in my practice.

I believe that in order to understand something fully, one needs to have a good grasp of the context within which it operates. I have tried to blend the practical with the conceptual, thereby offering a model of the consulting process which readers can build with or modify according to their own needs. Above all, I am attempting to share my knowledge and experiences, along with my opinions and values as a consultant in the hope that I will contribute to the growing community of consultants in a positive way.

Many people have played important roles in the development of this book. I can name only a few here, but many colleagues have shared their experiences with me, and numerous clients have encouraged my efforts. Many times in the course of my reflections as I sought basic principles and anecdotes with which to punctuate the text, my mind went to my own early mentor, the late Richard Loftus, who helped me cross over from being a bright college kid to a practical professional. His greatest praise was when he discovered that I had "unlearned" something. My good friend and colleague, Gabe Shelley helped by sharing experiences that earmark changing principles in client-consultant relationships. John Vanderheyden, with whom I have worked over the past three decades, advised me on the practices and intricacies of international work, and in particular working with the International Financial Institutions. Doreen Sanders, formerly editor of the University of Western Ontario Business Quarterly and now in her own communications business, gave me enthusiastic endorsement for this book and helped me address the challenge of publication.

On a more personal note, I have had an advantage few other writers can claim. My wife not only put up with my focused attention as I faced my computer for long periods, but she played a material role in the book itself. She read every page with the critical eye of an academic and refused to let me say anything she did not understand. Her qualification for this task is unmatched, because Betty Jane Punnett, Ph.D., is a leading professor of international business, and, what few people know, began her academic career with a degree in English literature. Her vital contribution in all aspects of this book is immeasurable, and without her support, it might not exist at all. Lastly, my on-going cheering section comprising my son, David and my daughter, Jill and their families kept me energized, and, as any parent knows, this kind of support serves to heighten the bar as well.

We all benefit from good consulting; we are all diminished by poor work. It is my hope that this book will contribute to the success of consultants, and by so doing the profession as a whole.

INTRODUCTION

The Technology Century

The twentieth century is often referred to as the technology century. The pace of change has increased unrelentingly and, in the past two decades, we have witnessed a revolution in the way business is conducted in much of the world. Computerization is enabling more people to do more things faster and with less effort. At the same time, the quantity of information accessible in databases and via the Internet is almost unlimited. In business, the result has been a reduction in the ranks of administrative personnel and middle management, an increased pace of change, and a truly global business environment.

Business is being forced to find new, more effective ways of doing things. Most large organizations have now restructured, "flattening" organizational structures so they can be more responsive to the rapidly changing and increasingly competitive environment. Small players are joining forces to compete against larger players and large players are merging to compete in global markets.

In Canada's public services, over-spending and a ballooning public debt has led to similar results. Every department has faced downsizing and/or privatization, throwing thousands of skilled professionals out of work and leaving government management ranks decimated.

In this highly competitive and streamlined environment, both private and public sectors need the flexibility and expertise that can be provided by consultants and contract workers, hired on an "as needed" basis. The assertion that "We have become a nation of contract workers" is not far from reality. Outsourcing is now an everyday part of doing business and recent years have seen a dramatic expansion in the consulting sector in response, both in terms of the number of consultants and the variety of the fields in which they work.

Consulting has become an attractive career choice for a wide range of people with a variety of training, talents and experience – from managers, trainers, scientists, professors, computer experts and other technical specialists, to doctors, lawyers and other professionals. Some work part-time, from their home offices while carrying another job, as is common with college and university professors. Some have set up shop at home or in a small office to provide specialized services based on expertise and experience gained when they were employed by an organization on a full-time basis. Others are recently graduated from college and employed by a firm of consultants, perhaps a small, specialized firm, or perhaps one of the giants that provide services around the world.

Today, supported by vastly improved and affordable computerization and telecommunciations, the independent consultant working out of his or her home office can provide a level of service and communication that in the past was available only from a large firm. Many of these new independent practitioners have never run their own businesses, however, and they are uncertain where to begin or how to develop their expertise into a consulting practice.

This book is a handbook for the new consultant, whether part time or full time, sole operator or employee of a small firm. It will guide the consultant through each aspect of starting and running a consulting practice, from writing proposals to setting fees to marketing and expanding the business.

The earlier chapters provide an overview of the consulting business – how it began and how it evolved to its current structure – which will help new consultants to understand fully the field they are entering and the discipline required to develop a consulting practice. Subsequent chapters explain how to get started, the secrets of marketing and selling professional services, of expanding the client list and the business, and much more.

Although consulting is not new, it is clearly expanding in both the range of services provided and the number and variety of Canadians moving into the profession. The work is demanding, challenging, and at times, frustrating, but it can also be satisfying and very rewarding for those talented individuals who are prepared to devote the effort and discipline required to succeed in this new career.

ONE

The Essence of Consulting

Consulting Defined

Organizations make changes only when managers make decisions and take action. And with the pace and competitiveness of the current global business environment, poor decisions can quickly lead a solid company onto shaky ground. It is not surprising then that businesses of all types are turning to outside professionals for input in their decision making. This is the primary role of the consultant – to help clients make actionable decisions that are consistent with their interests.

All consultants – the consulting orchardist advising a farmer on plant breeding and propagation, the consulting engineer recommending the design of a town site to a town planner, the consulting physician providing advice to a nursing home operator, and the corporate strategist making recommendations to an executive – have one thing in common: they are trying to help their client *decide* to take some particular action. The farmer, the town planner, the nursing home operator and the executive are all part of the management of their enterprises.

For this reason and because management consultants make up such a significant proportion of the consulting industry, the model of the management consultant is frequently used throughout this book. However, what is true for management consulting is also true for consulting in a wide variety of fields. All consultants, for example, face issues of establishing their practices, marketing their capabilities, setting fees, selling, proposing and performing their work. The basic principles of interacting with clients answer to the same challenges, and communication skills in all kinds of consulting are of paramount importance. A significant amount of consulting is purely research – sometimes hard sciences, sometimes social sciences – and this book addresses the need for consultants to understand the various techniques and principles of research as well.

■ *Advisor versus Expert*

One of the most difficult hurdles for new consultants to overcome is the tendency to confuse being an advisor with being an expert. Most consultants are accustomed to being right more than they are wrong. In addition, their training may have conditioned them to think in terms of problem-solving and or finding the "correct" answer. This can lead them to form judgements early in the information gathering and processing stage and to stop their work when they believe they have the "right" answer. Their role, however, is to advise, to help the client "be right" within the context of what the client wants to accomplish. The consultant's challenge is to prove or demonstrate his or her conclusions based on good information and analyses, rather than opinion, regardless of how well founded or "right" that opinion might be.

The role of consultant as expert is at times appropriate, for example, when the consultant brings special knowledge and/or experience to a situation, possibly to resolve differences in opinion or to help a client make choices among options. The expertise, nevertheless, is only valued when the client believes in the consultant's objectivity. The credibility of consultants, whether advisors or experts, rests on keeping their personal agendas separate from those they are advising.

Machiavelli's effectiveness as a consultant to fifteenth century Florentine kings was not due to some magic he possessed, nor even to his own first-hand experience with the power systems he seemed to understand so well; it was due primarily to his abilities as an observer and a chronicler of human behavior. His interpretations of events and actions were accepted as accurate, and all that needed debating were his logical arguments associated with them. His own beliefs and opinions, while often sought, remained basically unknown. Machiavelli also said, "A prince who is not himself wise cannot be wisely advised. Good advice depends on the shrewdness of the prince who seeks it. . ." This suggests that the client is at least as important as the consultant in making a relationship successful – a message the consultant should always keep in mind.

The effectiveness of the consultant depends, therefore, on the skills applied to gathering and interpreting relevant information and in communicating the results to the client who will make decisions based on the consultant's work. The particular strengths of a consultant, be it from specialized knowledge, training, or years of specific experience, can differentiate the consultant, but do not differentiate the *process* of consulting.

In summary, while the concept of advisor seems to simplify the description of what a consultant is, the notion of a professional advisor involves much more than merely providing advice. Professionals are dedicated to providing helpful advice, and in order to be helpful, it must be believed. In order to be believed, it must be based on credible information, knowledge and expertise. Further, the advice must be useful, and therefore must reflect the client's goals and priorities, rather than those of the consultant, because it is the client who must manage the results and take the risks of uncertainty. The consultant's role is to help the client make good decisions and take the appropriate actions resulting from those decisions.

Figure 1-1 depicts the decision-making process that consultants seek to support.

The top element of Figure 1-1 shows the combining of the experience and collaboration of interested parties with research appropriate to addressing an opportunity or challenge. This combination produces data which are combined with knowledge and insight in order to produce information. The information, in turn, reveals the hitherto unknown and provides an element of discovery leading finally to actions founded on a logical and

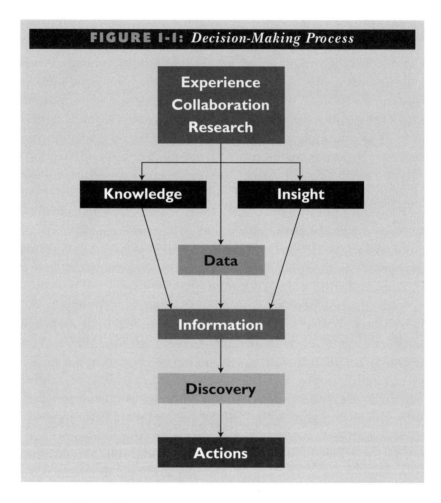

FIGURE 1-1: *Decision-Making Process*

informed base. The consultant can play a role in each of these elements, and perhaps more importantly, the consultant can support the entire process to help clients arrive at good decisions. This model can apply to all decision making, whether in a scientific laboratory, a retail store, a government bureau or a corporate boardroom.

Focus on Professionalism

Simply stated, consulting comprises the following four elements:

1. **THE CLIENT** what the client wants, needs and expects

2. **THE CONSULTANT** special qualifications and capabilities, and the skills to use them

3. **INFORMATION** from within and from outside the client

4. **THE CONSULTING RELATIONSHIP** based on mutual trust and respect, supported by common expectations and open and effective communication

The professional consultant surrounds these four elements with discipline and integrity. The discipline is evident in the way the work is carried out. The investigation is thorough, the analysis is rigorous and the communication between client and consultant is clear. Integrity involves trust and the total commitment by the consultant to the client's agenda. It is this integrity and accompanying commitment to ethical conduct, which eventually separates the consultant who can develop and sustain a practice from one who can not.

Evolution of Consulting

Before dealing with the practical aspects of developing and running a consulting practice, the history and ethical characteristics of the profession should be appreciated in order to put the consultant's role in context. Many of the principles reflected in the marketing, selling and performing aspects of consulting have their roots in this context.

▇ *In the Beginning*

Consulting is probably one of the world's oldest professions. The ancient Greeks went on long and arduous journeys to consult the oracle high in the mountain at Delphi, who, it was said, could foretell the future and provide warnings for those who could interpret her trance-induced riddles. And medieval wizards and priests, who supposedly possessed great powers, were early consultants to kings and princes.

Not only was Niccolo Machiavelli a trusted consultant to Florentine kings in the fifteenth century, as mentioned earlier, he was probably the best known consultant in the modern sense and was author of definitive works on the subject of power and its use. Even today, his dispassionate view of organizations, individuals, and the exercise of power are the touchstone of generals, industrialists and politicians. Machiavelli was imprisoned for much of his career, apparently because his influence was too great. Perhaps this attests to his effectiveness as a consultant.

■ *The Rise of Modern Consulting*

Although consulting as a profession can be traced back to antiquity, in the modern sense it has its roots in the industrial revolution, which gave rise to two major phenomena. The first was the development of factories and the resulting change in relationships between owners and managers and the workers they employed. The second was the separation of management from ownership created by the rise of joint stock enterprises (corporations). The former gave rise to the development of scientific management concepts and techniques, and an appreciation of the need for objective and accurate information to support effective decision making. The latter gave rise to the need for public auditors whose role was to ensure that shareholder interests were served by the managers. Two distinct professions evolved in response: industrial engineering and public accounting.

The first of these, the industrial engineering profession, is usually accredited to Frederick Winslow Taylor, the father of scientific management. Taylor's work at Bethlehem Steel in 1889 focused on workers shovelling pig iron. He calculated the optimum combination of load and shovel size and recommended changes which led to a fourfold increase in worker productivity. Their wages, however, increased only 60 percent. Taylor thus demonstrated that work was worthy of scientific measurement and evaluation. He also demonstrated the power of incentive pay, but this went largely ignored until labor markets tightened after the Second World War.

The second professional group, the public accountants, developed in response to the need for shareholders to have objective and reliable information about their investments. Independence and integrity were of the utmost importance because these accountants were privy to all aspects of the enterprise that they examined. Their authority came from the board of directors, a body elected by shareholders to represent their interests, and their investigative powers were substantial. Due to their training and objectivity, they soon became important advisors to management as well, and their investigative and analytical capabilities were helpful to managers wishing to improve their decision making.

By the time Taylor died in 1915, the concept of work measurement and scientific management had grown to become industrial engineering, personified by the hated time study (or "efficiency") expert with the stopwatch. Others such as Henry Gantt and Frank and Lilian Gilbreths expanded the study of labor productivity and the mechanistic view of management thrived.

The study of worker productivity gave rise to the Hawthorne experiments conducted in General Electric plants during the 1920s. It was found that things such as improved lighting markedly increased worker productivity. But when these results were tested through reducing the lights to their former levels instead of the expected reduction in productivity there was an increase. The conclusion was unmistakable: workers were responding not to the better working conditions, but to the changes themselves, which indicated to them that they were being noticed by management. This led to studies of motivation, worker morale, and the impact of the human factor, or management, on productivity. The profession of industrial psychology was born and with it, the consulting industrial psychologist.

The Second World War saw the large-scale use of consultants by government. Productivity was a priority, as was training and leadership development, particularly in the armed forces. Operations research and large-scale simulation studies were developed and, with the advent of the computer, sophisticated information systems were put in place. Financial integrity was essential as well. The accounting profession was called on to provide financial controls and analyses, as resources were allocated on a massive scale among competing demands for vital war effort enterprises. The consulting profession developed engineering, financial and human resource specialities; the profession was coming of age.

The post-war years saw rapid growth in the size and breadth of the consulting industry. As described by the International Labor Organization (ILO), the total number of full-time management consultants was assessed at 100,000 in the United States by the end of the 1980s, six times the number that existed in the mid-1960s. Many consulting engineering firms expanded during the post-war period as well and broadened their range of services into new areas such as environmental assessments, community surveys and management consulting.

The term consultant today includes a wide range of advisory activities, covering an expanding range of areas of special knowledge and expertise. In addition, there are now a large number of consultants working part-time: university professors, scientists, technicians, specialists in a multitude of disciplines. To this can be added the emerging role as interim or contract employees in a range of activities, and as managers and providers of outsourced service programs.

Today, professional consulting is a response to the changing needs in the market for advisory services. It continues to evolve as technologies change and societies adjust to them. One needs only to compare the early form of consultant/expert represented by the efficiency expert stereotype with the many and varied roles of today's consultants to appreciate the degree to which the profession has evolved during this century. The following is just a partial list of the many ways the modern consultant may be called on to provide services:

- obtain and provide information
- provide specialized expertise on a short-term basis

- provide independent advice
- explore opportunities in confidence
- provide expert opinion
- diagnose a situation from a special point of view
- develop and recommend action plans
- design systems and processes
- act as a catalyst to accomplish changes
- provide personal counseling
- develop and provide training
- assist in consensus building
- plan and facilitate meetings, particularly retreats

Industry Structure

How does the new consultant fit into this diverse and expanding industry? The evolution and structure of the management consulting industry, arguably the largest part of the consulting industry, provides a context within which the individual or independent consultant operates. The following sections of this chapter trace the structural development of management consulting.

Large Accountancy-Based Firms

The consulting industry structure reflects the varied roots from which it has sprung. Chartered accounting firms occupy a large, possibly dominant, position in the management consulting field. Most accounting organizations provide some consulting to their clients, and the majors, such as the "big five" (Deloitte & Touche, Arthur Anderson, Ernst & Young, KPMG, and Pricewaterhouse Coopers), have large, full-service consulting divisions, which operate internationally, employ thousands of professionals and serve organizations of all sizes and descriptions.

As the demand for a wider range of consulting services grew, the accounting firms needed to attract a wider range of specialists to provide them. They hired professionals with a broad range of business skills and experience in disciplines other than accounting, such as psychology and engineering. The newly graduated MBAs from a number of prominent universities in the US and Canada were particularly attractive due to the broad range of analytical skills they brought with them.

Expanding their consulting activities and attracting this broader range of skills to perform consulting services presented the accounting firms with other challenges. Consultants typically work for management, while an auditor's prime directive is to protect the interest of shareholders. Should the interests of managers diverge, or even appear to diverge from those of the shareholders, the auditor's objectivity may be compromised.

A new business structure was required. Some accounting firms formed separate consulting firms to enable the accountants to maintain their independence while providing an attractive organizational structure to attract top quality consultants from a range of backgrounds and disciplines. In Canada, for example, Touche, Ross, Bailey and Smart (a predecessor firm to Deloitte &Touche) created a firm called Payne-Ross Ltd. in 1958. Four years later, an interlocking partnership formula was developed which maintained the needed separation and avoided the potential conflict of interest presented by the accounting firm's ownership and close association with the limited company and Payne-Ross Ltd. became P.S. Ross & Partners. This partnership model became the standard for the industry until the 1980s.

The industry continues to evolve and mature. Competition has driven the larger firms to rationalize and restructure to retain global clients. The large accounting firms generally have absorbed their consulting firms as divisions and now provide the full range of professional services under a single name through many divisions and offices. A few giant firms now dominate the industry, with many, many small firms also providing consulting services.

■ *Large Operations-Based Firms*

Another group of large consulting firms emerged from roots established during the early part of the twentieth century. The

Hawthorne experiments of the 1920s had demonstrated that employees would respond to management's leadership. The work of the efficiency experts also demonstrated that work could be measured and, through measurement, analyzed and reduced. Management as a science was born, and schools of management sprang up at Harvard and other universities in Canada and in the US. Management practices arising from industrial engineering and related disciplines, including psychology and finance, provided material which could be taught and which provided a field of research.

Consultants like J. O. McKinsey and Edwin Booz formed successful firms in the 1920s, which have become the giants of today. They provide services similar in nature to those of the leading accounting firms, but their roots in industrial engineering and work measurement are still clearly visible in their approach to problem solving. The database of analyses for these firms is often established through measuring client operations and activities directly and recording field observations that influence results. Operating improvements and implementation are frequently the prime concern for these consultants. In contrast, the accounting based consultants frequently focus on financial and systems information, augmented with interviews and discussions with responsible managers and executives. Objectivity remains a key characteristic of both.

In practice, the industrial engineering and accounting styles have converged to yield similar results; they provide essentially the same range of services, and employ similar people. Nevertheless, the engineer is more common in one, and the accountant in the other.

■ *Independent Consultancies and Federations*

According to some estimates, 40 large consulting firms account for as much as half of the worldwide revenues, but the vast majority of consultants are employed in small, frequently one-person, firms. The recent trend toward corporate downsizing, coupled with the power of personal computer technology, has given rise to a large and growing number of independent consultancies. Often, a group of independent consultants will band together in small or medium-sized federations to try to take the best from both worlds – maintaining the individual freedom and independence of the independent consultant while pooling resources to enable them to more effectively pursue major consulting projects.

These federations operate under a single name, such as Western Management Consultants, or RMC Resources Management Consultants Limited, to choose two Canadian examples. They combine the promotional resources of their member professionals for greater impact, and they work in teams specifically structured for client situations to provide the cross-functional expertise needed. Some small federations require that all consulting work carried out by members be under the common federated name, while others permit members to carry out some work under individual firm names, when the work is not attracted by the federation. All have a formula for sharing common administrative and promotional costs and for distributing profits.

As these federations grow over time, they take on the characteristics of single firms, with members conceding increasing amounts of independence to realize more of the large-firm benefits. Success in a particular area of consulting tends to generate similar work, and professionals can gradually become more specialized. As administrative requirements increase, roles become more defined and policies and procedures become more elaborate. More resources are made available with growth, more consistency is desired in the federation's marketing program, and the promotional focus changes from individual qualifications to strengthening the firm image and reputation as a whole.

The character of the practice usually changes with growth as well. With a small firm or federation, each project is unique, shaped by the make-up of the team and the individual client. The consulting relationships will be personal, with every member of the team in direct contact with the client. Each consultant will be aware of, if not actually working on, all professional projects active at a given time. When a firm or a federation comprises fewer than seven or eight professionals, each will be called upon to perform at a professional level in several skill areas. In a small consultancy, for example, the same professional may be carrying out interviews in a marketing research project for one client while assisting in evaluating the information system for another.

As the firm or federation grows from 10 to 20 members, it is no longer practical for each member to have intimate knowledge of every active assignment and the work others are performing. Individuals find they are asked to participate on assignments by other professionals when the work is similar to the work performed for another client on another occasion. Similarly, they seek out assistance from other professionals based on their past experience in similar situations. Consultants become further specialized by this selection process. The consultant who may have served clients in both marketing research and systems development when the firm was smaller, now finds that all the work is in just one area.

As the firm or federation grows beyond 20, the need for more formalization increases. Performance appraisal for purposes of distributing profits as well as confirming long term relationships becomes more formal, and new information regarding individual contribution to the firm's performance is developed. Most larger organizations develop an information system to help members stay aware of the ever-changing client list and projects. Weekly reporting of activities and billings, expense reports, business development reports, client contact reports, and so on are common in larger firms. Administrative overhead is added and financial budgeting becomes more important in tracking the performance of the firm. Consulting by its nature is essentially focused on cash flow. One chief executive of a large consulting firm was quoted as saying, "No matter how big your firm is, in this business, you're only three months away from bankruptcy." As the organization accumulates additional professionals, each with a relatively fixed monthly requirement in terms of income, concern increases for maintaining a constant flow of new business. Professionals are formed into groups, based on a specific type of business common to each (systems consulting, marketing consulting, the automobile industry, tourism, etc.). This is usually done to enable members to develop more business of the type they have been doing successfully.

■ *The Pros and Cons of Small versus Large*

The professional consultant working successfully in a small firm is decidedly different from one in a larger enterprise. The large firm requires professional specialization, where the small firm requires professional breadth. The large firm encourages the development and promotion of techniques and solutions that can be employed in many situations for many clients and can be provided by one or more of a group of qualified professionals. The small firm builds its business on personal relationships and close identification with individual client needs and situations and the development of unique solutions for each client. The large firm promotes the firm's reputation and assigns qualified professionals to assignments based on their availability. Consulting teams in the small firm are drawn from the pool of existing consultants plus externally contracted specialists. The small-firm consultants rely more on the professional reputation of the individual than that of the firm. Large firms are sometimes criticized for switching professionals on projects to optimize utilization of their professionals. "What you see is what you get" is the slogan many small firms use to describe their differences from large firms.

One element of consulting that is shared by both small and large firms is its growing international nature. Large firms have traditionally worked for multinational clients, often addressing global issues, or at least issues with global dimensions. Increasingly, small firms and independent consultants are being called on to serve clients with international interests and, as areas of specialization narrow, an individual consultant can find his or her expertise in demand worldwide. In addition, work with the international financial institutions (IFIs) is increasingly attracting individual professionals in all specialties, and government bodies continue to commission specific international studies for which smaller specialized firms are often preferred. Even small consultancies with localized practices can find their expertise sought out by larger international consultants patrolling the Internet for expertise and/or opportunities for expansion.

Professional Designation

These two groups – the giant accountancy-based and operations-based international firms, and the small and medium-sized independent or federation – are thought to share roughly equally in the market for management consulting. To this should be added the many other disciplines which now serve as the basis for professional consulting, including engineering, industry specialties (such as health care or agri-business, transportation or local government finance) and generic specialties such as training, motivational program development and so forth.

While this large and heterogeneous group can all call themselves consultants, not all can be considered professional. In response to the need for clients to have some assurance that consultants are capable of performing in a professional manner, some groups have formed professional associations. The engineers provide the professional designation P.Eng. (Professional Engineer) and place restrictions on who can call themselves an engineer. The designation CMA (Certified Management Accountant) has been added to the accounting profession to augment the venerated CA (Chartered Accountant), and its American counterpart, the CPA (Certified Public Accountant). Management consultants have a similar designation – CMC (Certified Management Consultant) – which is recognized internationally and awarded by a formally chartered Institute of Certified Management Consultants (ICMC). These and other comparable professional designations indicate a standard body of knowledge and a dedication to quality and ethical performance by the profession's certified members.

Until relatively recently, there was little training available to individuals wishing to become consultants or improve their consulting effectiveness. However, more and more universities are now offering courses relating to consulting (especially within MBA programs), and the large consulting firms provide substantial in-house training. For the independent or new consultant in Canada, the CAMC (Canadian Association of Management Consultants), formerly the Institute of Certified Management Consultants of Canada (ICMCC), is increasing its program of professional skills development and broadening its reach to include non-members. These efforts are in response to the growing number of individuals entering the consulting field and the diversity of their backgrounds.

There are no obvious limits to the size and scope of the industry, and it continues to be an individual service relying on self-discipline for its ethical integrity and quality performance. However, as the industry continues to develop and mature the level of professionalism will keep pace with the efforts of its members.

TWO

Getting Started

Consulting is an "easy entry" business in that anyone can get started with little investment. The modern consultant can operate out of a home office and, with available low cost technology, can perform sophisticated research and produce professional documents inexpensively. Whereas most businesses need working capital with which to grow, consulting is a cash-generating business – it actually generates cash as it grows. Often, billings can be timed to coincide with business requirements by arrangement with clients. During the valleys when billings are low, ongoing business development efforts can require investment in travel, printing, mailing and other costs; but these are generally much lower on a daily basis than fees. In short, effective consulting is a relatively low-risk business with comfortable returns. The key, however, is to be an "effective" consultant.

Anyone who considers becoming a consultant should first look carefully at the profession – what it is, and what it isn't. This chapter identifies some of the main aspects of the consultant's job and suggests steps to take to get established initially.

Do You Really Want to Be a Consultant?

People get into consulting for many reasons and in many ways. Some choose consulting as a bridge between employers; some become consultants by responding to requests for help from former employers and other business associates; others, notably teachers and professors, make use of special expertise on a part-time basis to earn extra income; still others, upon retirement after years with an organization, decide to try self-employment. Increasingly, young university graduates are selecting consulting as a career early in their working life.

While the number of consultants is growing worldwide, the consultant's life is not for everyone. Those considering consulting work frequently approach practicing consultants for information. Let us look at the following three concerns that often crop up.

What Makes a Good Consultant?

Perhaps the single most noticeable attribute of effective consultants is their expressed desire for independence. Effective consulting requires consultants to be independent in three ways: thought, operations and business.

INDEPENDENT THINKERS Consultants must be independent thinkers. They must be able to appraise critically all relevant aspects of their client's situation including their own work and conclusions. Clients value the objectivity that consultants provide, as well as their special expertise.

INDEPENDENT OPERATORS Consultants must be able to operate independently of supervision. At times, they may be members of a team, with teammates depending on them to perform the assigned tasks on time and within prescribed and agreed upon budget limits. The actual work itself is frequently performed alone or with client personnel, but it is coordinated with others during team meetings and by means of memos. Consultants must be able to manage their own time and have sufficient self-confidence to be comfortable operating alone. Frequently, consultants will be conducting assignments for more than one client at the same time. Whether they are on their own or employed by a firm, they will be faced with broadly stated requirements, timing and cost parameters. These need to be broken down into activities that can be scheduled and carried out according to their own timing and availability. Client and team deadlines and project requirements are sacrosanct, and each member of a team must respect each other's schedule. In this case, too much independence can affect professional performance adversely.

INDEPENDENT BUSINESS-PEOPLE In a way, consultants are even independent of their own business or employers because they balance the needs of their clients with the needs of their own businesses. Consultants must focus on client requirements and at the same time, manage for profits. The requirements of the business (those things needed to build and maintain the business, make profits, control costs and keep track of fees and expenses) need to be balanced with a given client's current wish to pay for the services. The consultant wants to provide the service, but the business requires that the consultant be paid. The consultant may

INSIDER'S VIEW

Be careful – "freebies" can get out of control as inexperienced consultants, eager to develop new clients, give away their services. Much money has been lost on free consulting in the name of potential business. Keep track of this time and include it into the nonchargeable time recorded for other purposes such as administration and promotion. There are only 24 hours in a day, and the key decision for a consultant whose main stock-in-trade is time, is how it is rationed.

> ## INSIDER'S VIEW
>
> There is an adage, "Them as can, do; them as can't, teach." Add to this, "Them as won't, consult."

adjust the service to accommodate the client's budget and at times, may decide to provide services without charging in hopes that the client will pay for other services in the future. These decisions (to bill or not, how much and how) are business decisions. Consultants make these decisions for each assignment, and they need to be resolved so that the value provided to the client is not compromised.

Some people seem to be inherently more independent than others. A former newspaper editor, after a few months on contract with a large consultancy, remarked, "In this business, it seems every man is an island." One industrial psychologist, who had the responsibility for screening all applicants for a large consulting firm, remarked that in his experience, most good candidates had something "unusual" in their career choices. He cited examples of individuals who had chosen to leave university before graduating, returning to complete their degree some years later; former clergy and other students who switched courses to gain technical and management skills; those who had chosen a period of military service between more conventional types of employment; and so on. Perhaps these people were demonstrating personal independence of thought and action which, while mildly unconventional, resulted in valid personal career choices. In any case, according to this psychologist, there was something a little different about consultants.

■ *Defining Your Consulting Services*

It is one thing to have specialized skills and knowledge; it is quite another to describe them as professional services. The operative question is, what will clients pay for? Clients buy results or outputs, not efforts and other inputs. Technical know-how is valuable to clients only when it is applied to achieve results for them. It needs to be converted to the client's specific purposes before it is valid as a professional service for which fees are justified.

The first step in defining the services you will offer is to examine the nature of the special skills and knowledge you feel you possess as a consultant. Marketable consulting services arise from many different directions. The following six types of services illustrate the different sources for consulting expertise.

1. **INDUSTRY-BASED SERVICES** Many former executives in a consulting capacity want to provide generalized organizational and managerial advice based on their extensive experience. Usually their experience relates to a specific industry, and may not be credibly transferred to other industries. It is their industry experience that is often most important to potential clients. There may be many sources of management skills but few with the extensive industry and special technological knowledge and its attendant network of contacts. Examples include automotive industry "knowledgeables" and petroleum industry specialists.

2. **KNOWLEDGE-BASED SERVICES** Some consultants are scientists and scientific researchers. Some are highly trained and experienced in technical fields such as information technology (IT). Potential clients may be relatively specific and perhaps limited in number for this type of consultant, but because the consulting service is highly valued by these clients, it can be a very lucrative form of consulting. Knowledge-based consultants often have concerns for conflict of interest because they are privy to client's proprietary information, which often is protected technology. This frequently leads to secrecy agreements, whether expressed in formal documents or merely implied on an ethical basis. Conflict-of-interest issues of this type can limit the consultant's availability to accept engagements from competing firms. This limitation may be taken into account at the outset of any

engagement and appropriate measures taken to limit the penalty – possibly a fee surcharge and a time or geographic limit to the restriction. Consultants can be found in many scientific areas ranging from orchardry and opthamology to solid waste management and psychology.

3. **TECHNIQUE-BASED SERVICES** Some consultants develop and market a specific technique with which clients can address specific needs. Packaged training programs and services for time management, Total Quality Management (TQM), some process re-engineering, continuous improvement and performance management programs, negotiation skill development seminars, inventory control, and an array of personal development approaches using special meditational and other methods are among the products provided by these consultants. Some of these packaged services are relatively low in cost and rely on highly structured and programmed approaches and a high volume of clients.

Technique-based consulting can be very lucrative, but it usually requires a substantial investment in marketing. The techniques can help some clients, but because they are not custom tailored to suit the individual needs of clients and address only the technique itself and not the unique context of the individual client who might want to use it, they are frequently limited in their value. If they can be applied to an organization directly, they may be beneficial; if they require customization, they may not. They can sometimes be solutions looking for problems – a reversal of the usual problem-solving orientation of the consultant.

4. **PROFESSION-BASED SERVICES** Some consulting work is undertaken because it requires certification by a professional. Engineers, municipal planners, medical and paramedical specialists, accountants, lawyers and the like possess recognized qualifications to perform and certify

certain types of work. Considerable responsibility comes with this special certification power. Not only can professionals face discipline by peers through professional institutes (medical associations, bar, engineering or chartered accounting institutes etc.), but they are liable under law for the competency with which they perform their work. When an engineer certifies a building or bridge as safe, it better be in proper conformity with all appropriate specifications. Similarly, when accountants certify an annual report as conforming to generally accepted accounting principles, they face significant liabilities if their auditing procedures and practices are found wanting. Profession-based services may be lucrative for the qualified, but they are not for the faint of heart.

5. PRODUCT-BASED SERVICES Consultants associated with telecommunications and systems applications are growing with the number and types of new personal computer-based services. Consultants specializing in certain software packages or in-home office computer applications now join the others selling telecommunications technology and related products. A possible conflict of interest and loss of objectivity may arise when consultants receive compensation for the products they sell as well as (or in place of) fees for professional services. Special care is needed on the part of the consultant to ensure the client understands any limitation the consultant has as to the recommendations that may be forthcoming from the consulting work. Either the consultant is a consultant or a salesperson, but not both at the same time.

6. INTERNATIONAL SERVICES Consultants who offer their services internationally are growing in number due to a number of factors. Their clients are expanding internationally with the freeing of international commerce encouraged by World Trade Organization agreements and NAFTA, as well as other global and regional conventions.

The International Financial Institutions (IFIs) continue to commission substantial consulting work. The Internet is beginning to provide opportunities for consultancies advertising on the Web. Many consultants combine their specialties to offer an international dimension to their services and, as international travel increases, the opportunity to meet collaborators grows as well.

These are some of the major service categories which some consultants define as their professional practice areas. They are specialties which command a market value. One of the most difficult challenges for new consultants is to identify how their particular skills and knowledge can be translated into a specific saleable service or set of services. Typically new professionals are not accustomed to project work and cannot readily identify specialties for which there is a demand, and for which there are potential paying clients. New consultants need to examine their employment history in detail and find significant personal accomplishments and ways of describing their capabilities in terms of delivering observable benefits, not merely performing work effectively and efficiently. In short, they need to perform their own personal SWOT (Strengths, Weaknesses, Opportunities and Threats) analysis. This is a process in which the individual lists his or her personal and experiential strengths and weaknesses, and examines them in context of the situation itself, as either opportunities or threats. There is a considerable body of self-assessment and career planning literature which has been developed within the outplacement or relocation counselling industry to which you can refer to guide you through this process. Suffice it to say that the challenge for consultants is to define and describe themselves and their practice in terms which promise real benefit to clients and at the same time differentiate them from the large number of other firms and practitioners serving similar markets.

Personal characteristics would include education and specialized training, special skills, such as language and unique knowledge, as well as personality factors, such as those needed for selling and presenting. Verbal and written fluency, for example, are important skills for consultants. Work experience, particularly including special assignments and internal projects, should be itemized with a view to narrowing in on possible specialties (not broadening as when looking for employment). Industry knowledge is particularly important, both in terms of a consultant's special skills and lexicon, but also in terms of developing marketing plans and networking capability. Consultants with experience with consulting firms can readily focus on their potential for differentiation from established practitioners. These consultants may have strong local contact, for example, and some experience in collaborating with others; as independents, they can combine efforts on a project-by-project basis with anyone they choose.

Situational opportunities and threats which face most new independent consultants include the challenges and processes of setting up a small business and implementing marketing programs with limited resources. The market for consulting services is growing generally, but not all segments are equally attractive and many are faced with client bases under severe fiscal restraint. The new independent should identify and focus on segments within the general markets of interest which are currently experiencing the most pressure for change – growth, restructuring, cost containment, etc. These are the areas most likely to need outside help by clients. High growth areas are always changing rapidly and usually offer the greatest opportunities.

Defining a basis for a consulting practice is necessarily an individual process. As such, it is often difficult to muster the objectivity needed to perform SWOT rigorously enough to result in a clear path on which to proceed. For those independents struggling with this process, it is best done with the help of a friend or counsellor who can provide objectivity. The process of answering probing questions posed by another person forces clear articulation and can lead to more definitive statements of how the practice

INSIDER'S VIEW

As one survey respondent said, "How do I know what my answer is until I tell you?"

will be developed and who might be willing to pay for the services to be offered. Checklist 2-1 summarizes the process:

CHECKLIST 2-1: *Defining a Saleable Service*

1. Recruit a Counsellor/Friend

2. Conduct a SWOT review of yourself and the situation:

   ✔ Strengths – for example, personal characteristics, network of contacts, special skills and knowledge and special work experiences

   ✔ Weaknesses – for example, inexperience with selling and presenting, running a business, possibly a low level of confidence, or limits to knowledge

   ✔ Opportunities – for example, growth areas in familiar industries, areas of current industry concern and change

   ✔ Threats – for example, curtailed spending by potential clients, direct competitors, new technologies or market developments

3. Summarize specific client needs identified which you can help satisfy and articulate clearly the realizable benefits you can provide, then test these conclusions with market research.

Once you have considered the services you have to offer, the next step is to define them from the client's viewpoint. Consultants should begin their market research with discussions with potential clients and other business contacts about how these special abilities might help clients achieve better results. By developing an appreciation of where and how your services can help clients, you will be better prepared to make decisions regarding pricing and setting marketing priorities of various services. The key to success at this stage is extensive networking of friends, business contacts and accessible industry spokespersons (trade association members and staff, for example). Bureaucrats in government agencies that serve industry segments of interest to the consultant can often provide valuable insight and relevant documented material. Ask questions and when those are answered, ask some more. The process of doing this research can be as valuable as the research itself as you reorient your thinking to look for services that you can provide and build skills in interviewing, networking and objective thinking.

For some prospective consultants, the best way to define their focus is to join a consulting firm and find the area of the practice to which they can make the greatest contribution. The large international consulting firms have offices in major cities, and listings of firms can be found in business directories and Yellow Pages. Associations and professional institutions, like the Canadian Association of Management Consultants, can provide information on the location of consulting firm offices as well. Most professional firms have literature describing their organization and practice, which will help you determine your fit with a particular firm.

Firms of consultants are often organized in a structure that reflects the services they offer. Groups of consultants who specialize in the same fields – industrial engineering, financial management, information technology and so on – are formed into organizational units with responsibility to develop specialized consulting services that focus on their technologies. Sectoral specialists – government, automotive or health care, for example – are also grouped together. In general, professional firms are structured to gain the advantages of grouping professionals to develop their expertise and service offerings and to meet market needs. Firms are interested in professionals who can demonstrate or at least describe a potentially profitable market for their skills, and many firms of professionals resemble a group of cooperating practices, with independent, yet shared, responsibility for practice development.

It is important for consultants wishing to find employment with an established firm of professionals to be able to describe themselves in terms which are meaningful to the firm. Recruiters within the firms know how to seek out the appropriate information from prospective employees and many have sophisticated questionnaires and psychological testing procedures to help ensure that mistakes are minimized. By performing the SWOT review described earlier and testing the markets for the viability of services the consultant might offer, consultants can be better prepared to respond to recruiters' probes. By undertaking these exercises, new consultants will have begun the difficult process of shifting their basic paradigms from the processes and programs of an employee to characteristics of projects and services, more appropriate for consultants. Most consultants find the services they offer are constantly evolving. They blend the most recent experience with their basic skills and techniques to provide an improved set of tools to address changing client needs. For the new professional, it is as important to develop expertise in the process of consulting as it is to develop a clearly defined professional service or product.

■ *Benefits of Becoming a Consultant*

There are several real benefits to the consulting profession.

Consulting is seldom boring

Every client is different, and therefore, every situation is different. Whether the consultant is concentrating on a specific set of systems or techniques to implement (for example, ISO, TQM, team building etc.) or attacking complex, one-of-a-kind technical issues, there is ample variety. Consulting assignments are as different as the people participating in and affected by them. Variety is one of the most rewarding aspects of consulting.

Consulting is a constant learning experience

Just as every assignment is different, so is the information the consultant collects, analyzes and disseminates. Equally, every time a consulting team is employed, the dynamics that produce new shared experiences with peers, client personnel and other professionals is a source of stimulation and satisfaction.

Consulting is a helping relationship

There is significant reward in seeing the client's appreciation for the help provided. Many assignments come from former clients or referrals from them. When these tangible results occur, consultants can take justifiable pride in the ability to provide real help. This feeling of professional accomplishment more than offsets those occasions when consultants feel disappointed in not being able to share in the success of the recommendations, which often occurs after the consultant's assignment is finished.

A recent assignment in a small manufacturing plant on a Caribbean island was particularly gratifying as the local management became excited as new techniques of using information began to markedly improve their company's performance. These were essentially unskilled people with little training in managing, yet they were succeeding in performing to the high standards required of them by their US parent. As they continue to improve, it is important that they take the ball and run with it on their own.

◼ *Misconceptions of Becoming a Consultant*

There are many benefits associated with the consulting profession, but equally there are also many misconceptions, and the beginner consultant should be aware of them. Some of these are:

Consultants make a lot of money

Some consultants are successful and earn a comfortable living, but they also work long hours, travel extensively and endure the stresses of a peak and valley business. Some high-profile consultants do make a lot of money, but stories of astronomical earnings from consulting are largely overblown. When a consultant charges $150 per hour, this is frequently compared with the $40 per hour charged by a tradesman, and the conclusion is drawn that the billing rate is exorbitant. The hours billed represent only a fraction of the total time consultants spend at work. A substantial portion of their time is spent in administration, marketing and building clientele. These activities cannot be directly billed to clients, but are reflected in the billing rate. Independent consultants can expect to average as much as half of their time developing business, at least initially.

Life is always good

It is often said, "If it looks too good to be true, it probably is." Consulting can be a frustrating and disappointing experience for those who attempt it without the ability or commitment to selling their professional services. Life is good for a consultant as long as the work is billable (a client is paying for it). It is the valleys, between assignments, which are stressful and call on extra emotional reserves. Not being in demand, even for a relatively short time, can threaten self-confidence just when self-confidence is most needed to address new possibilities and potential assignments. Competition is fierce at times, and valleys between assignments can seem interminably long. More often than not, the next assignment comes unexpectedly as a result of consistent and broad-based marketing efforts rather than from targeted sales efforts. Both broad-based marketing efforts (the shotgun) and targeted sales approaches (the rifle) should be part of the marketing plan. The latter often takes longer to develop, while new client opportunities can occur almost serendipitously as a result of word of mouth, a published article or a speech. Consultants must be alert to these unexpected opportunities and ready to respond quickly.

INSIDER'S VIEW

The spouse of a consultant once remarked, "There is no one more miserable to live with as an underutilized consultant!"

Consultants visit exotic places

Most consulting requires traveling, either to a client's location or to key contacts and other sources of information – specialized libraries, government offices etc. – needed in the course of the work. To some, this may seem glamorous – consultants are often seen going to or coming from distant, sometimes exotic, places. The reality is quite different. Consultants usually fly regular fare and always seem to be in a hurry. Most consultants would agree that the notion that consulting is a glamorous life is another myth. It is hard work and calls for a high level of sustained energy. Two days' travel each way to Bangladesh or China, plus the lost time there and the jet lag on your return is hardly glamorous – even if you avoid stomach problems. You really have to *want* to do it. Some find it stressful because of the amount of time and effort required for marketing and selling, and the travel involved usually provides little time for sightseeing. Many independent consultants accept "red-eye specials," eating in restaurants, sleeping in hotels and missing their children's birthdays as part of the price one pays for the satisfaction derived from performing the work.

> **INSIDER'S VIEW**
>
> "Join the firm and see the world through a hotel window," as one wag put it.

Consultants just give advice and then leave

A common misconception about consultants is that they sell advice. True, some consultants do accept roles as counselors, but even in those cases, their advice must be defensible and grounded in fact and logic that can withstand challenge. Consultants sell time, not advice, and time is needed to gather information about a client's specific situation, analyze it and communicate it. Most clients do not want advice. Rather, they are looking for help in making choices, and they need a fresh, independent viewpoint supported by fresh information. Often this is accomplished by recasting information with which the client is already familiar but which the consultant analyzes and reinterprets.

Consulting takes place in an atmosphere of impending change

> **INSIDER'S VIEW**
>
> What a consultant believes is worth little; what a consultant can prove or demonstrate is often worth a lot.

that has its proponents and opponents in a client organization. Whenever consultants venture an opinion on a sensitive matter in a client meeting, they can be challenged by someone who has some facts that refute their opinion. If consultants cannot defend their position by other facts, or a better analysis of the same facts, they go down in flames, and their credibility suffers a significant blow.

Understanding the true nature of consulting – that of selling time, not simply advice – is particularly important to those considering entry into the profession based on years of specialized job experience. Many become consultants with the expectation that clients will pay simply for advice based on this experience. While this may happen in very special circumstances (such as scientific second opinions, for example), in most cases, these experts are disappointed. They soon find that to apply their experience in consulting, they must adjust their thinking to develop specific projects and use their knowledge to help clients understand their situation better.

Projects have a beginning and an end. Consulting assignments generally take the form of projects and the thought process in describing an ongoing process as a series of projects takes practice. Consultants can visualize opportunities to help clients when they develop this project-oriented thinking. It is a skill that can be learned with practice. This thought process will be discussed more fully later in this chapter in the section "The Consultants' Paradigm."

Consultants can do a better job than the client

Effective consultants never presume to know the client's business as well as the client does. The consultant is simply staff support and knows more about gathering information and how to use it in support of decisions, but not what decision is best for the client. This position stems from a common error many new consultants make – believing that there is one "right" answer to the client's situation. It is entirely the client's prerogative to decide what the firm wants to achieve. In the business sense, it is the client who must choose the level of uncertainty and risk to accept when making choices. It is the client who decides whether to hire or fire an individual, regardless of ability and performance as documented by the consultant. In short, the client has the right to be wrong. The consultant can only recommend.

A decision to become a consultant because it appears to be the only avenue available to an early retiree or an individual laid off or unemployed in middle or late career can be risky. The work is hard and at times, tedious and unglamorous. It is rarely a place to salve bruised self-esteem or recover lost status among peers who may view consultancy as an admission that you can't get a "real" job. Those emotional bruises need to be addressed before an effective commitment to consultancy can be made. Consultancy, with its flexibility and personal freedom can be lonely and stressful at times. A fragile ego or a self-esteem weakened by the trauma of rejection from a forced retirement can seriously impede an individual's ability to present a confident and positive attitude.

CHECKLIST 2-2: *Do You Really Want to Be a Consultant?*

✔ Assess your competancies.

✔ Compare yourself with attributes of effective consultants.

✔ Examine the costs and benefits of becoming a consultant.

✔ Reflect on the misconceptions of a consultant's life.

✔ Determine whether you have the attitude, energy and abilities to handle the stress, and the ups and downs of consulting.

✔ Research and define the services you will provide.

✔ Orient your thinking to projects and client-centered perceived needs.

Effective consultancy requires a positive attitude toward oneself and one's skills and abilities. Effective consultants believe that what they have to offer is truly valuable in order to justify charging a relatively high fee. Further, much of consulting is selling, which is an emotional process that most people find stressful. The key part of selling – asking for the order – is virtually impossible for some. A positive attitude is vital in gaining the trust and confidence of a client.

In contrast, there is no more powerful elixir to help a person put the past where it belongs and get on with a productive life than securing that first consulting assignment through one's own efforts. To the effective consultant, the fun is finding a world full of opportunities and challenges. Anyone can find problems. Run through Checklist 2-2 as you consider if consulting is for you.

The Consultant's Paradigm – The Project World

A paradigm is a particular way of looking at the world. It is a complex product of an individual's knowledge, training and culture, yet it can often change as new information is encountered and new insight gained. Most people are conditioned to see the world in which they live and work as a set of ongoing processes. At work, these processes comprise sets of routines and activities designed to maintain a part of the organization and enhance its progress along defined lines to achieve a stream of results. Frequently rewards are related to the ability to maintain and enhance these processes. There is no stop or start to these processes. Rather, there are achievement milestones and a feeling that things are running smoothly, or not. Projects are relatively unusual in this environment. Task forces, study groups and the like are seen as exceptions to the daily job requirements and are often viewed as add-ons. These project groups are generally temporary in nature and have defined deadlines.

In contrast, consultants live in this exceptional world of projects, and they learn to see the world that way. This is the consultants' paradigm. Effective consultants think in terms of projects, rather than processes. They are able to envision the service they offer in terms of defined beginnings and endings. This makes it easier for clients to use consultants because the basis of the relationship is the provision of a specific service for a fee. The assignment is a specific project with predetermined tasks and agreed outcomes and timing. There is a start and a stop to the project, and it is often designed to change the processes in a client's enterprise rather than to maintain them.

When clients describe what they are trying to accomplish, professional consultants will translate the information immediately into the array of projects which could be performed and which would help clients achieve the desired results. It takes some time and practice, but it is possible to develop this translation skill. One exercise is to ask yourself with respect to each client situation, "What can I do to help?" The answer will invariably be a set of actions which you can perform and which will define a project designed to change things. Eventually, when the paradigm change has taken place, consultants begin to see project-oriented thinking as the natural way to look at situations and define projects to help clients. This paradigm will become a tool of the trade. A client chief executive officer, reviewing a consultant's recommendations, remarked, "I understand what's needed, but how do I do it?" The consultant listed the various tasks which needed to be accomplished, their timing and the responsibility for performing them on the client's whiteboard. The consultant found mapping out the "change projects" this way to be simple; the client thought it was exceptional.

Most consultants treat all client arrangements as projects with stated goals, milestones and deliverables. Even if this is only an internal discipline for the consultant, it is an effective means of tracking the accomplishments of the program and value to the client. Without some structure of this type, there is a danger that the expectations of the client will diverge from those of the consultant, which is probably the most common cause of breakdown of a consulting relationship. It is a common cause of misunderstanding between client and consultant regarding the value of the consulting service. Because effective consultants think in project terms, a project-based type of client management discipline is usually maintained, even in assignments using nonproject arrangements.

Not all relationships with clients are in the form of projects. Sometimes clients prefer unstructured consulting programs such as retainers and straight time (*per diem*) arrangements. These nonproject relationships can serve several purposes. They may ensure the consultant's availability on short notice to provide on-call services. They may be to engage a consultant to perform a series of related tasks that benefit from the consultant's intimate knowledge of the client and the client organization: sitting in on key meetings; counseling specific employees; evaluating candidates for employment; checking references or other specific information; facilitating workshops and discussions; providing presentations; leading in-house discussions concerning specific concepts and principles with which the consultant is familiar; and providing planned, progressive interventions in the clients' on-going operating or planning processes.

These unstructured relationships with clients are not uncommon, and many consultants find them particularly attractive because of the even flow of revenues over the term of the assignment. As clients become more familiar with specific consultants and become better informed through their own use of Internet resources, loosely structured nonproject types of arrangements can be expected to increase in frequency. Experienced consultants will work increasingly in partnership with their clients in addition to performing projects for them.

▉ *Finding Clients*

Obtaining clients is the key issue for any consultant. Having expertise may be sufficient for the problem-solving part of consulting, but it is not sufficient for building a consulting practice. The ability to identify and attract clients is a skill essential for success. A starting point for new consultants is to list a number of potential clients who can benefit from their help and who would be willing to pay for it. These are typically drawn from their network of business contacts such as former employers, suppliers and customers of previous employers, colleagues and other associates. The list should be as long and inclusive as practical.

Not all former business contacts are available as clients. For example, in the case of some public sector employers, there are prohibitions against "double dipping." In other words, retiring with pension and immediately becoming retained as a consultant may be barred. Some private sector employment contracts contain clauses restricting post-employment consulting activities as well. Former competitors may present ethical and legal problems if working with them might constitute a conflict of interest. Consultants must be cautious about revealing sensitive information from a former employer or client.

Once a list of potential clients is developed, this preliminary planning work sets the scene for the more extensive final on-going marketing research described in Chapter 3. New consultants can begin to categorize the markets to which their services should be directed by reviewing the nature of the contacts on this list. In addition, they can begin to understand the networking process required to access and maintain these contacts and develop them as clients and leads to other clients. In short, this list will provide the basis for developing an initial plan for marketing your business.

■ *Setting Fees for Services*

What to charge for consultant's services is one of the most common questions asked by new consultants, and there are no easy answers. Most professionals say to charge "what the market will bear," which is the real question.

Unfortunately, there is no ready way for most independents to determine what the market will bear. Some consulting "products," such as regular surveys, seminars and training workshops have well-developed markets, and an examination of competitive literature can provide some guidelines for pricing, but most consulting involves developing unique projects to serve unique client situations. Further, while consultants in firms of consultants can be identified in terms of their expected billing rate relative to others in the firm, this is still a distant surrogate for "what the market will bear." In addition, consulting services are not always price-sensitive, and successful consultants frequently define their specific proposals to suit a particular client such that the expected benefits so far outweigh the consulting costs, that the latter are of little significance. Even in competitive bidding situations, this can be the case, and there are many instances in which a client has significantly increased the amount set as the consulting budget when a new and better approach is proposed by a bidder. Clients buy results, usually described as benefits; and they are willing to pay for them when they are effectively sold.

When independents begin their own practice following a period as a member of an established firm, they have already worked with a billing rate and know what clients accepted when they were representing a firm. They usually use that as a base and make a judgmental decision to set their fees based on it. It may be slightly lower because they no longer have the established reputation of their previous employer with the goodwill associated with it, but sometimes they will attempt to maintain the same rate, or even a higher one, depending on the particular client base they serve and their reputation within it.

But what of the new consultants starting their own practices who do not have this market knowledge? These consultants may be able to find out from a colleague or a client what standard billing rates are characteristic of established firms, but they must still relate these rates to their specific situation. Should they compare themselves with juniors in a big firm? Does their special experience and knowledge make them more comparable to senior consultants, or even partners, in a firm? Some large firms hire retired or outplaced executives in special categories and assign them special billing rates until their performance is demonstrated. Others retain former executives as associates, building them into the budgets of projects at fixed amounts without establishing a formal billing rate.

Given this variability and the lack of generally useful market information, many new consultants look for a formula which they can use to provide a rate which is reasonable and relatively competitive. Many consulting organizations track performance by relating revenues realized from professional fees to salaries paid to the fee-earning consultants. This so-called "factor" or "multiple" is the ratio of fees earned to salaries paid as follows:

$$\frac{\text{Total fees earned}}{\text{Salaries}} = \text{Factor}$$

According to the International Labour Organization (ILO),[1]

> *The normal value of this ratio in consulting firms is between 2.3 and 3.5, but ratios higher than 3.5 are not uncommon in larger firms. . . . A single practitioner can often achieve a lower ratio by operating with lower overhead expenses. For example, if he or she spends 27 per cent of the 225 "days available". . . on marketing, administration and other non-chargeable activities, total annual income may be $150,000 (salary $85,000, social charges $20,000, various overhead expenses $30,000 and profit $15,000) to be earned in 165 chargeable days. The per diem fee is $910, while the multiple is 1.77. . .*

This model reflects single practitioners serving institutions such as the IFIs (International Financial Institutions) which maintain a database (DACOM, as described in the next chapter) of individual professionals and specialists registered to serve them. There is little marketing effort required of these consultants, other than keeping their registration information up-to-date and responding to published opportunities of interest. In comparison, most consultants operating an independent practice in Canada need to spend much more time on marketing and other non-chargeable activities than

---

[1] *Management Consulting – A Guide to the Profession*, 3rd (revised) edition, Milan Kubr (ed.) (Geneva: ILO, 1996), pp. 560 and 561.

this IFI-based illustration infers. Consequently, the per diem fee and multiple would need to be higher to provide them with a reasonable business base. When consultants have examined the market for their services and wish to use a formula to calculate a reasonable hourly billing rate, the following formula is often used:

$$r=S/(250x8)x(2.5x1.3)$$

where r is the billing rate and S is the salary the consultant expects to receive from the business. Most consultants can define a salary level that they feel is appropriate, given the last salary they received from a former employer. The salary is then converted to an hourly rate by dividing it by 250 days and by 8 hours. The result is multiplied by 2.5 to provide for overhead and profit coverage from the consulting business. The 1.3 further increases the billing rate to take into account the fact that consultants expect to be "billable" only approximately 65 to 70 percent of the available time. For a consultant who has been accustomed to receiving a $75 000 salary, for example, the calculation would be as follows:

SAMPLE BILLING RATE CALCULATION

- **S** (salary) = **$75,000**
- Converted to an hourly basis (dividing by 2000 hours – **250** days @ **8** hrs/day) = **37.50** per hour
- Increased for overhead etc.($37.50 x **2.5**) = $93.75 per hour
- Adjusted for expected utilization factor (65–70% – a multiplier of approximately **1.3**) the billing rate = **$122** per hour

This suggests a billing rate of about $125 per hour or $1 000 per day, based on a standard 40-hour week.

This billing rate may be only a guide at times as the consultant assesses the client's ability to pay, the competitive situation and the attractiveness of the assignment. It may also serve as the basis for quoting on a fixed-charge basis, attractive to some clients who want a set price for a planned result.

The most common basis for setting fees is to plan the project, estimate the amount of professional time required to perform it (possibly including an allowance for contingencies) and bid based on that estimate. In practice, the estimate becomes the maximum fee unless changes are agreed on between client and consultant in the course of the work. Expenses (travel and living, long distance charges, and items purchased on behalf of the client, such as books and reports) are usually billed as extra, typically at cost as incurred. Estimates of expenses may be required, but usually expenses are small relative to the total cost, and a rough estimate is acceptable.

The First Steps

The preceding parts of this chapter have dealt with the principles to be addressed by a person considering becoming a consultant. It focused on the attitudes, benefits, misconceptions, thought processes and basic preparedness issues. The balance of this chapter addresses some of the practical considerations of starting a consulting practice. Having gone through the process of making sure motives are appropriate, thought processes are flexible and some potential clients can be identified, the prospective consultant has a choice: work for a consulting organization as an employee or set up as an individual consultant. There are many good books on how to get a job, and it is not this book's intention to duplicate that information here. Suffice it to say, do your homework and look for network connections to provide more information and perhaps arrange for introductions.

■ *Working for a Consulting Firm*

Consulting firms are many and varied as to their size, scope and areas of practice. There are large international firms like EDS and McKinsey, accountancy-based firms like KPMG Peat Marwick & Partners and Deloitte & Touche, mid-sized specialty firms like The ARA Consulting Group Inc., who perform international public sector projects, and a myriad of others ranging from local independents to smaller and medium-sized regional firms. Each has its own position in the market, and each provides a range of services involving many skills and specialties. They provide excellent career paths for some and equally excellent training in the field of consultancy for others who eventually set up their own independent practices. In general, large firms and smaller independents differ significantly in terms of their strengths and limitations and therefore the experiences they offer to the new consultant. Some of the key differences are outlined in Figure 2-3.

FIGURE 2-3: *Comparative Advantages*

Large Firm	Small Independent
• Reputation and prestige	• Flexibility of service and responsiveness to each client's multi-dimensional requirements
• Full range of services	
• Capacity for large projects	
• Global network of associates and clients	• "Who you see is who you get" – work is performed by the consultants whom client meets
• Substantial support services component – training, advertising and promotion, research and development, possibly some advanced technology	• Local community ties – consultants live with the results of their work after the assignment is finished
• Financial stability – not as seriously affected by swings in chargeable activity in any particular sector or location	• Can access as partners the best talent in the world – not restricted to the best available in the firm
	• Possibly lower cost base and rates

Even as a member of a consulting firm, each consultant is expected to develop a practice which contributes to the total firm portfolio of services; therefore, the attributes valued in a consultant are essentially the same whether the consultant is recruited by a firm or beginning in his or her own practice. The most significant difference is the training available from the firm and the opportunity to learn how consulting is performed and managed from experienced colleagues. Established firms have a fairly constant series of client opportunities as a result of their on-going programs of marketing and client development. Consequently, new recruits will likely be assigned to a project in some capacity early in their employment. Most of the large firms have formal training programs as well.

The internal structures of firms and their administrative procedures quickly focus new employees on the business of consulting and the need to keep close track of time and expenses, a useful discipline in any case, but particularly for consultants who subsequently decide to open practices of their own. Generally, professional firms are organized around specialties, and new recruits may find that although their qualifications suggest more than one specialty area, the firm is not organized to accommodate this. Also, the larger the firm, the more structured it tends to be, which can reduce a consultant's opportunity to build a broad base of skills based on widely varied client experiences.

■ *Setting Up Your Own Consultancy*

There are also many good reasons for consultants to begin their own practices. Their time is their own, the results of their efforts are clearly attributable to their own energies and judgment, and there are substantial tax and income advantages for small business entrepreneurs. If self-employed consultants could realize a billing rate close to the large firms, achieve a utilization rate of close to 80 percent, and limit their vacation to one month, their income, after taxes, could be as much as four times the salary a consulting firm might pay them. In practice, of course, these dimensions are rarely attainable. Independent consultants rarely achieve the billing rates of the large firms, and usually have much lower utilization rates. Typically as much as one third to one half of the available time for independents in a new practice is consumed by nonbillable activities such as marketing and administration.

Equally, there are many cautions. As with any start-up entrepreneurial enterprise, one must be prepared for periods of initial losses as business development expenditures exceed early revenues. Financing is based on consultants' own resources since lending institutions are not supportive of new entrants in the service industry. Debt financing should be minimized in any case because it merely adds the risk of fixed overhead commitments. Apart from the risk, sole practices can be lonely. While consultants' time is their own and the successes are the results of their own efforts, so too are the setbacks and unsuccessful proposals theirs alone. Colleagues with whom consultants can discuss their businesses are essential. However, client issues are confidential and must not be shared without due regard for this responsibility.

■ *Joining a Consulting Group or Federation*

Joining a consulting group is a compromise worth investigating. Many groups are formed by sole practitioners who wish to share administrative and marketing expenses with like-minded colleagues. They often operate like a federated group of individual practices, sharing work on a negotiated basis and marketing the group under a common name to reduce individual marketing expenditures.

Some groups permit members to undertake work under their own individual name as well, but the terms under which this will be permitted must be clearly set out in the agreement to cooperate. When an individual practice is maintained, a group member can usually retain the tax benefits of being a sole practitioner.

This compromise form of start-up – group membership – comes at a price. A typical group requires a 25 to 40 percent share of billing revenue from each member, participation in the administration of the group and a commitment to marketing the group identity. Some also require an initial financial investment in the group.

■ *First Order of Business*

Whether you begin on your own or in a group, the first assignment is the highest priority. It not only provides the start-up revenue and a feeling of satisfaction that the business is under way, but it provides the shakedown for the administrative process. Invoices will need to be rendered, accounting routines have to be started and maintained and the consulting practice will begin to develop as an entity of its own – an independent business.

If you choose to begin your practice on your own or to join with a group of independent consultants under an umbrella organization, there are a number of routine setup functions that can and should be completed as quickly as possible. These include the following:

1. Discuss Your Plan with Your Accountant

Select an accountant who is nearby and who is properly qualified and accustomed to working with small businesses. Your accountant will prepare both company and individual tax returns as well as help you set up your initial bookkeeping and management systems. There are a number of good, user-friendly software packages available that can be learned quickly. A bit of time invested in training at this point, probably with the help of your accountant, will pay off significantly later. In Canada, you will need to register with Revenue Canada to set up a GST account. Your accountant can also help you with this and any other required registrations.

2. Select Your Corporate Form

Again, your accountant can help by describing the tax consequences and liability issues associated with unincorporated proprietorships, partnerships, small groups of independents working together and sharing administrative and marketing costs, incorporated companies etc. Corporate charters are simple to obtain and cost little. They can provide a number of benefits from a convenience point of view, particularly with respect to taxes. Your lawyer can advise you on tax issues as well. Tax advice from a lawyer may provide a different perspective from that of an accountant. Lawyers' advice is privileged, and therefore protected from public scrutiny or use as evidence. Accountants' relationships are different and their client files may be called as evidence in some circumstances. Your lawyer may be able to discuss your intentions with respect to your specific taxation and other issues more freely than your accountant. In addition, your lawyer can advise you regarding the pros and cons of incorporating or operating as a sole proprietor and can arrange to obtain a charter for you if you decide to incorporate. If you incorporate, your lawyer can also provide the needed corporate secretarial services.

3. Give Your Business a Name

For many consultants, the tendency is to use their own name or some derivative. It is important to remember that a business name, like a brand name or a label, can be a contributing part of the marketing program for the business. Many clients respond better to names which carry with them some image of the business being conducted. The name Edsel never did much for Ford, but Mustang evokes a concept and stimulates an expectation of value and performance.

You may need to search several names through the appropriate government agency before settling on one which you like and which is available. Again, your lawyer can help.

4. Set up Your Office

It is important to establish office space. Your office is a place where you work, where you can leave files and papers with a knowledge they will be undisturbed and where you can locate the support equipment you need to run a business. Most importantly, it must be a place you like to be and in which you look forward to spending considerable time. Constructing a complete office in your basement could produce a dungeon-like atmosphere not conducive to long hours of desk work. Most consultants fare better in an office where there is some natural light and fresh air. One option may be a designated space in your house that can be reasonably isolated from distractions, yet that is comfortable and well lit, with ample room for your desk, shelves, office equipment, a coffee table and extra chairs.

It is probably a good idea at this point to consult your accountant on the various options for charging business items to the business as legitimate expenses deductible for tax purposes. Even if your office is in your own home, an appropriate portion of the costs of maintaining your home (heat, light, power, mortgage interest, maintenance, etc.) can be charged against the business. This might require substantial additional personal record-keeping, but it can amount to important tax savings. An alternative is to establish an annual square foot rental charge to the business which reflects these costs. Some startup costs may be capital investments and warrant depreciation. Computers and related equipment may have multi-year write-off provisions. Each case is unique and what is best in one case may not be in another; best to seek professional advice where taxes and required record keeping are concerned.

Another option is to rent space from an office-rental complex. Many of these complexes provide support services and equipment for copying and faxing. Some have boardrooms and other meeting rooms as well. A variation of this is to secure the necessary office space as part of a group of related professionals sharing common interests and agreeing to share common office and administrative costs. It is usually easy to arrange. This will get some of the start-up details out of the way quickly.

On occasion, you can rent an office for a large project during its duration. This way, you have the advantages of a full formal office when it is needed without adding overhead costs to your business. Remember, for the independent practitioner, the revenue stream (fees) is usually variable; it is important to avoid as much fixed expense as possible, and office costs and other administrative expenses tend to be fixed. By managing these costs such that you incur them largely only when you are billing on assignment, you can reduce the leverage risk of your consulting business.

The rapid growth in independent consulting practices is enabled, in part at least, by the availability of low cost high technology. In-home offices can produce professional results with affordable computers, printers and related equipment. By the same token, in order to compete effectively in this environment, all consultants need to meet the expectations of the market for professional output – described later in chapters on presentations and proposals – and effective performance. The latter is supported by effective use of telecommunications technology (e-mail, Internet, voice mail, digital cellular systems, etc.) and necessitates for equipping your office with an integrated technology system and equipping yourself with the knowledge and practice needed to use it effectively. Most components interface readily and are user-friendly. It need not be as intimidating as it once was, and besides, sometimes the convenience they provide and the scope for self-expression is actually fun!

You will also need basic office supplies and some equipment including a computer and printer (you probably won't need a copier initially), probably a second (or even a third) telephone line and fax machine, staplers, a file cabinet, folders, paper clips etc. Buy these at an office supply store, where you will get commercial grade products. These are not school supplies – you need them to last and stand up to the full demands of office use. You can design your own letterhead and produce stationery as you need it or obtain a supply from a stationer. A good instant printer can provide quality business cards.

5. Develop Descriptive Literature

Early in the process of marketing professional services, it becomes apparent that the dual question "Who are you and what do you do?" needs to be answered. Established firms have a family of brochures and pamphlets produced for this purpose. Most independent consultants respond by developing a brochure that describes the business they are in and their qualifications. Increasingly, consultants are setting up their own Web sites on the Internet. E-mail is fast replacing faxes, and as more electronic networking becomes possible, the Web is becoming a necessary part of professional service marketing.

Effective marketing materials (including Web sites) contain information that responds to the marketplace and addresses the following marketing questions from the point of view of the potential client:

- Why have I received this, and who is it from?
- Why should I read it?
- Why should I care what it says?
- How can these people help me, and how do I know they are qualified?
- How can I find out more about them?

Chapter 3 will discuss marketing your services in greater detail.

6. Set up Your Auto Log

Your car will become your second office. Keep a small pad on the front seat as an auto log. Each time you get into the car, consider where you are going. If it relates to business, make an entry in your log with the date, the purpose (client or potential client, post office, bank, lawyer, accountant, stationer etc.) and the mileage. Most of your trips will be similar, and you will be able to develop standard mileages for most purposes. For unusual trips, use your odometer and enter the mileage after the trip. Eventually, making an entry into your auto log before you start the car will become as routine as fastening your seat belt.

7. Set up Your Communications System

Most consultants spend a significant portion of their time out of their offices, often in their cars, on client premises or in airports. This time is valuable time, and should be made as productive as possible. Modern telecommunications greatly facilitates the notion that you travel with the basics of your office with you. In particular, you should have a fully equipped laptop and a cellular telephone. Not only can you conduct business when you are on the move, but you can maintain up-to-date records and accounts at the same time.

Laptop technology continues to evolve rapidly and increase in speed and power. Modern operating software (Windows 98, for example) includes a full range of applications enabling the user to communicate in a variety of modes, from e-mail – an essential in today's world – fax, and voice. Visual communication is possible as well with some additional systems, but this is yet to be widely used. As laptops become faster and more powerful and versatile, many users are replacing desktop computers with "docking" systems which convert a laptop into a cpu (central processing unit) by simply plugging it into a configuration containing a keyboard, monitor and telephone line.

Most good laptops (but not all portable printers) will operate internationally and can handle a range of voltages and currents. Global standards are in place in most major hotels around the world, and they are rapidly adding the necessary telephone jacks and outlets in their rooms to accommodate business travellers and their "offices." Limitations still exist, however, and batteries in laptops and portable printers run down after only an hour or two of use in most models. Also, the outside line needed for e-mail and Internet access cannot be accessed through the telephone systems in use in most hotels and many offices which pass through central answering stations.

A car phone, a specific type of cell phone (usually more powerful

INSIDER'S VIEW

Fax machines need outside lines, but most office administrators and hotel managers will allow you to plug into the fax jack for a short time to do your e-mailing when you run into problems with the phone system in your room.

and therefore more reliable), is essential. Your car phone will not let you procrastinate. On-the-road time can be used to think, plan and hold meetings with yourself. Invariably, you will recall a former client you have been meaning to visit or some other call you have been meaning to make but never seemed to get around to when you are in your office. You can clear at least a month's backlog of telephone calls the first week of having a cell phone. For the modest investment involved, it can pay for itself many times over. A hands-free system is recommended (and required in some locations if you use the phone while driving). It is also recommended that you pull over to the roadside before engaging in any complex telephone conversations. If you are not accustomed to a cell phone, take some time to practice for your own effectiveness and safety.

Cell phones are inappropriate for some calls. It is important to remember that while they look and behave like regular telephones, they are really radios, and the conversations for which they are used are not private. Credit card information and other confidential matters should not be disclosed on the cell phone; there have been a number of high-profile cases where people operating scanners have intercepted cell phone conversations with potentially serious and embarrassing consequences. As the cell phone industry converts to digital technology, these problems will be eliminated, but one should always err on the side of caution, particularly when using rented or borrowed equipment which may be analog, not digital.

If you are just starting your practice with anxiety heightened by having been downsized, you may need to adjust your work style after years of pressure to do everything immediately. Take one step at a time. Spread the tasks over a few weeks, and take some time to go for a walk or sit in the sun. You're the boss, now, and nobody can tell you when to work. The world will unfold as it should.

Most of these setup decisions are not necessarily permanent and can be changed later. Therefore, it is more important to put the structure in place than it is to make sure everything is perfect at the outset. This is particularly important for new consultants who are fresh from the trauma of unplanned early retirement or other unexpected severance from a previous employer. These individuals are frequently heavily stressed and find that even normally simple and straightforward decisions are difficult as they struggle with shaken self-confidence. It is important to begin work as soon as practical, but don't worry excessively that everything is not correct and in place. Most things can be changed over time at little cost and with few concerns. Checklist 2-4 reviews the steps in starting your own consultancy.

CHECKLIST 2-4: *First Steps*

✔ Consult your accountant and your lawyer

✔ Set up your company – give it a name and address, including e-mail and fax

✔ Set up an office with supplies

✔ Develop some literature and possibly a Web page

✔ Set up your auto log and other expense records

✔ Get a car phone or a cell phone

✔ Prepare for your first assignment

First Assignment Challenge

There is nothing like the thrill of the first business assignment; it provides the shakedown for all your procedures and processes. The following issues arise when you are first invited in to meet the client and discuss your services.

■ *Who Is the Client?*

In most cases, identifying the client is straightforward. The organization which commissions the work is the client, and the individual with whom the consulting program is discussed is the principal contact. The consultant should confirm this, however, because in some cases, the individual is not empowered to commission the work or the budget for the type of work discussed has not been approved. Sometimes, the individual describing the consulting work needed is not the individual whose requirements the consultant must meet. There may be several agendas at work at the same time. For example, the chair of the board of a large group of companies might commission a consulting project on behalf of one of the companies the group controls. The invoicing would be done to the subsidiary company, and the key contact would be that company's president. Early in the process it is important to identify who is the real client, because the president's agenda may be different from the chair's.

Sometimes there actually is no client when a project begins, and the consultant needs to help those interested in having consulting work performed identify the internal steps they need to take in order to become a client. Very often, consulting opportunities arise when a group of people with a common business interest discover they are interested in pursuing an opportunity or stimulating some kind of a change. The need for consulting help is identified, the consultant is called and all parties agree on what should be done. Before expending much more effort, however, the consultant must first determine who the client will be. A project needs a sponsor – some organization, or possibly an individual, who will pay the consultant for time and expenses. Sometimes, a joint or group of clients can be assembled to commission and share the funding of an initial validation study to examine the feasibility of continuing further. The important concern is that there be a client, not just a clear need for a consultant.

Many a consultant have wasted time, energy and emotion on interesting causes, only to find that in the end there is no client – no person or organization willing to fund the work.

■ *What Will You Deliver?*

Very quickly, as you discuss the nature of services you will provide, clients express a wish to know just what they will get for their money. One way consultants address this is to discuss the "deliverables" resulting from the work. Anything tangible resulting from the professional work can be considered a deliverable. Usually the key deliverable is a report of some kind, and the client wants to know what will be covered in that report and at what level of detail. Sometimes the consultant will supply equipment or software or something else to be purchased in the course of the work. Information in the form of charts, tables and so on may also be deliverables.

Time, in itself, is rarely considered a deliverable, but the results from applying professional time to a project are. These deliverables are the tangible things the client gets for his or her money.

■ *What Will You Change?*

Even veteran consultants are constantly looking at the fees that they charge to determine their fairness and competitiveness. For the new consultant, the challenge is intensified because of the lack of suitable reference points. Most new consultants undervalue their services by underestimating the time required to do the work for the client, but practice and perhaps some hard lessons will provide the reality check needed.

This is where the billing rate you have calculated earlier comes in. By examining the work to be done and its work-time content, the cost can be calculated by applying the billing rate you have established. The billing rate will be only a guide for many consultants. It facilitates estimating the costs of a project, but the actual pricing and billing arrangements may be a separate decision. The pricing may reflect the consultant's assessment of the strategic attractiveness of the project, the value to the client as well as the client's ability to pay the full rate.

Billing arrangements may take into account the client's administrative preference as well as the cash flow consequences for the consultant. It may be quoted as a fixed fee, a series of equal payments or progress billings linked directly to the time expended. A growing practice is benefits- or results-based billing, a derivation of contingency billing, in which the fee is paid only when specific results are achieved; the size of the fee may depend on the magnitude of specified measurable results (e.g., savings or profit growth). While intellectually appealing, in practice this can give rise to a host of problems by appearing to focus the consultant on achieving specific near-term observable results, possibly at the expense of longer term concerns for a client's overall welfare.

Contingency fees have been one of the most controversial issues in the practice of management consulting and for many years were banned by consultants' codes of ethics. These codes have largely been modified in line with current practice, but they still seek to limit the degree to which billing arrangements appear to place consultant interests above those of their clients. They will be discussed further in Chapter 8 which deals with professional ethics.

On other occasions, particularly for some public sector institutions, the client specifies the billing rate to be paid, and all bidders must agree to that before submitting their proposals. Some government contracts contain a clause that requires the consultant to certify that the rate quoted is the consultant's "best rate," and that nobody receives a better one. For this and other reasons, you may decide to decline consulting opportunities at reduced rates. You may wish to price your work on a "fixed-fee" basis, in which case the billing rate is irrelevant to the client. Consultants should nevertheless have their target billing rate decided in order to determine whether to accept the client-defined rate or to pass on that particular opportunity. In any case, market forces prevail.

■ *Be Clear on Handling of Expenses*

The basic convention for professionals is to charge clients with any expenses incurred directly in the course of performing the work on behalf of that client (fee-plus-expenses basis). When the engagement is accepted for a fixed cost, including expenses, the issue does not arise. If you offer services for a fixed amount, be explicit as to how expenses are to be treated. If possible, keep them extra, at cost. Otherwise, you may have a client unexpectedly ask for 150 copies of a report at the end of the assignment, a cost you might have to absorb if your price includes expenses.

A variation on the at-cost-as-incurred practice is the use of per diems and standard charges. Most large organizations and government agencies publish a set of standard charges including mileage, meals and, in some cases, accommodations allowances. Many consultants use these charges in place of actual costs. Certainly, standards are more convenient and less controversial, and actual costs can be limited to miscellaneous out-of-pocket items not covered, such as long distance telephone and parking charges. Major expenses, such as significant travel costs or the purchase of equipment or services, should be cleared with the client in advance of incurring them. This kind of client involvement is good client management practice. Expenses are usually a small part of the total consulting costs, and most clients need to be assured only that their treatment is fair and defensible.

In some businesses – for example, the advertising industry – expenses are typically related to contracted activity such as producing a commercial. In these cases, the agency may mark up the costs by a percentage deemed to reflect the supervision necessary in performing the contracted production service. Consultants, however, normally find that marking up expenses can constitute an apparent conflict of interest since there is an implied incentive to incur unnecessary expenses.

■ *Establish Invoicing Details Up Front*

Some clients find it easier to process invoices for a regular (i.e., monthly) predetermined amount. Others prefer a schedule of progress billings based on the time and expenses incurred to date of invoice. Issuing invoices on the tenth of the month following the month-end cutoff date for accumulating charges is typical of the consulting industry. The consultant should be flexible in arranging the invoicing schedule to suit the client provided the cash flow consequences are fully understood.

Since few clients have a budget for consulting, it may be prudent to note the client's budget year-end timing so that the payment schedule can spread the burden over more than one budget. Also, clients frequently agree to an initial billing early or at the beginning of the assignment to cover the start-up activities and to "exercise the system," or, in other words, to make sure the accounting department has made appropriate provision for the nonstandard, probably nonbudgeted expenditure on consulting services.

Government assignments often contain provision for a holdback of some portion of the fee until the client releases a final approval. In these cases, consultants can usually protect their interests by negotiating a deadline for such a final release after which the holdback will become payable in full.

All invoices, checks and assignments should be numbered for control purposes. The invoice itself can be a very simple document as sample Figure 2-5 demonstrates. It contains information about the amount, the assignment it covers, the terms of trade (typically, due when rendered) and, in Canada, the GST included and the consultant's GST number when applicable. (Not all revenue is subject to GST – foreign earnings are not, for example.)

Clients vary as to the amount of detail they require, particularly with respect to expenses and their need for receipts. The level of detail required on invoices should be worked out with the client at the beginning of a project to ensure that there are no unnecessary delays, as should the terms of billing and payment. Payment delays and processing difficulties should be addressed immediately and brought under control before any meaningful deliverables have been provided, regardless of the size or nature of the client. If the client is reluctant (or unable) to pay the first invoice, you may have to stop work until the situation is clarified. Usually the client is just as anxious as the consultant to remove administrative complications from the consulting process.

FIGURE 2-5: *Sample Invoice*

URA **Consultants**   Phone (700) 738-4877
423 Consultant Way,   Fax (700) 738-9180
Somewhere, Earth ZIP/Postal Code   e-mail ura@server.ca

International Foods Division
Capital Foods Limited
2100 Ladel Street
Toronto, Canada M2T 4N1

ATT: A. Mometer, President

November 18, 1998

INVOICE NO. 5698

Progress Billing for professional services in connection with **Sales Force Improvement** project for October 1998:

Professional Fees		$12,400.00
Expenses:		
Mileage to Toronto and return	800km @ $.34	$272.00
Per diem re Toronto		55.90
Hotel charges in Toronto		88.84
Parking charges		3.50
Mileage incurred in local interviews	480km @ $.34	163.20
Long-distance Charges		47.47
Printing		23.62
Courier		14.93
Stationery and other office supplies		63.20
Miscellaneous administration expenses		140.00
	Total Expenses	$872.66
	Total Fees & Expenses	$ 13,272.66
	Plus GST @ 7%	$ 929.09
	Total this Invoice	CDN$ 14,201.75

Terms: Due When Rendered   **GST# 738974561**

A Division of **I. M. Okeh Inc.**

■ *Learning Process*

Successful entrepreneurs and businesses are constantly learning and evolving to accomplish continuous improvement. Consulting practices are no different. They need to evolve as well to ensure that the services offered and the processes by which they are marketed and sold are competitive and relevant. Following a decision by a client to commission you as his or her consultant, there is an important opportunity for feedback. This is equally true for clients who decided not to hire you. Most clients are quite willing to provide information about which particular aspects of your approach they found most favourable to their decision and which they found least favourable. They appreciate your attempts to improve. A file should be maintained containing memos to yourself based on these feedback discussions. This file should be reviewed on a regular basis.

Perhaps the most important part of completing the start-up stage of a new consulting business, or in achieving a professional goal within a large firm, is to learn to enjoy the business. It is hard work and at times, can be frustrating and lonely, but the successes make it worthwhile. Don't forget to celebrate your successes!

> **CHECKLIST 2-6:** *The First Assignment Challenge*
>
> ✔ Target the client – know exactly who will be paying the bills
>
> ✔ Know what specific deliverables are expected
>
> ✔ Agree on cost, including provision for expenses
>
> ✔ Understand the invoicing procedure
>
> ✔ Build in a learning process
>
> ✔ Exceed the client's expectations

When your first assignment materializes, you will experience a series of emotions: first the knowledge and understanding that your development work has paid off, and that your selling efforts have succeeded. That is satisfying. Then comes the moment of terror when you realize that you now have to deliver on all that you have promised. At this point, go for a walk, take a break.

When you return to a calmer, more relaxed state, you can begin to plan for the activities your proposal has described. Your confidence is high. You know that you can do as good a job as anyone because you have the special skills and experience that are needed. You've started! The next step is to expand beyond that first assignment. That's where marketing comes in.

THREE

Marketing Your Consulting Services

Perhaps the most asked question by new consultants is "How does one get business?" It is simply not true that those who can benefit from your services will come calling once you develop a consulting specialty and announce its availability. It just doesn't happen that way. The better mousetrap theory went the way of the buggy whip. You have to help clients *want your* services, not merely *need* services like yours. It is a sobering thought that most potential clients do not even realize that they may need a consultant – they may know they need something, but most do not automatically translate their problem into a need for a consultant. Few organizations budget for the use of consultants the way they do for other services such as advertising or auditing.

Even when clients recognize that a consultant might provide some benefit, many have difficulty in determining what kind of consultant to retain, and on what basis. It is up to the consultant to show potential clients how they can benefit from using a consultant, and more to the point, a specific consultant. There is no magic wand that automatically translates the consultant's skills and experience into client benefit; it is up to the consultant to make that connection. The process of making that connection is marketing.

What Is Marketing?

Marketing is a term that means different things to different people. To some it means advertising, to others it means selling, and to still others it means carrying out a set of activities designed to place a particular product or service in the mind of a potential customer. There is an element of marketing in all of these popular definitions, but none of them provide the total picture and there will be disagreement from marketers on each of them. *The Oxford Dictionary of Current English* defines marketing as, "sell; offer for sale; buy or sell goods in market," but most marketers would disagree with this limited usage.

Perhaps the best definition is that marketing is not a set of activities in itself, but rather an *attitude* which renders a set of marketing activities effective. That attitude is one of concern to satisfy the needs or wants of a potential customer or client. It is customer or client needs-driven. It is not driven by supplier or consultant products or services. This client-oriented attitude permeates all effective marketing and selling.

The marketing function is organized differently in different industrial sectors. Industrial marketers (automotive parts suppliers, for example) normally include marketing as a part of their selling organization, where those staff activities associated with marketing (market research, advertising, promotion, pricing, positioning and product development) are performed to support sales activities. In contrast, consumer marketers (packaged goods manufacturers such as the cosmetics, food and soap companies) generally regard market research, advertising, promotion, pricing, positioning and product development as distinctly separate from sales. To consumer marketers, the end consumer is not their direct customer, but the customer of their customer, the retailer. This difference is reflected in the relative importance placed on direct sales efforts in reaching the final customer by different types of marketers.

Most consulting does not deal directly with consumers at large. It focuses on specific services for specific clients/customers. It is generally a form of industrial marketing, with the emphasis on understanding and responding to the needs of the people and organizations to which the services must be sold. The marketing attitude begins with the question, "What do you want?" It then leads logically to, "What do you need in order to get what you want?" and "How can we help?" It is other-directed and inquisitive. The effective marketer of professional services is a questioner and a listener.

Marketing internationally has its own set of pitfalls. Cultural variables can differ widely from country to country and what is acceptable and effective in promoting your service or product varies with these differences. In China, for example, the profit motive,

Another Perspective

MARKETING AUTO PARTS BY THE CHINESE

During a meeting in Shanghai attended by leaders from a number of Chinese automobile parts manufacturing companies, the spokesperson asked the visiting Canadian consultant and the Canadian Trade Officer a straightforward question. He asked, "How can we sell parts to the North American auto makers?"

The consultant responded that the North American purchase requirements are quite clear. "You have five conditions to satisfy:

1. The right product
2. The right price
3. The right quality
4. On-time delivery
5. Consistent performance

"If you can satisfy these, they will be interested in speaking with you," he said.

Expecting the normal response – "If we try, we can do it" – the consultant and Trade Officer were taken aback by the response, "Why?"

It finally occurred to them that in China, all sales of this type are directed by the state. These executives were expecting the Canadians to request the Canadian government to require Ford, GM and Chrysler to buy from them.

which we all take for granted in commerce, may not be at play at all.

Marketing effectively internationally requires some research regarding the markets to be addressed. Canada's foreign trade officials are regarded as among the best in the world in terms of information in support of Canadians attempting to market. It is a good idea to visit the local Canadian trade officer when in a foreign city; they are usually well-informed about local customs and marketing practices.

■ Challenge of Marketing

Many books have been written on the subject of marketing professional services. Numerous seminars and workshops are available and large firms expend substantial resources on training their professionals how to market their service. Yet many professionals claim that marketing is the most difficult part of being a consultant. Why do many consultants have difficulty marketing? Perhaps it is because marketing is an emotional process. To some consultants, it feels like bragging, something that, as children, we are taught not to do. Consultants are more comfortable with facts and logic, the framework upon which their experience can be mounted to provide solutions to problems. Emotions are a different thing; they are private and subjective, and for some consultants, to express them is in conflict with the detachment of professionalism.

Marketers risk rejection when they attempt to respond to the emotional aspects of client feelings and wants, but such is the essence of marketing because they hope for acceptance and success. Translating consultants' offers and their genuine desire to help into marketing terms is the professionals' challenge. Some have difficulty reconciling the notion of self-promotion with professionalism. They would prefer to let their accomplishments and credentials speak logically and professionally for themselves. Building a prosperous consulting practice, however, requires something more. It requires effective marketing.

Therein lies the conflict. Many professionals have difficulty marketing, yet they want to use their talents and skills to help others. To professional consultants, marketing is a process by which they can let potential clients know of their services and their availability to provide them. It is also the life blood of the business, and an ongoing marketing effort is essential if a consultant is to reduce the impact of the peaks and valleys of the business and expand the practice over time. The key to effective professional marketing, therefore, is for consultants to focus on marketing

> **INSIDER'S VIEW**
>
> Believe in the validity of what you can do, and don't be confused by who you are. Clients want what you can do. Your ability to build on-going professional relationships will come as a result of doing what you can do well.

the services offered by the business while maintaining the personal passion for the services offered. The emotional component can be turned to the marketer's advantage when the adrenaline is focused on the promise of an opportunity to help and be paid for it. Once professionals develop the professional sense of self and embrace the marketing attitude, they are ready to market consulting services. The balance of this chapter examines the principles and practices of effective marketing as they can be applied to professional consulting services.

■ *Preparing for Effective Marketing*

Consultants need to learn to do those things that attract the attention of potential clients. They need to do so in a way that offers potential clients help in achieving what they want. To attract clients, consultants must understand their market – its principle characteristics, its key players and their roles, their expressed current wants and needs and how to communicate with them in the marketplace. The following are the steps that consultants can take to prepare for marketing their services.

Determining Your Target Market

The first job for any marketer is to identify the target market. Consulting markets come in a variety of dimensions depending on the nature of the consulting service offered. By reviewing the nature of the consultant's skill and experience, it is possible to isolate some characteristics of the potential market for the services. The first question to address, then, is, "Who is your target market?" The more precisely this is defined, the more effective the marketing strategy and the communications process will be. Not everyone is a potential client. For most consultants, potential clients are a small subset of society that can be defined in a few dimensions such as industry, technology, client type, organizational focus and geography.

■ *Industry*

Some consultants are specialized by industry such as the automotive, food or women's fashion industries.

■ *Technology*

Some consultants cross industry lines with a common technology such as computer systems, marketing, plant breeding, graphic arts or communications.

■ *Client Type*

Some consultants specialize in small businesses, while others have services useful only to large organizations with budgets for such things as training and research. Some focus on public sector clients such as local municipalities, government departments, nonprofit organizations, boards, commissions etc.

■ *Organizational Focus*

Some consultants provide services to top executives, while others focus on line and department managers, first line supervisors or owner-operators.

■ *Geography*

Markets can be local, regional, national or multinational and rely on contacts, knowledge and possibly citizenship of the specific area. Others are global, within the limits of language abilities, and still others are global without limitation.

Defining the primary target market helps in identifying the parameters of the research needed to understand that market.

Understanding Your Target Market

After you have identified your market and its dimensions and characteristics, the next step is to understand how it works and what it needs now. This usually means doing some market research. This can range from the informal analysis of one's own experience supplemented by some personal conversations with knowledgeable friends, business contacts and colleagues, to commissioning market research companies to conduct formal research projects. Individuals and small firms usually rely on less formal research, whereas large consultancies, institutes and trade associations frequently carry out formal survey research. The decision as to how much effort is justified for an individual consultancy depends on the amount of additional information needed and the resources available. All consultants, whether with a large firm or not, should carry out some market research to learn about and stay abreast of their target markets.

Sources of Information

Some of the sources of information are: publications, government, Internet, conferences, conventions and trade shows, surveys and personal networking.

■ *Publications*

The periodical publishing industry is large, ranging from consumer groups with special interests, and trade and industry groups, to professional and academic groups. These periodicals serve the information needs of particular segments of society just as most consultancies do. These segments are the industry, geography or some other grouping of organizations with which the consultant's area of professional competency relates. A key source of market intelligence and general information for the consultant is that set of publications that relates to the business of current and potential clients.

Some publications are broad in their coverage, such as general business dailies (for example, *The Wall Street Journal,* The *Globe & Mail's Report on Business* and the *National Post)* which serve general managers and other business executives in all industries and sectors. Others are much narrower in their focus and serve more specialized segments, such as *Canadian Grocer,* a monthly trade publication for the retail food industry. Some publications are extremely specialized, targeting a very specific audience. *Keywords* is a quarterly publication for users of SPSS, a specialized software for use in sophisticated statistical analysis. Similarly, some segments are broad in scope and include a large number of individuals and organizations such as management and industrial engineering. Some are narrow such as orchardry and marine photography. Nevertheless, most segments are served by periodicals.

Some industries, such as the women's fashion and the advertising industries, rely heavily on current information, and these are served by many and frequent publications. For example, *Women's Wear Daily,* as its name suggests, publishes every day, and *Style,* which serves a Canadian segment of the women's fashion industry, publishes 14 times a year plus an annual buyers' guide. Similarly, *Advertising Age* and its Canadian counterpart *Marketing* publish frequently and are the bibles of the advertising industry. Other segments are served by monthly or quarterly trade and industry publications, often also with buyer's guides and/or annual statistical issues. Professional organizations – the Institute of Certified Management Consultants, the Canadian Institute of Chartered Accountants, the Engineering Institute of Canada and trade associations too numerous to mention – produce regular publications and newsletters generally for their members, but usually available to interested nonmembers.

Consultants should be familiar with the array of publications serving their target markets and should read them regularly. The editors of these publications are in the business of knowing what is happening in the world affecting their readers, and the articles published in them are usually focused on topics their readers are interested in and concerned about. They are a good source of market intelligence for consultants serving or wanting to serve those specific segments.

■ *Government*

In addition to trade publications and other private periodicals, government agencies at all levels frequently attempt to make suppliers, including consultants, aware of their current and future needs. Most have instituted computer-based information systems, including Internet Websites. For example, the government of Canada and various provincial governments initiated an OnLine Bidding System (OBS) that disseminated information about a range of government purchasing requirements. This system is now called MERK and is run by the Bank of Montreal. Some provincial listings are included. The World Bank, a major user of consulting services, provides a number of detailed publications and is accessible through its website: *http://www.worldbank.org/html/dec/home.html*.

■ *Internet*

As illustrated above, the Internet is fast becoming the medium of choice for many organizations, and all consultants should become familiar with it and the use of the various search engines (Yahoo, Alta Vista etc.). A few hours' surfing can yield a number of key information sources that you may wish to consult regularly. There is no shortage of information; on the contrary, the challenge is often to be able to sort through the plethora of information and information sources now available through the Internet. More and more, consultants will be expected to have this information at their fingertips – literally.

■ *Conferences, Conventions and Trade Shows*

In a manner similar to publications, most market segments are served by shows, conferences and/or conventions. These are occasions, generally held annually, during which hopeful suppliers of goods and services display their wares. Colleagues and competitors meet to hear presentations of recent research or the experience of industry leaders and other "knowledgeables." They generally discuss current affairs affecting their market or segment. Networking is particularly important at this time, as this is often the only time many participants find during the year to make new contacts and renew standing ones.

The programs provided often list the topics on which the group will focus and the title and identity of the keynote and other main speakers. These programs in themselves can be a source of market intelligence and may justify attending to meet others whose interests are similar and to gain more understanding of the issues being addressed. In addition, these gatherings sometimes result in "Proceedings" that publish the papers submitted. They may be available from the organizing body and can be a valuable source of market information.

Many of these gatherings are open to the public; some charge an (usually modest) admission, while others, notably academic conferences such as the Academy of Management, require registration and are usually designed for member groups. Most are interested in attracting more participants and welcome new attendees. Costs vary, from free to several hundred dollars. Attendance can be useful in terms of potential client contact and networking, but there are many conferences, conventions or trade shows from which to choose, and each should be evaluated on its own merits.

■ *Surveys*

Market research surveys can be expensive and involve issues of survey design and administration best left to the experienced researcher. They can also be time-consuming. Consulting markets differ widely, and developing a list of possible respondents to a telephone or direct mail survey is not an easy proposition for most amateur researchers. The design and pretesting of the questions on which the survey is based is critical to the validity of the responses, and they are beyond the skills of most amateurs. Finally, the professionalism with which the survey is conducted can have a significant bearing on the response rate and therefore on the objectivity and reliability of the results and on the cost. For these reasons, small consultancies rarely carry out formal surveys as part of their market research, and, if they do, they are very limited in size and scope.

Larger organizations do commission surveys. The purpose of these surveys is usually to assess the nature and strength of the firm's public image or the demand for some of their specialized consulting services. Some consulting services develop around specific techniques, systems or programs, and the demand for these can be measured through surveys.

These large firms also provide the more traditional customized consulting projects that are uniquely defined in each case for each client. Research on the demand for this type of professional service is more difficult and more expensive to conduct. Therefore, it is less common.

Smaller consultancies are often focused on either standardized services, (such as ISO certification consulting), specialized seminars and training programs or customized services in a defined area. Formal market research surveys might be justified if the consultancy is based on a product-type specialty where the principal marketing effort is broad-range advertising and direct mail promotion. The marketing program will require a sizable resource commitment, and a survey to confirm the demand and pretest the approach may be good business practice to reduce the risk. If the consultancy is a custom service, however, the marketing approach will likely be focused on public relations and personal contact, and the cost of survey research may be hard to justify.

■ *Personal Networking*

Most consultants, whether they are with large firms or operate their own practice, rely heavily on personal contacts for market intelligence. When starting out, consultants are urged to discuss their plans with former employers, colleagues and business acquaintances when designing their service offering. As they proceed to develop their practice, they expand their circle of contacts in the course of their work, both on assignment and in the process of marketing their services.

These contacts can be further extended by membership in local business organizations, (such as chambers of commerce), local chapters of professional societies, service clubs and so on. All of these contacts offer opportunities to discuss market events, trends, patterns and their implications. As well, they provide some opportunities to discuss new and different consulting approaches and services.

Consultants should develop the habit of writing "contact reports" to save the information provided by important contacts. These can then be reviewed periodically to provide new insight and refresh the consultant's marketing approach. Contact reports should be simple and straightforward because their use is entirely internal. Figure 3-1 illustrates a format that might be used. Keep a few of these forms handy at your desk and the master on your computer to fill out at the end of each day. It only takes a moment, but it captures useful information.

FIGURE 3-1: *Sample Contact Report*

Date:	(of contact)
Contact:	(person's name and affiliation)
Occasion:	(Conference luncheon, chance meeting, scheduled
	meeting in connection with an assignment or some
	other event)
Message:	(A brief note for future reference)

On-going Market Research

Market research should be considered an ongoing process, with each opportunity to offer services, whether successful or not, a potential source of additional market intelligence. Before presenting proposals or statements of qualifications with respect to particular opportunities, consultants should inquire about the background leading up to the request for consulting assistance. This inquiry should include the following:

- What were the factors in the potential client's environment which led to the need for change?
- How did the potential client experience these factors?
- Why was a decision made to do something now rather than last week or next year?
- How was the decision made to seek consulting help?
- How was the list of potential consultants developed, and how will the selection be made?[1]

---

[1] Some of these questions also form part of the selling process which will be discussed in Chapter 4.

A journal or file that records the answers to these questions can be reviewed periodically to identify trends and patterns of response. This will add useful market information on an ongoing basis.

■ *Focus of Market Research*

The focus of market research is to identify the potential market for the particular services the consultant wishes to offer and to understand the needs being expressed in the marketplace, particularly the language with which they are being expressed. For the marketer, the key is to answer the needs with products and services that satisfy needs directly. This is called "selling the benefits," as opposed to "selling the features." This is a critical dimension of marketing, which is the difference between providing what the customer (client) wants versus trying to sell what you can do.

Professionals with different specialties (accounting, engineering or human resource management, for example), who have a broad contextual understanding of their specialty, will tend to define similar problems when they focus on understanding the needs of their client rather than focusing on their own technology and what it might achieve. Their proposals will seek to achieve similar results, albeit probably by applying different problem-solving approaches. They will know when their own skills are needed and when to introduce their client to a colleague with different, more pertinent expertise to meet the client's current needs. In other words, despite their differing specialties, when consultants focus on providing benefits to the client in the client's terms, they will tend to see similar problems and offer similar solutions. Effective marketing is helping customers define what they want and then giving it to them.

For example, a client may be experiencing a decline in competitive position, and sales are beginning to suffer. A consultant who offers to provide market research because it will give the client better information about his competitive position is not addressing the client's expressed need. To some consultants, better information automatically means better performance, but clients rarely assume that to be the case. To many clients, better information is merely that – better information. Better performance comes from changing behaviour, and better information, while it may help point the way to better performance, it is not automatically synonymous with it. Better information can be considered a feature of the service the consultant is offering; better performance is the benefit the client is seeking. Effective marketing makes that connection for the client and offers to provide a service that will lead the client to better performance, not merely better information.

In short, the process of effectively marketing your professional services requires market knowledge, gained through a combination of research and experience and understood from the prospective client's point of view (see Checklist 3-2). It is focused on presenting the services in the language of benefits, not merely by features of the consultant's qualifications and abilities. International markets require more information in order to present benefits that are important in the foreign culture. Simple mistakes can be more costly in the international arena. Such things as referring to "North Korea" instead of the "People's Republic of Korea" can exclude you from accessing markets. Local sensitivities are important, particularly to marketers of services that call for judgment and integrity, such as consulting.

CHECKLIST 3-2: *Preparing for Effective Marketing*

- ✔ Identify your target market in terms of industry, technology, client type, organizational focus and geography

- ✔ Understand the information serving your target market – publications, government sources, Internet, conferences, conventions, trade shows, surveys and networking

- ✔ Research your market on an ongoing basis – reflect on and review your experiences in the marketplace

Tailor Your Marketing to Your Market's Needs

Why might a client want to hire a consultant? Clients seek consulting help for many reasons. Some believe the hoped-for benefits or solutions to their problems will come from the application of specialized expertise, some look for objectivity, a fresh viewpoint and independent advice, while others want temporary staff assistance, and still others hope their viewpoint will be confirmed by a credible authority. Each of these reasons has its own justification, but any or all may form the basis of a marketing position.

■ *Specialized Expertise*

In order to market specialized expertise, the consultant must be able to show highly focused and advanced credentials in the specialty. Technical specialties require evidence of relevant education and training with recognized diplomas or degrees and some years of experience of working in the field. In addition, some related publications in appropriate technical journals as well as membership in technical organizations support the claim of a professional level of competence.

■ *Objectivity and a Fresh Viewpoint*

Theoretically, any third party can provide this, but consultants marketing on this basis will have to show experience in providing this as a service. They will need to provide evidence of skill in conducting independent research and analysis for established organizations and be willing to supply references. This might be a former employer in which the consultant performed special studies. A related service – facilitation, in which the consultant becomes a mediator to help a group critically examine complex and possibly emotionally charged issues – will require some evidence of group or task force leadership, brainstorming and consensus-building experience.

■ *Temporary Staff Assistance*

Frequently, a client needs help for a period of time during some transition or the implementation of changes. Retaining consultants is often cheaper than hiring employees at the level of expertise and experience needed. Furthermore, when the task is completed, they will no longer be needed. Unless the client wishes the consultants to continue with additional work, they leave and consulting costs cease. Computer programmers, interim managers and supervisors and other contract workers are becoming common consulting roles in the current trend of outsourcing.

There is growing concern that some contract work and consulting is merely a ruse by which some employers switch otherwise full-time staff to part-time, thereby avoiding paying normal benefits. To that extent that this is true, public pressure may require that part-time employees become eligible to participate in the same benefits as full-timers. There is also growing evidence, however, that many employees are seeking to change to a contract status, notwithstanding the need to provide their own benefits, in order to take advantage of the tax benefits and freedom associated with being their own boss. It is a two way street.

■ *Confirm a Viewpoint*

Frequently, organizations or groups within an organization need to defend publicly a position based on internal research, and, rather than trust their own credibility, they retain a consultant to review their position and verify their findings. The consultant must be publicly respected and possess the appropriate credentials to evaluate the client's position. Such an assignment does not relieve the consultant from rigorous and critical analysis, and sometimes the consultant finds the client's position in need of qualification or that it is actually unsupported. This is the principal risk associated with such an assignment, and this risk should be clearly understood by all parties concerned before the assignment is accepted.

In some countries, consultants perform as lobbyists and champion specific points of view on behalf of clients. In other countries, including Canada and the US, this can present an ethical dilemma and be considered unprofessional. Taking a position creates a potential conflict of interest for the consultant, who can no longer present an objective position on the subject nor ethically accept assignments from clients which espouse alternative viewpoints. (See Chapter 8 for more detail on Ethics.)

Communicating with Your Target Market

Potential clients communicate in a number of ways. In the course of performing the market research (as discussed earlier in this chapter), the consultant will identify the key publications, organizations and events that serve the target market. These publications, organizations and venues become the vehicle through which the consultant can market to potential clients.

■ *Publications*

Most organizations subscribe to periodicals and news publications in order to stay informed about trends and happenings in their industry that may affect them. These may be highly specialized trade publications and/or the general business press. Sometimes they include regional and local publications or international magazines. Periodical indexes available at any reference library and the search engines on the Internet are sources for developing lists of key periodicals serving the target market and reviewing current articles describing specific issues and organizations involved with them. Consultants can contribute articles to these publications as part of their marketing effort.

■ *Organizations*

Trade and industry associations, specialized research groups, professional institutes, regulatory agencies, chambers of commerce and national organizations which promote international trade and development provide communication forums for their members. These are some of the types of organizations to which potential clients may belong. Directories of these organizations can be found in the reference libraries, and the Internet will yield relevant interest groups and their Web pages as well. Consultants can frequently contribute to the discussions of these organizations as part of their marketing programs.

■ *Venues*

Many organizations participate in annual trade shows, research forums, industry and academic conferences and other similar events of interest. More generally, many service clubs attract people who work within potential client organizations and meet regularly to cultivate business and personal relationships and perform community service. Consultants are frequently invited as speakers at these venues.

Marketing Tools

Regardless of its size, the consulting firm needs a well-orchestrated and on-going marketing program if it is to thrive and prosper. Large consulting firms have resources committed to formal advertising and public relations programs that promote the firm, but because of the personal nature of the professional relationships involved in consulting, the activities of individual members of the firm are also critical to the ongoing marketing program. Smaller firms rely almost exclusively on the personal marketing programs of the individuals. A consultant's chief marketing tools are registration, advertising, articles, speeches, networking, public relations, brochures, Web sites and referrals. Each can yield important results, but when combined in an effective way, they can be the key to cost-effective professional practice development and to a successful total marketing strategy.

■ *Registration*

Some organizations, notably government departments and agencies which make frequent use of consultants, have formal registration procedures by which consultants can become identified in their files. The World Bank and other international financial institutions (the Caribbean Development Bank and the Asian Development Bank, for example) maintain registries of individuals and consulting firms and catalog them according to specialty and geographic experience as well as other attributes. CIDA (Canadian International Development Agency) maintains similar listings, as do many departments of the federal and provincial governments in Canada. While some large individual government departments accustomed to regular use of consultants maintain their own records, these tend to be subsets of the more general central registry maintained by the coordinating government department. Nevertheless, they may require separate registration. Frequently Public Works and Government Services Canada, the government's purchasing department, is given responsibility for developing and maintaining the central registry of suppliers, including suppliers of consulting services.

Some bidding procedures restrict potential bidders to registered suppliers, and while being registered does not mean consultants will automatically be asked to bid on a project for which they are qualified, not being registered will make it even less likely. A little time devoted to contacting the government agencies and large firms which might be potential clients to inquire about registration procedures is well warranted. The Internet can help. Most large organizations have Web pages that contain e-mail connections.

> **INSIDER'S VIEW**
>
> If you wait until you learn of an opportunity by it being listed, you are already at a competitive disadvantage to those who have maintained closer contact. If you hear about it and are not registered, you are at a double disadvantage.

Once registered, it is essential to maintain regular contact with officials within the various departments of organizations. This is still a necessary part of marketing to that organization, and it should be considered a basic part of the marketing program.

■ *Advertising*

This is the most expensive marketing tool, and, for many consultants, it represents a high-risk investment. Advertising investment is always a matter of faith. One develops the best approach one can, based on the best information one can develop about the target market and its needs, commits the necessary resources and hopes for increased business opportunities as a result. The resource commitment may be substantial; too small a commitment is wasted. Advertising needs to be pleasing, differentiated, obvious and repeated in order to be effective. Nobody has yet devised a reliable way of evaluating the effectiveness of advertising; its effects on sales growth cannot be distinguished from the many other influences. For that reason, advertising investment is a matter of faith and may involve a resource commitment too large for many smaller firms to justify. "People don't read advertising. They read what they like, and sometimes it's advertising," is a statement often attributed to David Ogilvy, the advertising guru.

Large consulting firms now advertise substantially in the business press and relevant trade publications, and occasionally on television. Some sponsor professional sporting events to gain visibility among potential clients. Smaller consultancies or independents can sometimes achieve greater volume by advertising in specific trade publications that target a specific population. For example, if you are a computer consultant, you can reach your target audience more effectively by advertising in one of the many computer trade magazines.

The potential provided by the Internet as an advertising medium continues to attract interest among firms of all sizes. For many smaller consultancies, which find that traditional advertising requires too much investment to be justified, a relatively inexpensive Web page may be the answer.

Advertising is rendered effective when it succeeds in answering the basic questions, "who do I want to see this, why should they look at it, and what do I want them to do?" In other words, a website should be designed with the same care one would use in designing a print ad. As in developing an ad, most consultants find it best to engage a professional to design and develop their website. Professional web design and management services are widely advertised and cost little to use. As technology continues to evolve and as web traffic continues to mushroom, the number of technical and near-technical factors to consider multiplies. Issues of compatibility among browsers, standards revisions, privacy and confidentiality of information and speed are among those best left to the professional web manager.

Effective use of graphics, animation, audio, photographs, etc. are all important in website design and marketing. Your website manager can help you incorporate design characteristics which download quickly and yet are attractive. You may also wish to include hypertext links which provide the website visitor with direct access to additional information you wish to feature either on your own site or others.

Merely posting a website, while relatively inexpensive, is not necessarily effective advertising. The website needs to be "merchandised" to maximize the number of appropriate visitors it attracts. There are a number of inexpensive ways to do this, such as:

- Be sure your website address is on all your stationery and business cards.
- Include the site address on all other advertising and promotional material, with an invitation to visit it.
- Make sure the site is registered with several key search engines, particularly those that feature web page searches.
- Negotiate links with key organizations whose activities relate to yours and your clients and who maintain active web pages. These may include colleagues with whom you cooperate professionally, as well as domestic and international trade and professional associations.

- Make sure your site is interesting and encourage repeat visits by including items of current interest to your clients, such as recent industry executive career moves, critiques of selected articles and publications of interest, scheduled events of interest to the industry you serve, etc.
- Encourage interactivity such as salary surveys to which respondents can contribute information and receive survey results in exchange. This provides content for your site and at the same time helps build your contact and mailing lists.

These are but a few ways to increase the visits to your website. As with most marketing, a bit of creative thought can yield a never-ending stream of ideas for making your website interesting and active. Remember also to provide e-mail access to visitors so they can get in touch with your firm.

Advertising is not selling, and a lot of the current literature on web commerce focuses on selling products or definable standard services, such as life insurance. Consulting is a personal, face-to-face service and is not likely to be sold over the Internet and paid for by credit card. Consultants may sell survey results, articles and specialized published training material, however, and some services may be sufficiently standardized (research in support of recruitment, for example) to be saleable electronically, but, for most consultants, the web is an advertising medium, and a potentially exciting one, where they can introduce and explain their services to prospective clients.

■ *Articles*

Consultants develop interesting concepts and techniques in the course

> **INSIDER'S VIEW**
>
> Stewart H. Britt, an advertising consultant, said, "Doing business without advertising is like winking at a girl in the dark. You know what you're doing, but no one else does." (*New York Herald Tribune*, 1956, as reported in *The Pan Dictionary of Contemporary Quotations*, London, 1989).

of their work, and these provide good material for articles that can help promote the consultant's business. The focus of these articles should be the sharing of new approaches and technologies that the consultant develops or uses in the course of professional work. The selling value should be indirect in that the article should be of interest to potential clients. They should not be construed as sales pitches because they lose their appeal and credibility with excessive self-promotion.

Some consultants worry that they will be giving away their technologies by writing informative articles. More likely, they will impress readers by demonstrating that they have the techniques and know how to use them. In most cases, the risk of giving away something will be more than justified when one assignment results from an inquiry stimulated by the article. Editors of trade publications will accept articles from writers who have legitimate contributions aimed at their readers. By becoming an important source of information, consultants will often receive requests for articles, or even regular features from editors.

In preparing for their marketing, consultants learn about the publications which cater to the markets they want to reach. The information on the publication masthead provides all that is needed to make contact and express your wish to become a contributor. If convenient, a visit with some of the editors is an effective way to identify topic areas and issues which may be of current interest as well as to gain an understanding of the parameters (length, typeface, graphics, editorial features and departments etc.) for material the publication can use. Persistence pays off when finding and following up on opportunities to provide articles.

Writing in a professional style is a skill that consultants need to master as part of their professional set of tools. Consultants call on these skills when they document their work concisely and unambiguously in reports to their clients. Writing articles requires a different set of skills from writing reports and proposals, however, and can be quite time-consuming for a consultant. Some consultants prefer to retain the services of a copywriter for article writing, however, a copywriter should not be expected to understand the content as well as the consultant. The services of professional copywriters need not be expensive if they are instructed well and given enough time to understand the content and the publication for which an article is intended. Two one-hour sessions with a good copywriter, coupled with a day or so of the copywriter's time, can produce a publishable article in two weeks. Even smaller firms and individuals can often justify retaining a good copywriter.

Choosing the subject, however, poses a different challenge. Many professionals who are willing to write articles find defining a topic for publication difficult. Three good sources of topic ideas are editors, colleagues and clients.

Editors

As suggested above, editors of trade and general publications are constantly searching for new material for their publications. Similarly, executives of relevant trade associations that issue regular publications to their members and/or to the general public need a constant flow of new articles and commentaries. They can indicate topics of current interest, identify feature sections in their publication that relate to the consultant's work and discuss the schedule of upcoming feature editions and the opportunities they present. They can also indicate deadlines, desired format and length of articles.

Colleagues

Colleagues and other professionals can help. Often a consultant will be too close to a situation to grasp the significance of the approach developed and applied during a particular assignment which might form the basis of a good article. Others who understand the technology and are familiar with the work have a more objective viewpoint and can be less modest about the accomplishments. They can identify possible article topics with relative ease.

Clients

Clients frequently welcome an opportunity to collaborate on an article for the trade. They often find the publicity favourable and like to demonstrate their progressiveness and willingness to experiment with new techniques and make effective use of professional services. In addition, working with client personnel in developing topics provides an excellent opportunity to improve the consultant's understanding of the work from the client's viewpoint.

■ *Speeches*

Consultants make presentations and should develop good public speaking skills. (Chapter 6, "Effective Presentations," describes principles of effective speaking.) Trade association meetings, conferences and industry study groups provide forums for new contributors. Service clubs are often looking for speakers on topics of interest to members. Organizers of these events can help in developing topics and scheduling engagements. Public relations organizations often provide or coordinate with speakers' bureaus and speakers' agents. These are usually too general in focus to be of much value to consultants, but they can sometimes provide leads to organizations constantly searching for speakers.

When the demand for a consultant as a speaker exceeds the time available for speaking, the consultant will charge a fee high enough to ensure the time spent in preparing and delivering a good speech is valued and compensated. As a rule of thumb, a one-hour speech will require a full day of preparation. This fee is often waived when the occasion fits directly within the consultant's marketing objectives.

As with most of the individual components of an effective marketing strategy, speeches can be "merchandised." A speaking engagement offers more marketing potential than the single event of the speech itself; it provides an opportunity to distribute hard copies of the speech to attendees and to business contacts. In addition (as will be discussed below in the section on public relations), it may provide a press release opportunity, which can lead to media exposure and further distribution. The platform from which a consultant speaks is important, but often not nearly as important as the larger audience to which a public relations effort can be directed.

■ *Public Relations (PR)*

Consultants who wish to focus additional resources on their marketing efforts and have an understanding of how public relations professionals work are increasingly making use of this service. At the same time the number of independent PR professionals seeking out consultants for clients is growing. Although most large consulting firms retain the services of PR professionals, many independents prefer to conduct their own promotional activities.

PR professionals are selected for their familiarity with particular target markets and the communications processes that serve them. They can provide advice on topics of interest for articles and speeches, assist in arranging speaking engagements, writing articles and arranging for their publication and in preparing press releases. For instance, if a consultant finds that articles in trade publications are effective marketing devices, he or she can use their own time and effort to visit appropriate editors and canvas for topics of current interest and produce appropriate articles for publication or purchase the services of a PR professional to perform the same tasks.

Perhaps their most unique contribution to a consultant's marketing program is their skill and experience in managing media relations and securing appropriate press coverage for their clients. Effective PR professionals will be in close contact with all the key editors and be very familiar with their requirements. They will have gained the respect of the editors by providing them with usable and interesting material in such a way as to minimize the editor's additional work in converting the press release into an article for publication.

Many PR professionals are consultants themselves and their services can also include strategic marketing and management plans. In effect, they are marketing consultants to consultants. They can do as much or as little as you tell them to do. Of course, the more they do, the higher the monthly cost will be. The costs may be as low as $1000 per month and range upwards with the performance requirements and amount of time purchased from the PR specialist.

However, one positive mention in the media can return a multiple of this cost in new business to the independent consultant.

PR professionals are frequently drawn from the marketing or journalism industries. Their effectiveness when operating on behalf of consultants is a combination of their ability to write in a journalistic style, as opposed to the formal professional or technical style that consultants use, and their talent in strengthening their client's reputation in the desired marketplace. Some PR professionals have gained considerable knowledge in the course of serving similar clients, some of whom may also be in the consultant's target market. With sufficient research, guidance, input and discussions with their clients, PR professionals can develop the entire content portion of speeches and articles. An added benefit is their objectivity and fresh approach. In addition, their responsibilities include making the content easy to understand and interesting, and, more importantly, positioning the topic so that it is of interest to the specific group being addressed by the article or speech. They should be able to discover the newsworthiness of a speaking occasion and frame a press release with enough content to be interesting to the target media as well.

■ *Brochures and Web Sites*

We have already discussed the importance of descriptive literature in Chapter 2, "Getting Started." Although the marketing impact of brochures and Internet Web sites is a matter of continuing debate, consultants are asked routinely to provide information about their qualifications as a part of their marketing efforts, and most agree that some standardized material is helpful. Large firms develop brochures to feature individual product and practice areas, as well as more general information about the firm, its origins, values and clientele. Being able to respond to these and similar general questions with effective literature will not, in itself, win consultants new clients; however, not having any will hurt their credibility. Many experienced purchasers of consulting services expect proposals to contain company material in formal brochure format to be bound into the proposal document when it is submitted. This suggests that there may be a positive reason for having prepared material.

Although many small firms and sole practitioners make use of current PC technology to design and develop their own brochures, this task can also be given to PR or marketing professionals. They can ask the same questions a potential consulting client would and develop the answers in strong format and style. In addition, professionals have resources such as artists, designers and graphic technologies to produce impressive professional material that need not require a significant investment in either time or funds.

Many consultants are setting up Internet Web sites that contain much the same material as their brochures and pamphlets, as well as copies of recent articles and press releases. Web sites can be found using the major search engines, such as Yahoo and Alta Vista and have e-mail links established for easy communication. Their marketing value is no more certain than that of brochures, but their importance is growing as more become established. To use them as marketing tools requires significant effort in that they must contain material which will be of interest to target market "surfers" and be constantly updated. Many local Internet service providers offer free or low cost Web site services, but the specific design and content are your responsibility. Again, the PR professional may be helpful in this regard, but specialists in Web site home page design and maintenance are emerging as the Internet gains increasing importance.

■ *Networking*

Most consultants have files and mailing lists of personal contacts. These comprise past clients, colleagues and acquaintances as well as personal friends. It is essential that these files be maintained and refreshed. Congratulatory letters in response to appointment notices and other achievements provide opportunities to maintain contact, as do periodic visits and luncheons. Notes pointing out an interesting article, a bit of relevant market intelligence and the like are usually appreciated by the contact person, and they demonstrate that the writer considers the contact to be important. These contacts can be helpful as sources of information and even as ways to gain access to potential clients and other sources of information. In addition, they form a mailing list which can be used to distribute reprints of articles, hard copies of speeches and press releases. Increasingly, these lists are becoming adapted to e-mail which makes informal contact easier.

◼ *Referrals*

A significant amount of consulting work stems from previous work. Past clients are a major source of new business, both directly and by referral. Increasingly, consultants are asked to provide potential clients with references, and there is no substitute for a reputation established through successful professional assignments. These referrals can occur from a variety of sources, and because they are a significant source of business, stimulating referrals should be part of the ongoing marketing strategy. An inquiry which comes from a referral should receive the highest priority response, and the consultant should always remember to promptly call and thank the source of the referral. This treatment is influential in getting the business and demonstrates respect for the referee as well. Referrals can be developed from clients, colleagues and institutions.

From Clients

Most clients respect consultants' efforts to market their services and are prepared to help, provided it is consistent with their own policies. A few firms have policies which preclude providing supplier references; others do not wish their public to know that they use consultants and so will not give references. Most clients, however will help and need only to be asked and given the necessary information about the inquirer and the requirements. Some clients will provide more generalized letters of appreciation for work done, and these can be used as references in many cases. Consultants should make a practice of discussing references and referrals with clients at the completion of their work and incorporating regular follow-up with past clients as part of their contact program.

From Colleagues

Peter Drucker is credited with coining the term "knowledge worker," referring to those individuals whose value derives from their own experience and specialized knowledge. Knowledge workers can be contracted on a project-by-project basis to accomplish specific tasks, after which the team disbands and its members go on to other teams and other tasks. Consultants often work in teams, collaborating with others to address specific client needs. With the rapid growth of in-home offices and independent consultants, the opportunities for collaboration have increased greatly. In addition, large firms frequently retain independent specialists for specific assignments.

Most experienced consultants develop networks of other professionals and firms, many of which they have worked with and whose professional skill and integrity they respect. The practice of referring clients to respected colleagues has always been an important professional practice, and it continues to be a significant source of business for consulting. These colleagues should be treated as valuable contacts and part of the marketing strategy.

From Institutions

Most professional consultants are technically qualified in some field, many of which are served by associations of similarly qualified individuals, such as the Institute of Certified Management Consultants of Ontario (ICMCO). ICMCO regularly receives inquiries from organizations seeking consulting help, and it has developed procedures by which it can make referrals to its members. Not all management consultants are members, but those who are can take advantage of this referral service. Consultants are well advised to become members of appropriate professional organizations and to become involved in their referral process.

A well-developed marketing program is much more than the sum of its parts and tools. (See Checklist 3-3 for a list of tools.) Articles yield reprints, speeches yield hard copy and press releases, press releases yield more reprints and networking yields an ever-growing contact and mailing list. The basic strategy of effective marketing is to make each of the elements of the marketing process

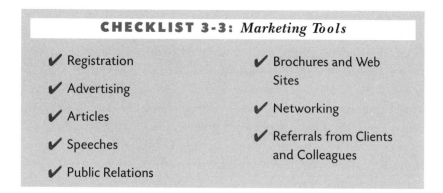

CHECKLIST 3-3: *Marketing Tools*

✔ Registration

✔ Advertising

✔ Articles

✔ Speeches

✔ Public Relations

✔ Brochures and Web Sites

✔ Networking

✔ Referrals from Clients and Colleagues

work as effectively as possible. In the case of professional services marketing, this means that each element should be capable of multiple "hits" on the target market. A program of regular mailings of reprints of articles and press releases ensures that the target market is aware of the consultant's activities and comments. It also demonstrates that the consultant keeps the list up-to-date. Figure 3-4 depicts a professional services marketing approach and illustrates the multiple hit dimension of the various elements.

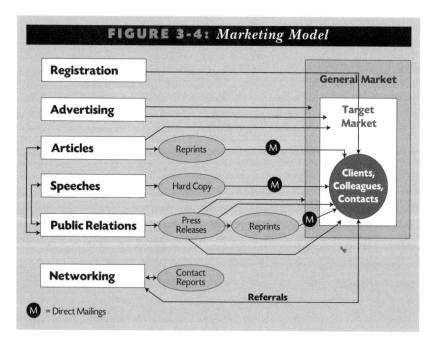

FIGURE 3-4: *Marketing Model*

Market Positioning

"Positioning" is a term marketers use to describe the way a product or service is presented to the market to differentiate it from other products and services. For example, a supplier may wish to be positioned as the lowest cost one, or as the highest quality one, or the one with the broadest line (one-stop shopping), or some other concept that relates to specific needs or niche the supplier feels it can satisfy and that the market values. Examples of consultant positioning might be as an expert in a particular technology or industry, about a certain country or region, or the best professional in a certain field in the local community. Whatever the positioning, if it is to be effective, it must link the demonstrable qualifications of the consultant with the needs of the market.

Furthermore, the needs of the market should be expressed in terms of benefits clients can expect from the use of consultants. The fact that a consultant can do something is not a benefit to the client. The results to the client in terms of need satisfaction and an improved ability to capitalize on an opportunity stemming from the use of a consultant may be a benefit. Effective marketers focus on how their services can be of real benefit to clients. Benefits, like beauty, are largely in the eye of the beholder. Benefits are those things that clients want that will help them realize their unique goals and objectives. For example, not all business clients are obsessed with short-term profit maximization, and not all share the same attitudes toward taking risks on new ventures. Not all clients have the same capacity for change. What a client perceives to be a benefit is what professionals must offer in order to market their services effectively. The marketing challenge for consultants is to select and articulate a positioning that reflects how they expect to provide benefits to clients.

Exploring the International Dimension

As the world continues to globalize, so too do opportunities for consultants – large and small. Canadian consultants have a particular advantage internationally because of Canada's image as a country

SHIPS IN THE NIGHT

This is reportedly an actual transcript of a radio conversation between a US naval ship and Canadian authorities off the coast of Newfoundland that took place in October 1995. The transcript was released by the Chief of Naval Operations on October 10, 1995.

> *Americans:* "Please divert your course 15 degrees north to avoid a collision."
>
> *Canadians:* "Recommend you divert your course 15 degrees south to avoid collision."
>
> *Americans:* "This is the Captain of a US Naval vessel. I say again, divert your course."
>
> *Canadians:* "No, I say again, you divert your course."
>
> *Americans:* "This is the aircraft carrier USS Lincoln, the second largest ship in the Unites States' Atlantic fleet. We are accompanied by three destroyers, three cruisers and numerous support vessels. I demand that you change your course 15 degrees north, that's one-five degrees north, or countermeasures will be undertaken to ensure the safety of this ship."
>
> *Canadians:* "This is a lighthouse. Your call."

of conservative, supportive people who likely do not represent large special interests as they travel abroad. We are pictured as similar to but different from Americans, as many favourite anecdotes of Canadians demonstrate. The fact that we are differentiated from the Americans has both helpful and limiting implications for Canadians consulting abroad.

■ *Differentiation in International Markets*

This close association with Americans and our ability to work with them while maintaining a position of objectivity and independence contributes to the ease with which Canadians travel the world. We are educated and trained equally well and, as the Canadian population base continues to diversify with the addition of new immigrants, we have many consultants who speak many languages and are familiar with many countries and their cultures. As a result, we find international opportunities for which we are uniquely suited. Canadians are respected for their abilities and their objectivity. They are seen as technical experts in selected areas and are frequently selected for work in areas traditionally important to Canada, such as telecommunications and transportation, power generation and transmission, resource management, agriculture, public sector organization and operations, health care planning and development and selected areas of computer software development.

On the other hand, American technology is more broadly based and generally respected around the world. In addition, American-based experience is attractive internationally because many of the world's multinational corporations are US-based, and their foreign divisions have little difficulty retaining consultants who are familiar with and known to executives at head office. For this reason, US experience is invaluable and worth pursuing.

Selling Your Services in the US

Many independent consultants find lucrative markets for their services in the US. The marketplace is similar, and the marketing principles and practices are essentially the same as in Canada. The marketing model illustrated in Figure 3-4 applies equally well in the US. There are some unique features which should be considered as well.

Most Canadian consultants need some Canadian experience before addressing American opportunities. By building a Canadian base of experience and therefore a clear understanding of what services and practice characteristics are most attractive to clients, consultants begin to focus their practice and marketing messages on the emerging client base which they serve best. Their marketing approach becomes both more efficient and effective.

The American market is well served by local consultants and competition is intense in most markets. The Canadian has the initial disadvantage of being an outsider in a business community which is proud of the American way of doing things. The Canadian must sell better and with greater focus on unique specialties in order to turn this negative differentiation into a positive one.

The US market is vast in comparison with the Canadian market and should be approached with focus. Most Canadian consultants focus on a specific industry, and within that on a specific group of companies or geographic region. Markets in the US are frequently delineated by specialized trade associations and publications, many of which serve geographic regions and greater metropolitan areas such as Detroit, Chicago or New York. As in Canada, these associations and publications' editors can be key sources of market intelligence and vehicles for marketing through articles and specialized conferences.

Some Canadian consultants add to their US efforts through networking from their Canadian clients to US subsidiaries, parent and sister organizations. Some supportive Canadian clients will arrange introductions with key suppliers in the US, as well.

Other Canadian independents establish formal linkages with US independents with whom they have established relationships, either from personal sources or through past collaborative work. The firms can then market jointly, sometimes even adopting the same name. In this way the Canadian consultant becomes less "Canadian" and more international. Joint ventures work as long as both parties believe they realize satisfactory benefits from the association.

The Canadian Department of Foreign Affairs and International Trade (DFAIT) has active programs in most major centres in the US in support of Canada-US trade in services as well as traditional products. They offer a number of workshops and seminars designed to help first-time exporters assess their markets and understand the details of dealing with US regulations and practices. In addition, they support Canada-US Business Associations in a number of communities where executives from both countries can meet over luncheons with featured speakers and become involved in activities intended to improve the ability of each to serve the other. Also, they maintain a WIN database which is used by trade commissioners to promote individual company capabilities to foreign buyers. As with any registration system, it may provide some leads from time to time, but it is not a substitute for the main marketing requirement – constant sustained personal effort on the part of the consultant.

The website *http://www.dfait-maeci.gc.ca* reaches DFAIT and serves Canadians wishing to export. By adding the further suffix, */ifinet*, it leads to substantial useful information regarding consultants and the IFIs, notably CIDA (Canadian International Development Agency). The website *http://www.infoexport.gc.ca* accesses the array of sectoral market studies produced by DFAIT's Team Canada Market Research Centre. While Canadian consulting experience is similar to that of the Americans, it is not identical, and this, along with the acceptability of Canadians in some markets not open to Americans (Cuba, for example) provides a number of bases on which some Canadian consultants can differentiate their offerings to international markets. Some areas of possible differentiation follow.

Strategy versus Technology

Due to the relatively small size of the majority of Canadian companies as compared to the US, the decision to engage consultants in Canada tends to require top-level approval. This has an important effect on the nature of consulting performed and consequently, on the type of experience gained by consultants in the two countries. Although consultants on both sides of the border gain similar experience in much of their work, Canadians generally tend to be more experienced with smaller organizations than their American counterparts. As a result, Canadians become involved at the senior levels of their clients' organizations.

Conversely, many large American firms, including those operating in Canada, contract for consulting work at the branch or divisional level where the primary concern is technical support in dealing with current operating problems. For example, productivity improvement at the division level may be concerned with work method improvement, transportation and physical distribution streamlining or systems upgrading and process redesign and reorganization. These are areas in which American consultants develop substantial experience and skill. This helps them develop highly marketable systems and approaches to addressing these operating issues.

Questions about matters such as marketing and strategic planning, global product development and international rationalization, financial management and control, executive staffing and organization change management are more likely to be addressed at head office and, while important, represent only a relatively small portion of US consulting work. They are, however, familiar to Canadian consultants because the bulk of their work involves top management issues with their Canadian-owned clients. Canadians develop a facility for addressing the special policy and strategy-based problems confronting their clients as they try to make improvements in their long-term viability.

Yet, it is dangerous and unwarranted to overgeneralize on this differentiation of experience. Consultants in Canada also perform a lot of work for their clients at the operational level and many US-based consulting firms are among the best in the world when it comes to wrestling with strategic change.

Consulting to Canadian Firms Abroad

It is a well-established pattern of international business development for a firm to expand into international markets and bring their traditional suppliers with them. American and European multinational firms frequently favour consultants who have experience with them at home. Similarly, Canadian consultants frequently find their international practice comes from Canadian clients operating abroad.

Sometimes being a foreigner has advantages, even in the US. A Canadian consultant was assigned the task of interviewing key senior executives in the distilled products distribution sector in several regions of the US. The client was a Canadian producer assessing the opportunities and risks of entry. On several occasions, local consultants marveled at the ease with which the Canadian gained access to these executives. The consultant was told by one executive that it was because he was from Canada and therefore, was considered important as was the Canadian client who was willing to pay for this international research.

The North American Free Trade Agreement (NAFTA) has eliminated many barriers to trade, including the use of consultants. Among its signatories are Mexico, the US and Canada. As the General Agreement on Trade and Services (GATS) and the World Trade Organization (WTO) continue to influence international trading policies and conditions throughout the world, the pressure to internationalize in order to retain and serve existing clients can be expected to increase.

IFI-Based Consulting

The International Financial Institutions (IFIs) provide a significant international consulting market and Canadian firms and individual consultants have had significant success in securing contracts throughout the world. The Canadian government is supportive of Canadian consultants pursuing international opportunities and many Government of Canada offices contain International Trade Centers (ITCs). ITCs are the logical first point of contact for Canadians interested in IFI-funded businesses and who are not familiar with IFIs, project cycles and procurement processes. The IFI contact person in the ITC can provide basic information about the IFIs and introduce consultants to other players in the network of contacts with respect to specific enquiries, sectors or markets of interest and federal programs relevant to IFI marketing policies. Outside of Canada, the Canadian government maintains a set of Offices of Liaison with International Financial Institutions (OLIFIs) in five locations:

- Washington, DC (for the World Bank and the Inter-American Development Bank)
- Manila, Philippines (for the Asian Development Bank)
- Abidjan, Côte d'Ivoire (for the African Development Bank)
- Bridgetown, Barbados (for the Caribbean Development Bank)
- London, UK (for the European Bank for Reconstruction and Development)

Consultants wishing to learn more about IFIs and the opportunities for them should start with the World Bank Web site at *http://www.worldbank.org*. This site will also describe DACOM, the central registry for consulting firms maintained by the World Bank and used by many of the IFIs to develop lists of consultants interested in certain areas of consulting. Individual consultants are also encouraged to register with the World Bank through their personnel department. The various publications available from the IFIs list upcoming and active consulting projects and some information about them. Interested consultants can express interest early and be kept informed.

Besides the World Bank Group, consultants can locate other opportunities through the United Nations Development Business Subscription Department in New York and the European Bank for Reconstruction and Development in London. New regional funding groups are forming to meet emerging needs, and these can usually be identified through the existing network of IFIs.

From a Canadian perspective, the Canadian International Development Agency (CIDA) is worth singling out. CIDA is well-known for its support programs around the developing world. It is an important source for Canadian consulting business abroad and has two types of programs in which Canadian consultants participate. The large IFI-funded projects which respond to requests from foreign governments, often call for the use of consultants. The consultants are selected by the foreign country with CIDA's approval. The second type of funding – Industrial Cooperation – is initiated by Canadians wishing to explore foreign partnerships. Consultants are frequently part of the initiating Canadian team.

Getting involved with IFIs generally requires spending some time examining the nature of the various institutions and their priorities and criteria for working with consultants. While their Internet-based information is helpful, personal visits to their offices and discussions with representatives are often essential in order to be in the active pipeline for current information on specific opportunities. For example, Canadian consultants might find it profitable to spend some time in Ottawa with CIDA representatives and become part of the information channel. CIDA can provide information about Canadian nongovernmental organizations (NGOs) and consultants active in the borrowing countries, and identify CIDA-funded projects or potential co-financing relevant to particular inquiries.

In short, marketing takes time, effort and money. Yet it can pay off in direct relationship to these variables, provided it is effectively focused. There are many opportunity areas for today's consultant and for some, an issue of overchoice. Marketing is the process that makes the telephone ring; Chapter 4, "Selling Your Services," deals with what to do once it does.

FOUR

Selling Your Services

Whether part of a large consulting organization or attempting to build their own practice, consultants are required to sell their services. Libraries are replete with books and videos about selling, and many focus on selling professional services. Many are quite thorough, and all professionals should supplement this book with some of the readily available material that concentrates on the topic. This chapter will attempt to capture the essence of the selling issues consultants face in developing their practices. The following account provides a basic model for exploring the selling process.

Case Study

Two young professionals from the consulting division of a big five accounting firm, along with 34 others from the firm, were selected to attend a week-long training retreat. All the others were accountants who were selected, as were the consultants, because of their potential to become partners in the firm. Recognizing the tension, perhaps rooted in stereotypes of each other's profession (the accountants envied the apparent glamour of the consultants' working life – lots of travel, consulting to top management etc. – and the consultants envied the security and prestige of the accountants' auditing relationship with their clients that continued year after year), one of the young consultants resolved to maintain a low profile for the week. He was *too* successful, and during an evening of beers, he was confronted by an apparent leader of the

accounting group with the question, "Just who are you, anyway?"
Few of the participants knew each other since they were drawn
from offices across the country.

The following dialogue then took place:

Consultant: I'm with the consulting group.

Accountant: What do you do?

Consultant: I'm in the marketing group.

Accountant: Oh! A salesman! (The attention of the whole group
now turned to the exchange between these two young men.)

Consultant: There is a difference between marketing and sales,
but we do work with sales organizations. Besides, what's
wrong with being a salesman?

Accountant: Salesmen are charlatans, always getting people to
buy things they don't want or need! (Nodding general
support from the other accountants.)

Consultant: I think you have the wrong idea. Salespeople are
helpful. They try to help people get what they want. What do
you think salespeople do, anyway?

Accountant: Salespeople are always telling you how their products are better than the competition, they tell you what to
buy, and they tell you to buy things right away, whether you
need them or not.

Consultant (rising to the challenge): I think you're wrong.
Selling isn't telling; selling is asking questions. I'll show you.
I'll sell you that table, but I won't do anything but ask you
questions, and you won't do anything you don't want to do.
Will you let me try? (The table was very attractive, and there
had been a number of comments from the group in praise
of the table and its workmanship.)

Accountant (feeling the pressure from his peers to play the
game): OK.

Consultant: First of all, do you like the table?

Accountant: Yes, it's a nice table.

Consultant: What do you like about the table?

Accountant: The table has some nice features. (The accountant
went on to describe several things which he liked about the

table, and the consultant continued to draw out the accountant with questions about the table.)

Consultant: Would you like to have a table like that one? (That
gave rise to the following.)

Accountant: Yes, we could use a table like that.

Consultant: How much do you think that table is worth?

Accountant: Oh, about $150. (His peers reacted to the low price,
and he modified his position.) Well, maybe $350.

Consultant: You'd pay $350 for that table?

Accountant: Yes, I would.

Consultant: Then, it's yours.

The accountant noted that the table wasn't the consultant's to
sell, to which the consultant replied that he would buy it and sell
it to the accountant for the agreed price. The accountant turned
to his peers and announced, "Point made! He sold me the table,
and all he did was ask me questions."

"And," added the consultant, "you didn't do anything you didn't
want to do." The table was sold twice more that evening as the
group demonstrated the principle.

This example contains all the key aspects of a selling situation.
The sequence of events can be examined and the basic technique
explored. Most importantly, the attitudes of all involved and how
they changed during the event need to be understood.

Interpersonal Dynamics

Selling professional services is a part of the overall marketing
process, as outlined in the previous chapter. As such, it involves an
important emotional component. Emotions are heavily influenced
by the specifics of the situation as well as by the relationship
between buyer and seller. Selling is a process viewed with suspicion
by some and misunderstood by many, perhaps because it cannot
be explained by a simple, logical, rational decision-making process.
Exploring the selling process, therefore, begins by looking at the
interpersonal dynamics involved in the selling situation.

Although greatly simplified, the table-selling incident described
above can serve as a laboratory for examining the selling process

in general. The attitudes and situations of the two principal people involved are:

■ *The Consultant*

The consultant believed that selling process was beneficial and ethical. He was not embarrassed by the exposure it required, and he was prepared to take some risk to demonstrate what he believed to be a helpful bit of knowledge. His choice of the table was not random. He selected it based on some research that had armed him with an understanding of how some of the group had remarked favourably on the table's features and had described the table's perceived benefits. In other words, he had confidence in his product and its ability to provide the benefits his customer wanted. This confidence in his product, in turn, provided him with the confidence that he was justified in selling the product to that customer.

The consultant was essentially alone in an environment that, while not unfriendly, was challenging. It presented a strong incentive for the consultant to succeed with this demonstration. In other words, the appropriate level of anxiety was present. You have to want the sale. The vice president of sales for a large door-to-door vacuum cleaner company claimed that he still knocked on doors when he found some spare time. He was no longer trying to sell vacuum cleaners, but rather, he was recruiting for the local sales offices. He commented that even after 30 years, "Whenever I walk up to a new door and knock on it, for an instant, I feel a panicky voice inside me say, 'Gee, I hope nobody's home!' Then the adrenaline kicks in and I know I'm ready to meet whomever answers. When that feeling is no longer there, I'll know it's time to give up selling."

■ *The Accountant*

The accountant was in the power position (as are most buyers), but he was also among his peers. This made the experience more realistic because his peers wanted to understand the consultant's approach to selling, and therefore, they put pressure on the accountant to play his role seriously. The accountant expressed a common cynical attitude toward sales, perhaps reinforced by the tension already existing between the consultants and accountants. He described selling in stereotypically aggressive terms in which customers are browbeaten by the salesperson until they give up and buy the product just to get rid of the salesperson. One of the other accountants offered the adage, "Selling is a simple three-stage process: find a happy person, make him anxious, then offer to cure the anxiety." The challenge to understand the question-asking process of selling was intriguing, so he accepted it.

During the exchange with the consultant, the accountant's focus changed to the product and subject of the sale – the table – and his attitude regarding the sales process and the consultant/salesperson was put aside as the two discussed the merits and benefits of the table. The consultant gradually moved the discussion from the table to the prospect of the accountant owning it, and the accountant found that idea desirable. The accountant's attitude changed from one of defensiveness at the prospect of being sold something, to one of agreement with the consultant on the benefits of the product.

The next step in the sales process was to agree on a price for the table. The consultant had the accountant suggest a fair price so there would be no disagreement on it (a technique to preempt objection to the price). Once agreed, the final step was to close the sale by confirming that the accountant could own the table merely by paying his own established fair price.

Becoming an Effective Salesperson

Effective consultants must also be effective salespeople, and effective salespeople understand the human dimensions of selling as well as the critical elements in the selling process. It is important for consultants to understand selling as a set of skills and practices to be developed and maintained in the same way they develop and maintain the other technical skills they use in their consulting.

To a few professionals, selling comes naturally, but for most, it is developed through training and experience. Some consultants develop the ability to critique their own sales performance, but many need help in building their skills and confidence. Most large consulting firms provide new consultants with some training and often use team-selling approaches to support the selling skill development of their employees. Actual field experience can be made more productive when the selling activities are shared with a mentor or colleague with frequent and frank feedback sessions immediately following a sales event. Many independent consultants find it helpful to include a colleague in some of their selling meetings, especially to obtain this feedback.

Sales training is one of the most extensive training commitments firms make, and millions of dollars are spent every year training salespeople. The myriad of sales training seminars, workshops and retreats, along with books and videos about various elements of the selling process, attest to its importance to firms and individuals. As well, this illustrates the widely held belief that selling is a set of trainable skills.

Most sales trainers agree that while salesmanship can be learned, not everyone can learn to sell. This is particularly true of consultants, many of whom have succeeded by virtue of their special skills, knowledge or talents rather than by their abilities to sell. In a given population, there will invariably be a small portion who will never be able to sell. They may be well-organized and technically knowledgeable, but their personalities are not suited to the selling process. Perhaps they are too shy, or they lack the aggressiveness to take the initiative in a selling situation, or maybe they lack the verbal quickness for the interpersonal interchanges that are part of the selling process. In any case, there are some highly qualified consultants who simply cannot succeed in the selling process. These are, however, a small minority. Conversely, there is probably an equally small portion who are natural sales people for whom training is largely unnecessary and who automatically do most of the right things. Training might help them to become better organized, but these people will sell effectively in any situation.

Most professionals are somewhere in between the natural salesperson and the never-to-be salesperson. These consultants can benefit from learning and practicing the various principles and techniques of good salesmanship. Most will improve their success in selling by applying sales principles in a disciplined fashion. The following is a brief summary of some key principles.

■ *Positive Attitude*

The salesperson needs to develop the right attitude. In the same way that marketing is an attitude as well as a set of activities, selling requires a certain attitude for the techniques to be effective. That attitude is complex and comprises several characteristics.

Optimism
Salespeople believe that the sale will be made.

Sincerity
Salespeople believe that what they are selling is of real benefit to the buyer.

Confidence
Salespeople are professional and comfortable in discussions about the client's situation, the services offered and the credentials that justify retaining that particular consultant (or firm) to provide those services.

Sensitivity
Salespeople help customers make an emotional decision by using a logical process. Salespeople need to develop skills in noticing and understanding the feelings and attitudes of others and responding to them in order to manage the selling process to reach mutual agreement.

Ambition

Salespeople want to make the sale and believe that each sale is important to them and their career.

Professionalism

Salespeople recognize that the relationship between salesperson and customer is friendly but nevertheless a business one, with responsibility to conclude a mutually beneficial business agreement.

Persistence

Sales, particularly of consulting services, which requires some relationship building, frequently demands a significant amount of give-and-take while the consultant and client search for and find the best mutual arrangement. This rarely happens on the first visit. Salespeople understand this and are prepared to pursue the sale until it is completed.

Focus

During the sales process, discussion will cover many topics – some specific to the situation, others more general about nonrelated subjects and still others somewhere in between. Although prepared to respond to topics raised by the customer, the salesperson needs to remain focused on the successful completion of the sale – for without the sale, everything else is irrelevant.

Persuasiveness

Although practiced at avoiding arguments and confrontations, salespeople use their verbal fluency and questioning techniques effectively to address both the logical and emotional aspects of the customer's attitude toward the purchase of the product or service.

Discipline

Although many appear to be casual and spontaneous, effective salespeople are well-organized and prepared for each sales opportunity and use disciplined selling techniques.

Resourcefulness

Effective salespeople have a positive attitude and see opportunities
and challenges where others see
problems. This enables them to
find benefits to counter objections
and develop imaginative solutions
to obstacles to the sale.

> ## INSIDER'S VIEW
>
> It has often been said
> that free advice is usually
> worth about what one
> pays for it.

■ *Belief in Value of Service*

Salespeople must believe in what they are selling. In order to want
to sell, consultants must adopt a business attitude that recognizes
the exchange of value as legitimate. They accept that their time
and services are valuable, and to provide them without adequate
compensation is to deny their value. These services justify a price
and the effort required to sell them to make a profit.

Consultants must believe that the service being sold will help
clients achieve desired results. Selling a professional consulting
service has an added discipline built into it because, having sold
an assignment, the consultant must then deliver the promised
work. This reality ensures that most consultants soon develop a
sense of honest and practical realism when they describe what they
will provide for the money they will be charging. At the same time,
this reality ensures that professional consultants believe in the
benefits of their service and their ability to produce results.

■ *Desire to Sell*

Salespeople must be willing to sell. Some consultants feel that selling professional services is unprofessional. This belief is founded
on the stereotypical view of salespeople as charlatans with the power
to persuade people to buy something they neither need nor want
at exorbitant prices (as the accountant in the case study believed).
It is true that pitchpersons, as are frequently seen on television
and at fairs, can be persuasive, but to attribute to them "powers"
is unrealistic and constitutes an insult to consumers at large.

Selling professional services is simply the process of informing prospective clients how the services being offered can help them achieve something they want. It is an offer of a business relationship which can provide value and in return, costs something. Many new consultants, who view consulting as an opportunity to help clients by applying their special skills and knowledge, seem to have difficulty feeling comfortable charging a fee for their time and work.

Further, some have the added difficulty of justifying aggressive promotion and selling as appropriate activities for professionals. They feel more comfortable remaining aloof from their markets and hope that clients will come to them on the strength of their reputation. Unfortunately, this reputation may not yet exist, and regardless of how substantial the expertise, if the market does not know about it, it doesn't count. In fact, when confronted with this difficulty during selling professional services seminars and workshops, consultants often reveal that they are simply unsure of their abilities to promote themselves and to sell because emotional interchange with prospective clients is involved. As the sales training proceeds, consultants realize that "professionalism" is a shield behind which they can hide when they don't want to sell. In short, like many people, they are shy. Once this shyness is recognized as natural, it can be overcome. Many consultants then succeed in losing their inhibitions regarding the selling process and become effective salespeople. They realize that selling their consulting services is justified, and even enjoyable, and is a necessary part of building relationships. These relationships are essential for consultants to make the contributions they are trained to make to the community they wish to serve. Once the consultant adopts this principle, wanting to sell follows naturally.

Checklist 4-1 reviews the qualities of an effective salesperson.

> ## INSIDER'S VIEW
>
> One experienced sales guru, in commenting on the breakup of a relationship, said, "Whenever a relationship breaks down, it is because someone stopped selling."

CHECKLIST 4-1: *Becoming an Effective Salesperson*

✔ **Positive Attitude, Comprising:**
- Optimism
- Sincerity
- Confidence
- Sensitivity
- Ambition
- Professionalism
- Persistence
- Focus
- Persuasiveness
- Discipline
- Resourcefulness

✔ **Belief in Value of Service**

✔ **Desire to Sell**

Critical Elements in Effective Selling Process

Sales happen when a buyer and a seller agree to make an exchange of goods/services for compensation. The buyer believes the transaction will provide certain benefits, and the seller agrees to the conditions of supplying those goods or services. During the selling process, the seller and the buyer have discussed the products/services, and the seller has helped the buyer understand how the benefits outweigh the costs of the purchase. The buyer, having understood the information the seller has provided, decides to believe and trust the seller sufficiently to make the purchase. It is at once a very simple but complicated process. It is simple in terms of the principles involved, yet it is a complicated interpersonal transaction in which values, attitudes, beliefs and judgment all play a part. Figure 4-2 illustrates the blending of needs and features to provide benefits to the client.

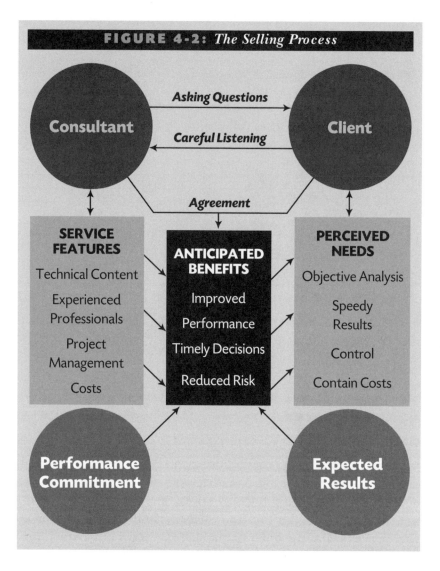

FIGURE 4-2: *The Selling Process*

The following are the key elements in the process.

Preparation

Effective selling requires preparation. Effective consultants never attempt to enter a relationship with a prospective client unprepared. Some situations arise with little warning, but consultants can address these, because, at a minimum, they are prepared to discuss the following:

- Clients' current situations, which become subjects for skilled probing by consultants
- Consultants' knowledge and understanding of the clients' current situation
- The specialties in which these consultants are trained
- The experience the consultants and their firms have in situations of this type
- The basis on which consulting services are offered, and how clients can avail themselves of them

More formal preparation is possible when the consultant has some advance notice of an upcoming meeting with a prospective client. With the Internet as a major information source, consultants are expected to be prepared with current information about the client's industry and the client itself if a Web page can be found. Articles in indexed trade journals and other periodicals can be located and studied at research libraries or in some cases, on the Internet. In the case of larger consulting firms, in-house libraries and files associated with related past work can add to consultants' information. Experienced consultants develop networks of colleagues and others who can often provide additional insights. This preparation focuses on understanding clients and the environment in which they operate. It helps consultants identify the needs and wants of clients in a context broader than that of clients' specific concerns.

Further, this research may provide some indication of the process by which clients make decisions to purchase specialized services. Criteria for assessing professional services are more complex than those associated with tangible products and services for which there are direct competitors. Professional services bear the stamp of the professional firm or individual providing them and, as a result, clients have to evaluate their confidence in the consultant as part of the buying decision. Part of the preparation is to anticipate this assessment by clients and be prepared to provide assurance meaningful to them. A few hours of preparation is a small investment, but it often means the difference between winning or losing an assignment.

■ *Purpose*

Every sales meeting needs a distinct purpose. A second part of the consultant's preparation for a selling situation is the setting of very specific sales goals for each encounter. These may include gaining acceptance in principle, gaining referral to the appropriate decision makers in the organization or obtaining a signature on a proposal or engagement agreement.

The initial exchange between client and consultant should establish agreed goals for the meeting. It is usually acceptable for consultants to announce their sales-related goal at the outset. Typically, clients will acknowledge that agenda and agree that it is acceptable. The frank and direct nature of this initial exchange sets the tone for what will follow during this selling encounter.

Both client and consultant want to do business if the right information is provided. In selling consulting services, that information includes the subtle interpersonal exchanges which establish mutual trust and confidence. Not all meetings have the goal of closing the sale. Some are designed to provide consultants with information needed in order to prepare a sales presentation, or to provide both parties with a better vantage point from which to understand the situation and their potential collaboration.

INSIDER'S VIEW

Moments before entering an office for a meeting with a client or prospective client, it is a good idea to repeat the specific objective for a meeting one last time to secure it in your mental agenda.

■ *Client Benefits*

The selling exchange should be client-centered. A basic principle of effective selling is to focus on benefits that clients want to realize. The classic distinction is between features and benefits. To the salesperson, the features of a product or service that differentiate it from the competition might appear to be benefits because they are attractive to many customers. To any specific customer, however, they are only features that might provide benefits, depending on the customer's needs or wants. For example, the fact that a given vehicle has air conditioning is not a benefit to purchasers unless they value it. If it is not a high priority, it is merely another feature of the vehicle to be weighed along with all others such as cost, size, colour and so forth. A house for sale may have an in-ground pool, but this feature may not be beneficial to a potential buyer who does not want to spend the time and money maintaining it.

Similarly, clients buy benefits, not the consultant's reputation or special techniques, which are merely a means to attain the benefits sought. They may buy quality improvement or market advantage, but not ISO-approved quality management systems and procedures for their own sake. While clients may be seeking specific techniques or limiting the search for consultants only to the large or high-profile firms, a client has some specific benefits in mind that the consultant is expected to provide. The selling challenge for the consultant is to identify and offer to provide those benefits. Sometimes that means providing specific features (techniques, formal credentials, for example), but always with an eye to the sought-after benefits.

In order to focus the selling process on benefits to the client, effective consultants/salespeople direct the discussion to clients' needs. Consultants need to discover (and often help clients discover) the true nature of the benefits sought. The client-centered nature of the discussion is characterized by consultants asking questions that will enable them to adjust their service to provide the desired benefits. By limiting the use of the first person (I, me, we, us) and emphasizing the second person (you) in their questions and comments, consultants can maintain this focus on client benefits. The features of consultants' approaches, techniques and credentials can be discussed subsequently and used to support their claim to be able to provide the benefits.

INSIDER'S VIEW

We all like to talk about ourselves and consultants are no different. We are proud of our accomplishments and our credentials, but we must restrain ourselves. Clients will ask for that information when they want to know it.

A special selling situation develops when the consultant is presenting a formal proposal to provide services to a client. Usually proposal presentations occur after meetings in which information is exchanged and the basic guidelines are established. Occasionally, however, proposal presentations occur without benefit of preliminary meetings. These latter usually occur in situations where client organizations (typically government departments or agencies) call for competitive tenders and are following strict bidding procedures that do not provide opportunities for initial discussions. They usually arise when the client is using a generalized tendering process, more suited to the purchase of standardized services (building a bridge, paving roads, maintaining sewers), where price is the most important criterion for selection. Fortunately, these situations are comparatively rare. They are not particularly well-suited to the purchase of professional services. If any selling opportunity exists, it may be in a presentation, if presentations are permitted. The key issues are building confidence and meeting specified price/value conditions. In these cases, consultants rely more on research results and presentation technique to conduct the selling process, but any opportunities for questions at the beginning of the presentation should be taken.

Presentations (see Chapter 6) imply much more consultant-directed communication because the consultant is in control of the meeting. Even when consultants have not had an opportunity to discuss the consulting situation prior to the presentation, they can usually begin the meeting by asking some well-thought-out questions. Some may be procedural in nature (for example, "How will you be making your final selection?" or "Why are you trying to obtain consulting help, and why now?"), but they may still lead to important information about the consulting situation. This will enable the consultant to adjust the verbal part of the presentation to reflect benefits to be derived by the client more precisely. On some occasions, these questions raise important unresolved issues, and the client becomes engaged in the discussion of them. When this happens, the formal part of the presentation may be scrapped or postponed, and the whole competition may be aborted. The client may choose to proceed with the consultant raising the key issues and defining a new assignment. When this happens, the consultant has been successful in selling the client what the client really needs, not what the client originally thought was needed.

■ *Questions*

Asking questions is central to the selling process. There is no substitute for intelligent questions in the selling process. Inquiry is accomplished through a mixture of open and closed probes. Open probes cannot be answered by a simple yes or no or only a few words. They require respondents to provide both information and insight on their values and thought processes. Closed probes call for short, specific answers, and they are used to gain specific answers. They can be helpful in opening the discussion and developing a rapport needed to make open probing more effective. Closed probes are used when the respondent is reluctant to disclose information or for some reason is difficult to engage in discussion.

In the case study at the beginning of this chapter, the consultant began with closed probes to start the accountant responding ("Do you like the table?"). The closed probe provides the respondent with few options: to not answer or to answer yes or no. This lack of options builds the tension between questioner and respondent and, unless the respondent chooses to end the discussion by not responding, effectively leaves control of the discussion with the questioner.

Once having received the signal from the accountant that he was willing to proceed with the discussion (the yes answer), the consultant then followed up with more open exploration of the accountant's values ("What do you like about the table?"). Open probes reduce the tension by giving the respondent a share in the control of the discussion by providing an opportunity to construct any answer the respondent chooses.

By continuing to ask questions and by varying the use of these two question types, the salesperson can manage the level of tension in the selling situation. The level of tension is important because the seller wants the buyer to make a purchase decision, which for most people is often difficult, involving commitment and personal choice. Furthermore, the salesperson wants the purchaser to make the decision to buy immediately. In general, closed probes can add tension but provide limited information. The rapid-fire type of questioning depicted in police dramas which feature "grilling" the suspect, or using "the third degree," is usually characterized by a series of specific questions of the closed probe type, deliberately used to increase the tension and anxiety of the suspect. Open probes provide much more information but tend to reduce the level of tension. Both types of question are important sales tools and form a critical part of the sales process.

As illustrated in the case study, selling is asking questions. The effective salesperson asks questions and the client/customer provides answers. Perhaps more important than any other set of skills, the consultants' ability to develop an effective questioning technique can lead to effective selling. It allows them to move from the general to specific, from technical to administrative, from high tension to relaxed exchange and from formal to casual and friendly. In short, it provides the consultant with the full range of persuasion techniques while not compromising the professional integrity of the relationship. The process is not so much to sell as it is to help the client/customer decide to buy.

Questions are important but only if consultants/salespeople use the responses. Developing listening skills is critical to the selling process because in selling services, these answers provide the information needed to develop an effective consulting approach. In addition to their value in providing information, they also serve to strengthen dialogue between consultants and clients and support this relationship. Relationship building and maintenance is an on-going and continual part of selling consulting services.

■ *Objections*

Objections need to be handled effectively. Genuine objections can be viewed as milestones pointing the way to the closing of the sale. As each one is overcome, the negotiations reach a step closer to agreement. Objections should be addressed directly and resolved before closing is attempted. Here, the consultant's primary tool is the question, "Why?" Why is the client hesitating? Why is a particular issue important to the client? Why does a particular feature of the proposal cause the client difficulty? And so forth.

One technique for dealing with objections is to acknowledge the objection by describing it in the consultant's own terms and asking the client to confirm that the understanding is correct. The consultant can then work with the client to develop a solution to the problem using impartial information and clear logic based on fact when possible. When countering an objection, the consultant must avoid arguments with the potential client, and rely on statements of observation and references that can be verified. One salesman once remarked, "You can slide a lot farther on grease than you can on sandpaper."

"Why is this of concern to you?" is a key question when encountering an objection and the principal tool in eliminating objections until there are none left and a close is possible. Some objections may be deep-seated, and the consultant must use sensitivity and probing questions to uncover them. One way to test whether a given objection is being stated accurately is to try a trial close. For example, if the consultant asks, "If I could solve this problem, would you give permission to proceed with this assignment?" and the client responds with a yes, the objection was probably genuine and can be resolved by a commitment to solve the problem. If the client answers the same question with a no or another objection, there is more at play, and the challenge for the consultant is to understand what is stopping the client from proceeding. More probing is required in this case.

Sources of Objections

Objections usually reflect unease on the part of the client. The nature of this unease needs to be understood before adjustments can be developed. These objections may arise from many sources, such as:

IT'S EXPENSIVE. Consulting costs money, and the benefits need to be understood as many times the cost.

IT'S RISKY. The benefits are not certain, but the costs of not proceeding may be more, and measures can be taken to limit the client's exposure should anticipated results not begin to appear early in the assignment.

USING CONSULTANTS IS A SIGN OF WEAKNESS. The client is proud of having achieved success in the past without help. This attitude can often be redirected to illustrate that many clients view the effective use of consultants as forward thinking and possibly providing added competitive advantages because some managers reportedly get nervous when they learn that one of their competitors is using a consultant.

CONFIDENTIALITY IS TOO IMPORTANT TO BRING IN OUTSIDERS. Consultants can implement special security measures in order that only those who need to know of the consultants' activities are aware of the project.

SOME CONSULTANTS ARE GOOD, BUT OTHERS ARE INCOMPETENT. The consultants' credentials may be good, but more references are needed. Requests for specific references are becoming increasingly common.

THE CONSULTANT WHO SELLS THE ASSIGNMENT MAY NOT BE THE ONE WHO PERFORMS THE WORK. Clients develop a sense of confidence in the consultant with whom the assignment has been discussed and developed, but there is concern that the consultant may not be accountable for successful project completion.[1] The client may need a more detailed description of how the project will be managed and who will be assigned to perform what work.

The fact that the consultant's "product" is usually being developed or customized during the selling process is a special characteristic of selling consulting services. It provides the consultant/salesperson with additional options in overcoming objections. In a consulting selling situation, the consultant/salesperson discusses objections in the context of all the flexibility the situation permits in order to overcome them. For example, scope can be modified, client involvement and contribution can be changed, the assignment can be modified into stages to give the client greater control, deadlines can be adjusted to suit client needs, payments might be deferred and so on.

Price

Discussion of price is one of the most sensitive parts of the selling process. The subject is usually raised by the client, and the consultant should generally defer this discussion until all objections are satisfied. The consulting service should be sold first on the basis of its ability to provide the client with desired benefits. All aspects of the service, its promised benefits, satisfying client objections and the relationship-building process should be complete before the price is addressed.

Professional services are rarely bought on the basis of price alone. When the selection of a consultant is based on price, it usually means that the client views all other aspects of the various consultants' approaches as essentially equal, and none has succeeded in differentiating from the competition. This is regarded as a failure in selling. Similarly, the sale of professional services is rarely lost because of price alone. The services and their providers are usually

---

[1] See Chapter 8, "Ethics and the Professional Consultant," for a discussion of "bait-and-switch" tactics.

sufficiently differentiated that price is not the main distinguishing factor. For this reason, discussion of price in the selling situation can generally be deferred until all other aspects of the potential professional engagement are discussed and agreement reached.

The consultant should wait for the client to introduce the question of price. Once price enters the discussion, attention becomes focused on this issue, and it is difficult to return to a further discussion of benefits, the primary object of the selling process. Benefits are what the consultant is selling, and price is not a benefit. When the client raises the question of price after all objections have been met, that is usually a signal that closing will take place immediately after and that the sales process is about to conclude. The consultant must be prepared to answer the price question when the right time to do so arises.

Although the client may want to discuss price early in the discussion, the subject should be deferred until all issues are resolved. It is usual for the consultant to request that a second meeting be planned at which the consultant will present a document (or make a presentation, if the project is complex) summarizing the first meeting for confirmation that all parties are in agreement. The consultant will then have had time to review the proposed project and its work content thoroughly and be able to provide a reliable estimate of price, which is the reason that the discussion of price is best deferred to the second meeting. Even then, discussion of price should still be deferred until all aspects of the project are confirmed and agreed to. If, during the second meeting, new issues arise, or old ones remain unresolved, the discussion of price should once again be deferred until the next meeting. In this way, when prices comes up for discussion, it is the only remaining possible source of objection.

Dealing with price as an objection is relatively straightforward when it is the only remaining issue. There are two basic options: reduce the work content or arrange payments such that the costs can be accommodated. The option of lowering the consultant's billing rate should not be considered. In effect, to do so devalues the consultant's level of professional expertise. Resourceful consultants can find considerable flexibility in revising consulting programs to reduce the work content without impairing quality. For example, projects might be divided into phases and some elements deferred until later, or client staff might be made available to perform some of the data collection and other research.

The relationship that develops during a selling situation, while friendly, is nevertheless a business relationship, and it is important that the business aspects of the situation be addressed dispassionately and precisely. Price can be stated in a number of ways that can ease the concerns of clients. Fees and expenses can be separated or combined and can be stated as a set amount per month. Billings can be spread over several of the client's accounting periods, perhaps even allocated over several budget years. They can be compared with other routine expenditures, such as the cost of a clerk's salary for a year and so forth.

■ *Control*

The salesperson should keep control of the selling process. Keep the ball in your court. Consultants/salespeople have responsibility for initiating, maintaining and concluding the selling process. The next step should always be theirs to ensure that the momentum is maintained over a series of meetings. To do this, consultants should end each meeting with a commitment with respect to the next meeting and its agenda, and they should always have something new to justify the next meeting.

A meeting should not close with the consultant saying to the potential client, "Give me a call when you have considered this." This is an invitation for the client to postpone. Rather, it should close with "I'll call you next Thursday to set up our meeting to discuss these issues." This way the consultant remains in control of the process but has the flexibility to adjust the work plan to suit the client. Similarly, the consultant should be in control in written correspondence, letting the client know what is needed and what to expect next.

■ *Closing*

Closing the sale is the most challenging aspect of selling professional services. Many consultants/salespeople can develop the client's expectations effectively, cultivate the relationship and display a keen understanding of the clients' needs with skillful questions but still not succeed in selling. They do not know how to close the sale; they neglect to ask for the order. Closing is a matter of timing and judgment. It occurs only when consultants/salespeople are confident that clients feel their needs are satisfied, objections have been met and resolved and the time for action has come.

Closing is direct and should be a confirmation of what has gone on before. It should contain no surprises, and it is the formal statement of agreement of the parties involved. The case study which began this chapter concludes with the simple statement by the consultant, "It's yours." In a professional selling situation, the closing confirmation may take the form of agreement as to timing and conditions of starting work. It should result in specific actions signaling the readiness of both parties to begin. Effective closing does not contain an invitation to continue considering the issues. It is expressed such that it confirms that the selling process is complete and the sale has been accomplished.

Early in the selling process, the consultant and client should agree on a schedule for decision making. While the best theoretical opportunity to close may be during the first meeting when the client's interest is at its peak, the closing may take place at the second or third meeting. The decision-making schedule helps bring some urgency to the situation. Generally, the faster the close, the better, because it signals to all concerned that there is agreement and a wish to move on and begin work. The longer the process, the more chance it will become bogged down with distractions.

Referral for Further Study

One particular distraction to be avoided if possible is a decision by the client that there is a need for additional technical input from specialists. Closing may be postponed indefinitely when the client

Another Perspective

HANDLING MEDICAL RECORDS A TECHNICAL ISSUE

Consultants are proposing a project to improve a large hospital's records management systems. The consultants are highly experienced in hospital records management systems, a very technical field, involving confidential material, off-size and photographic items and the like.

The client wonders whether the consultants' proposal should be reviewed by the head of hospital records before agreeing to proceed. The consultants are concerned that the head of hospital records may feel threatened by the proposed work and may recommend that the hospital staff perform the work themselves, without consultants.

The consultants need to reinforce the reasons for choosing experienced and objective professionals and focus on the benefits of change, avoiding any negative implications with respect to those currently involved in the hospital's records management practices. Further, the consultants might consider incorporating the records management staff in the early stages of the project and working together to develop and implement improvements. The consultants should try to avoid having the proposal referred to the records management staff.

decides that more study is needed before continuing to consider the consultant's proposal.

The introduction of additional people into the selling process, whether by the salesperson/consultant or the client, invariably leads to more objections and concerns. In addition, it often shifts the focus of discussion away from the benefits, which have already been considered and agreed upon. This can delay the process further and may discourage the client from proceeding at all.

Often the solution to a perceived need for more information is to agree on a preliminary project and begin the start-up stage of the work while a technical group collects the additional information, which can be reviewed in the course of the work program.

Sometimes the client is prepared to confirm a starting portion of the project, and that may be agreeable to the consultant in order to begin work. Once effective start-up has begun, many clients gain sufficient confidence to continue with the project. An important element in closing is to make the decision as easy as possible for the client.

"I'd Like to Think About It"

In the event that the sales meeting appears to be coming to a conclusion with the client announcing a decision to "think about it," the consultant knows that a sale has not taken place and that a new initiative is called for. One frequently successful tactic is to ask clients to identify the specific issues that they wish to think about so that both parties can think about them at the same time. Frequently, clients will then identify new or otherwise unresolved objections that might be dealt with immediately, thereby allowing for closing without further delay.

If deferral of closing is unavoidable, the consultant should immediately set up the next meeting and outline a focused agenda clearly centered on the specific issues that are preventing the client from proceeding with the assignment. The consultant can prepare additional information for presentation at that time.

Frequently, the "think about it" client position indicates that the question of timing has not been addressed fully. In other words, the consultant might have answered the question, "Why should we do this?" adequately, but not the second question, "Why should we do this now?" The first question addresses the merits of the project, whereas the second focuses on the client's decision-making environment. Probing this latter area may reveal other client concerns that may not have been addressed during the earlier discussions about the assignment characteristics.

Closing Signals

Closing signals from the client can occur at any time, and the consultant/salesperson must be alert for them. When they occur, the consultant should stop whatever process is occurring at that time and close the sale. Many successful closings, when they relate to consulting assignments, take the form of verbal confirmations, to be followed by a formal document, to ensure that the terms of reference and administrative details are unambiguously stated.

The discussion often becomes more summary in nature when an opportunity for closing arises. Agreement on what has been discussed and agreed to become the main agenda items between buyer and seller. The nuances of language become critical at this point. The consultant should use the inclusive first person plural (we and us) when summing up in preparation for closing. This reinforces the sense that the client and consultant are working together to accomplish a business transaction and beyond that, a business objective. Also, consultants should be positive in their language and refer to what they and client *will* accomplish rather than the conditional *would* accomplish. The former assumes a successful agreement; the latter that agreement is still uncertain. Comments like, "As soon as we complete the initial stages, we will do such and such," tend to move the discussion toward confirmation and closing.

As soon as the client displays an attitude with the underlying assumption that work is beginning, it is time to close and secure the agreement. When the client begins to be more concerned about administrative matters, such as the makeup of the steering committee, billing procedures, timing of work and the like, it is usually a signal to close. The consultant/salesperson should confirm the agreement with a series of short (closed probe) questions which anticipate the answer yes. Examples are: "Then we are agreed on that, are we?" or "You accept that, right?" or "Are we agreed on all the main issues, then?" Some complex situations call for a methodical review of all key aspects of the proposal in checklist fashion, with the consultant/salesperson asking for specific confirmation of agreement on each point. Once the client has agreed to all the main components, it will be illogical not to agree to the proposal as a whole.

INSIDER'S VIEW

Remember the salesperson's ABC: Always Be Closing.

Once consultants have asked for confirmation that an agreement has been reached (asked for the order), they should be silent and let the client make the choice of response. This silence creates a slight pressure that is important in order to help the client past a natural hesitancy to commit. If the consultant breaks the silence, the pressure is released, and the closing may be aborted. When the client speaks, the consultant should answer any questions directly, with a minimum of conversation, because the client is still making the commitment to accept the proposal. If the client becomes silent, the consultant should repeat the closing question and keep it central to the agenda of the moment.

Trial Closing

Closing the sale may be preceded by trial closings, during which the consultant tests to determine whether there are still unresolved issues that would forestall effective closing. A trial closing is a specific selling tactic in which the consultant attempts a closing (asks for the order) before all objections have been addressed. When trial closings fail, and clients do not confirm agreement on all key points, they usually present an objection. This may be only one of several unanswered objections which must be discussed. At this point, the consultant/salesperson undertakes further probing and restates and clarifies each objection as before. Adjustments in the proposed consulting program and a firm focus on the project benefits are the key selling tools in overcoming these remaining objections.

These trial closings are designed to elicit one of two responses:

1. confirmation that agreement has been reached and that the time has come to discuss details such as cost; or

2. a discussion of unresolved issues and objections is needed.

The consultant should be ready for either response and immediately pursue 1) closing or 2) further inquiry. Arguments are avoided. The consultant's persistence, resourcefulness and patience are all pressed into service to convert a trial close to a completed one. When questions such as "Are we agreed?" or "How soon can we start?" seem appropriate, another trial closing can be attempted. Several trial closings may be appropriate before the sale is concluded.

Trial closings don't always fail, so be ready for success if the trial close works. In that case, your objective has been achieved, and you should stop any remaining presentation, schedule the next step and leave.

False Closing

Sometimes the client sends premature signals, or the consultant misreads the situation and attempts to close before the client is ready. This situation is described as a false closing. The effect is the same as the trial closing, and it can be turned to positive advantage when it is used as a trial closing.

■ *Exit*

Once closing has been accomplished, it is time to make an exit. Consultants should thank the client, arrange the starting details, express appropriate eagerness to get started, gather up their material and leave. A common error inexperienced salespeople make is to stay too long after closing. The only thing that can happen after a successful closing is to reopen discussions and "unsell" the client. The temptation to remain and discuss the assignment further with the new client is natural, stemming from the relaxed feeling that one experiences after the negotiation is over. The consultant/salesperson needs to remain only long enough to thank the client, schedule the next contact and then leave. Relax with your colleagues or friends later. The sale has been accomplished.

See Checklist 4-3 for a review of the selling process.

Selling in the International Sector

People are people anywhere in the world, and the selling process outlined above is reasonably general internationally. Cultures differ, however, and values and behaviours differ along with them. What communicates sincerity and positive feelings in one part of

CHECKLIST 4-3: *Critical Elements in the Selling Process*

✔ Preparation – check your attitude; do research; set goals

✔ Purpose – for every meeting

✔ Focus – cite benefits, not features

✔ Questions – sell, rather than tell

✔ Objections – many sources – do not argue; understand them, work with clients to overcome them

✔ Price – keep to the last quote; and discuss it confidently

✔ Control – keep the initiative in the selling process

✔ Closing – help the client avoid procrastination by referral and postponement; recognize closing signals; attempt trial closes and ask for the order

✔ Exit – leave immediately when you have the order

the world may mean just the opposite in another. Words often mean different things when translated, and protocols can be minefields of offending actions.

Consultants selling internationally should be aware of major culturally based differences between Canadian behaviour and that in other countries in which they hope to do business. As globalization of business has expanded, so has the awareness that cross-cultural training can make the difference between success and failure in international dealings. Government agencies and a number of private organizations provide these services as well as language training. Canada is blessed with representatives from just about every country in the world, and many consultants discuss their upcoming visit to a foreign country with friends from that locale. Alternatively, many foreign cultures have local community groups that are usually pleased by requests to discuss cultural differences with Canadians who demonstrate the sensitivity to ask before venturing forth.

There are number of good books on the subject of international cross-cultural characteristics. David Ricks's *Blunders in International Business*[2] is comprehensive yet concise, and it is in its fourth printing since 1993. There are other sources as well as videos and films on the subject. Suffice it to say that there are many

INSIDER'S VIEW

The challenges of doing business internationally also arise when consulting in Canada across cultural lines.

simple ways to offend or to please international contacts, and they differ from culture to culture. International contacts will overlook blunders by tourists, but they will not be as forgiving to consultants who hope to do business with them.

Another Perspective

OFF TO INDIA

Before leaving on his first visit to India, a consultant sat down with an Indian colleague for a discussion about what to expect. During the discussion, the consultant noticed that his friend was moving his head in response to some of the consultant's remarks, a gesture that communicated, "well, perhaps, but I'm not sure I agree." This head wobble was frequent enough to cause doubt in the consultant's mind that he was understanding what his Indian friend meant. When he mentioned it, he found that this head wobble signified rather strong agreement and should be interpreted positively.

Later, in India, when a group of client managers were discussing his proposal among themselves, he saw the same vigorous side to side head movement. To the uninformed, it would have appeared that they were skeptical and perhaps disagreeing. This might have triggered an inappropriate response on the part of the visitor. The consultant knew better, however, and understood that he was succeeding with the sale.

[2]David A. Ricks, *Blunders in International Business* (US and UK: Blackwell Publishers, 1997).

Selling in the MUSH Sector

A special selling situation develops when consultants are presented with opportunities in what has become termed the MUSH sector by consultants. MUSH is an acronym for Municipalities, Utilities, Schools and Hospitals. These are large publicly supported non-profit institutions which represent specialized markets of significant size and are important purchasers of a wide range of consulting services. They tend to operate differently from most private companies and therefore present a special selling challenge. Some very large private sector firms have large bureaucracies and behave in many ways like the MUSH organizations. Occasionally, they use competitive bidding processes in much the same way.

While most organizations in the MUSH sector are concerned with productivity, they do not have the internal market pressures experienced by private sector organizations for cost reduction and increased efficiency. In addition, the services they provide are evaluated in terms of their social, as well as economic, value and quantitative measures of performance such as return on investment, stakeholder value and other productivity indicators are often imprecise and possibly controversial. For this reason, most MUSH organizations manage their operations through a series of administrative procedures and practices that centre around budgets that are developed and approved by their boards usually annually. Many consultants experience MUSH organizations as "budget-conscious" rather than "cost-conscious."

MUSH sector institutions are concerned with fairness in their purchasing practices. These institutions tend to be large, and they represent a significant and specialized market for many of their suppliers. In order to discourage unethical practices and to maintain processes open to public scrutiny, most have developed detailed and rigorous competitive bidding procedures that must be followed by would-be suppliers. Consultants wishing to sell their services to these institutions need to be familiar with these practices and develop selling tactics that can help them compete successfully.

In general, the competitive bidding process comprises some or all of the following modules, each of which provides selling opportunities.

■ *Announcement*

When an institution is seeking a supplier for a particular current need, it must first announce to potential suppliers that a bidding competition is going to take place. There are several ways to do this:

1. It may have a preselected or approved list of potential suppliers from which to choose.

2. It may post a notice in specific media that target the type of supplier it is trying to reach.

3. It may simply place an advertisement in an appropriate publication and invite respondents.

The choice of announcement method sends important signals to potential bidders. For example:

1. If the consultant receives a specific invitation to participate, it usually comes as a result of earlier marketing efforts by the consultant in registering with the requesting agency, possibly followed up with regular visits to officials in the agency to discuss current situations. (See Chapter 3: "Marketing Your Consulting Services.") Sometimes it comes as a result of the reputation of the specific consultancy in similar work. In any case, it should be regarded as high priority for response. Even if the consultant decides to forego this particular opportunity, it is important to acknowledge the importance of the specific invitation. Protocol is important to ensure that the prospective client understands that the invitation is valued. In declining to bid, the consultant should write a formal letter thanking the inviting party, giving the reasons for declining and expressing a wish to continue

to be considered for other opportunities. Documentation is particularly important in the MUSH sector. Even when personal relationships exist, all formal communication should be written and appropriate protocol observed.

2. With increased use of electronic communication systems such as MERX, the Web pages of the international financial institutions, such as the World Bank and specialized electronic billboards and publications, consulting requirements in a variety of fields are regularly publicized. Consultants scan these constantly for bidding opportunities in the MUSH sector. If the consultant learns of the opportunity from a specialized publication or electronic billboard and elects not to bid, a letter declining to participate is usually not required. All registered consultants will see this notice. It can be assumed, therefore, that competition will be keen for most projects, provided they are adequately funded. Consultants should respond to these invitations when they possess particularly strong and relevant credentials and/or can partner with associates whose specialty can provide a competitive advantage.

Other characteristics of the competition and required bidding procedures can influence the decision on whether to participate as well. For example, there may be insufficient time to prepare an appropriate response, or there are indications that consultants who have previously performed for this agency or are resident in a particular local jurisdiction will be given preference. Similarly, you may have particular knowledge, possibly gained from your visits to agency officials, that this type of work is characteristically awarded to one of a select group of consultants because of their familiarity with agency practice and policies.

3. Some organizations are required to advertise competitions in the general press but, in general, a broadly advertised competition should receive the lowest priority,

particularly when it requests proposals rather than statements of qualifications. These competitions can receive a large number of responses from a wide array of individuals and organizations, some qualified, many not. When consultants feel they are particularly well-qualified, they should immediately contact the advertiser and request an interview to obtain terms of reference and discuss the client's needs. If this overture is refused, consultants should probably forego the opportunity. Many large firms respond to these broadly advertised requests only if a member of their professional staff has peculiarly relevant qualifications and is willing to devote the time required to respond effectively. Alternatively, some submit standardized proposals which require little work to prepare but may succeed in getting them on a short list, at which time they will commit the necessary resources to compete vigorously for the project.

■ *Process*

Having reflected on the way the competition has been announced and decided to commit the resources necessary to win, consultants should now turn their attention to the content of the announcement to understand the process to be followed. There are two basic approaches in formal bidding processes:

1. The buyer issues only a request for qualifications (RFQ).

2. The buyer issues a request for proposals (RFP).

The RFQ approach signals that the client wishes to prequalify bidders and avoid the administrative work in receiving, evaluating and responding to a large and diverse set of bidders, many of which may not be adequately qualified. Consultants who succeed in qualifying will receive RFPs.

Many consultants prefer the prequalification (RFQ) option, provided enough information is made available on which to base specific and hopefully differentiated responses. The cost of preparing specific qualifications is far less than a full proposal. As a consequence, consultants will generally continue to pursue opportunities that adopt this process and frequently not those that require a full proposal before sufficient information is made available on which to base a competitive response. A critical variable in this decision is the opportunity to question the prospective client before submitting a response to the advertisement.

■ *Contacts*

A key determinant in deciding whether to pursue a MUSH opportunity is the opportunity to sell. Many bidding procedures are very restrictive as to how much access prospective bidders have to client personnel during the proposal preparation process. The more opportunity the consultant has to make these contacts, the better the consultant's true understanding of the project and its several agendas. As a consequence, the more effective consultants are at raising the important questions, the more opportunity they have of gaining the support of client personnel, and the better the chances of a successful bid. Conversely, many MUSH administrators are concerned that bidders may influence the staff unduly and gain unfair, possibly unethical, advantage in the process. Consequently, contact restrictions are often stated as part of the announcement information.

Most announcements contain information about how to obtain a copy of the terms of reference for the proposed project and identify an official to contact for further information. The material should be obtained and studied carefully, and the identified contact should be used as early in the process as possible. Ideally, the consultant can arrange a personal interview, in which case the consultant should frame two sets of questions to ask. One set is designed to obtain clarification on the substance of the terms of reference and to demonstrate the consultant's familiarity with the subject matter. The other is a set of general questions that focus on the business relationship to be established between the successful bidder and the client. These general questions include:

- Why is the work being done?
- Why is it being done now (not last month or next year)?
- Why was this particular method of notification used?
- How many bidders are expected to respond?
- Can interviews be arranged with others in the organization?
- Will there be an opportunity to make a formal presentation?
- How will the steering committee be comprised?
- What are the criteria for selection and how are they weighted?
- What is the budget for this project?
- Can the due date be extended? This may be a particularly revealing question in that it often provides information as to the concern the client has for the merits of the assignment. If the contact person can discuss an extension, this may mean that the assignment is responding to a genuine concern felt at a senior level of the organization to select the best possible consultant and not to be constrained by procedural issues. Alternatively, rigid adherence to the rules of procedure might indicate that there are reasons other than the merits of the project for commissioning this assignment at this time.
- What format and how many copies of the proposal or statement of qualifications are required?
- What are the key administrative procedures concerning billing schedules, expense reporting, interim deadlines, provision for holdbacks and so forth?
- How will the project be administered?

Frequently, agencies providing competitive bidding opportunities are reluctant to provide personal interviews to potential bidders. Instead, they provide a briefing session, and/or they require that all questions be submitted in writing, with the questions and responses then circulated to all bidders. Briefing sessions can be helpful, but, in general, they discourage questions because some bidders may feel that intelligent questions could reveal their competitive strategy. Nonetheless, the above inquiries and similar ones are still useful and can be managed so as to reveal little about the questioner's competitive or professional approach.

◼ *Presentation Opportunities*

Frequently, competitive bidding procedures do not specifically invite presentations from bidders, but they can be arranged on request. Usually, all bidders are provided with the same opportunities. Consultants who have developed confidence in their selling and presenting skills welcome these opportunities and should press for them. Hard copy provided at the conclusion of these presentations will answer the request for qualifications or proposals required by the bidding procedure.

◼ *Ideal Scenario*

The spectrum of opportunities associated with competitive bidding is broad. In general, the most attractive are those that provide the consultant with several opportunities to sell; the least attractive are those in which the consultant is asked only to submit a proposal in writing. Further, the most attractive ones permit the consultant to explore the opportunity through stages of gradually increasing resource commitment, such as the sequence that moves through the following steps:

- Initial briefing
- Prequalification to gain a position on a short list
- Thorough briefing and interview opportunities to understand the situation fully
- Opportunities for presentation responding to known selection criteria, including budget parameters
- Formal proposal submission, possibly as part of the presentation

Generally, clients that provide the most attractive bidding processes are those who are more experienced in working with consultants. Conversely, clients whose bidding process is rigid and protective are often inexperienced clients and are suspicious of consultants. Frequently, these inexperienced client groups within the MUSH sector are genuine in their wish to attract the best consultant for their needs, but, unfortunately, their rigid bidding process reduces their chance of success. The more experienced consultants may not respond to their invitation.

Rigid clients will require more work by successful bidders to gain their confidence and help them learn how to work with consultants. Consultants experienced in working in the MUSH sector develop skills and techniques unique to this administratively structured environment; for tips on selling to the MUSH sector, see Checklist 4-4. While many bidders may experience selling in the MUSH sector as constrained and limited, effective and confident consultants/salespeople will see selling in the competitive bidding environment as a special challenge to their resourcefulness and ingenuity. They will find opportunities to differentiate and sell in a large and potentially rewarding market.

CHECKLIST 4-4: *Selling to the MUSH Sector*

Recognize the preparation effort involved and assess the opportunity carefully by considering:

✔ Announcement – evaluate the method – invitation, billboard, advertisement

✔ Process – RFQ or RFP?

✔ Contacts – assess the opportunities and constraints in contacting client agency

✔ Presentations – will you have an opportunity to sell?

Decide whether to enter the competition, then if you are proceeding, decide to win and respond completely to the Terms of Reference.

Selling your services can be challenging, but it is essential to the process of building and maintaining a professional consulting

practice. Whether within a large firm of professionals or a sole practitioner, selling is the way the industry competes. Effective marketing programs that promote the consultancy and its competencies and achievements may result in opportunities to sell. Effective selling itself determines whether the assignment is obtained on acceptable (and profitable) terms.

Selling is a logical process of influencing emotions. Interpersonal relationships predominate, and, as with most human relationships, honesty and openness contribute positively to the experience. The key to selling for most consultants is to overcome their own fears and convert their attitude from problem-seeing and problem-solving (on which most of their training is probably based) to one of seeking out challenges and opportunities for themselves and their clients. It sometimes takes courage and some risk taking, but the rewards are substantial. It is essential, therefore, for consultants to develop effective selling skills and practices, and like any skills, to continue to maintain and build them.

FIVE

The Proposal

Perhaps the most important component in any consulting engagement is the agreement between client and consultant. The proposal contains all the elements of a contract and is the main document on which the consulting relationship is based. In some cases, notably public sector institutions, a formal contract is executed following acceptance of the proposal. Unlike proposals in other industries, a consulting proposal is not merely a sales pitch. It is confirmation of client requirements and a program to address them as expressed by the consultant. It describes each party's obligation to the other and details the parameters of the project such as timing, planned outcomes and costs. When accepted by the client, the proposal becomes a binding contract between the parties. It guides each party's activities and spells out their expectations. If it performs these tasks well, the proposal is an effective consulting tool; if not, it can become the Achilles' heel of the consulting relationship and a centre of dispute rather than a vehicle for cooperation. It is also the first test of the consultant's ability to understand what the client has expressed in the information provided and during any meetings leading up to its submission.

The proposal may take the form of a one-page letter or a multi-volume set of thick documents. Some government agencies and MUSH sector clients issue terms of reference that require extensive detail and separate documents to describe the technical and cost portions of the proposal. They can be very costly to produce. It may be a simple, informal confirmation of an arrangement already agreed between familiar parties, or it may be the first formal communication between a consultant and potential client, possibly in a competitive bidding process. Or it can be anywhere between these extremes. Even in the most casual of engagements, because some remuneration is involved, the consulting arrangement should be documented.

For most people, the act of describing a situation in written form forces both the writer and the reader to address and resolve ambiguities. These ambiguities often mask issues that are not resolved in the minds of the parties and, if left unresolved, they can cause disputes that might have been avoided had they been addressed at the outset.

The proposal is more than merely a formalization of the consulting agreement; it is a selling tool as well. Chapter 4, "Selling Your Services" discusses the relationship-building process as constant throughout a project. Each presentation, report and memo of communication between client and consultant presents an opportunity to build and maintain the relationship. The proposal comes at the formation stage of the professional relationship and should be viewed as an important selling document. Putting "sell" into a proposal is a major focus of this chapter.

Whether a proposal is a simple letter confirming a verbal agreement or a detailed and complex document, the basic elements are the same. Proposals need to establish expectations as to what each party will do, when and how much it will cost. Most contain information regarding the work to be done and what outcomes are expected. Some go into great detail regarding the work plan and expected results. It is usually helpful to reflect on important contextual forces that have led to the proposed work so the parties can recognize changing conditions that can occur during the work. Either party may want to adjust the assignment, and this is easier when a clearly articulated proposal is available for reference.

This chapter focuses primarily on what a proposal should contain. It is organized according to the sequence of elements that comprise a typical proposal table of contents, followed by a description of characteristics which distinguish effective proposals from mediocre ones. Some elements are combined in some proposals, others are elaborated in greater detail – notably the Proposed Work Program. The level of detail and format is a matter of judgment for the consultant and reflects the relationship with the client, and the stated requirements of the Request For Proposal (RFP), if one has been issued. The chapter concludes with some suggestions for ensuring that the proposal contributes as much as possible to the selling process.

Proposal Contents

Although effective proposals differ (sometimes widely) in their format, over the years, some standardization seems to have evolved. In fact, some government agencies and international financial institutions that commission a lot of consulting work may specify in detail the format that they require. For example, the Canadian

---

FIGURE 5-1: *Proposal Outline*

TABLE OF CONTENTS

Covering Letter and Letter of Transmittal

I. Introduction

II. Background

III. Project Objectives and Scope

IV. Proposed Methodology

V. Proposed Work Program

VI. Project Organization and Staffing

VII. Timing and Costs

VIII. Summary of Project Deliverables

Appendices

International Development Agency (CIDA) frequently provides specific outlines and format instructions, complete with maximum pages allowed for each section. One is illustrated in Figure 5-1.

The appendix at the back of the book contains a complete demonstration proposal written to a fictional client. Also in that appendix is a sample proposal letter that covers the same fictional situation, but which demonstrates the use of letter format for proposals where formal proposals are not required. The following is what each of the proposal elements should contain and accomplish.

■ *Covering Letter and the Letter of Transmittal*

These two documents are both in letter format and on letterhead, but there the similarity ends. The covering letter is a short letter attached to the proposal document, but not bound into it, which "hands" the proposal to the person designated to receive it. That person may or may not be the same one to whom the letter of transmittal is addressed. Sometimes the process calls for proposals to be delivered to a specific person by a certain time; the covering letter is addressed to that person and relates to the client's requirements for proposal delivery in specified format and in a specified number of copies. It confirms that these instructions have been followed.

In contrast, the letter of transmittal is an integral part of the proposal and is usually bound into the front of it. It is a formal communication between the client and consultant and identifies the key individuals responsible for the consulting engagement. It serves a purpose beyond these protocol issues by providing an opportunity to summarize the key benefits that the client can expect from this assignment, and it expresses the consultant's appreciation for the opportunity to contribute. The letter of transmittal provides the consultant's letterhead information, a handy reference for the client.

■ *Introduction*

The introduction should be a brief section describing the events that led up to this proposal submission at this time. For example, a request was made from someone to someone, perhaps to the consultant, and this proposal is the response. The request may have given rise to some preliminary work by the consultant (visits and discussions, research etc.), and the results of this preliminary work are used in this proposal. In other words, the introduction sets up the contractual context within which client and consultant have been drawn into this situation. It addresses the questions:

- How did we learn of this consulting opportunity?
- What have we done since learning of this opportunity to increase our understanding of the need for this work?
- How does our proposal reflect what we know and understand about the need for this work?
- Why do we believe we are particularly well situated to perform this work with excellence at this time?

■ *Background*

The background section refocuses the proposal on the client's situation and needs. It is an important part of the proposal because it provides consultants with an opportunity to show they understand what the client needs and why. It also allows consultants to distinguish themselves from their competitors by demonstrating superior knowledge of the technical issues involved and a keen understanding of the reasons the client is requesting these professional services at this time. A well-developed background section can be the most important factor in differentiating winning proposals from run-of-the-mill ones. Untrained or inexperienced consultants are frequently criticized for merely rehashing the client's recent history and information the client provided as part of the Request For Proposal (RFP) material. In contrast, a good statement of background provides a point of view and a specific interpretation of the situation and helps clients gain a perspective on individual consultants. All elements in this background section should be linked directly to the need for this work at this time and the special skills which are needed to carry out the work successfully. The background section should demonstrate that the consultant has asked and understands the answers to the following questions:

- Why does the client want this work done?
- Why now? Why not last week, next week, next year or last year?
- Why does the client think a consultant could help? Why not do this work in-house?
- Why is this the right project for the client to undertake, given the information they have provided?

These and other similar questions can provide the basis for a powerful background section. Chapter 4, "Selling Your Services" stresses that the key to effective salesmanship is asking the right questions. Some consultants tend to focus too early in the discussion on what clients say they want done. That question should be one of the *last* to be addressed, only after the consultant has gained a thorough understanding of the "why" questions (above) and is satisfied that the client is contemplating the right project.

Frequently, a proposal is successful because it is significantly different. It may describe a project that is different from what the client originally requested but, in fact, is what the client really needs to accomplish and what the client wants. When the client has defined a project that will not provide the results the client wants, experienced consultants recognize this as an opportunity to reopen discussions with the client and help revise the approach. When the consultant is successful, the competition is left behind.

Nevertheless, submitting a proposal defining a project or program that is significantly different from the RFP requirements is risky, and consultants should be sure of their ground before doing so. The client may have good (perhaps unstated) reasons for inviting proposals in a particular way and may dismiss out of hand submissions that do not conform to the RFP.

■ *Project Objectives and Scope*

Project objectives, the essence of what the client hopes to achieve by undertaking this work, should be a short, one-sentence statement. Ideally, it should probably not even be a complete sentence but rather an infinitive clause beginning with "to achieve," "to discover," "to implement," or some other phrase which completes the question, "Given the conclusions drawn from the background statement, why are we doing this?" Subordinate objectives may be included as well, but the statement of project objectives should be kept short, direct and to the point.

The statement of scope is often logically combined with the statement of objectives because it defines the limits of the project. Sometimes, it fits more appropriately with the methodology section, and occasionally, it is sufficiently complex and central to the client-consultant relationship that it justifies its own section. It focuses on the range of activities that will be carried out and, what may be as important, the limits to the proposed work.

A carefully articulated scope section can avoid serious misunderstandings which can arise later, about who is supposed to do what and to what extent. It should describe in definite terms:

- sources of information to be used in the course of the work – how information will be obtained and whose responsibility (client or consultant) it is to ensure that it is available
- organizations and people to be contacted in the course of the work, both within the client and outside
- work included and excluded in this proposed work program that establishes (and limits) the consultant's mandate

Two key parameters of consulting are affected by the scope section: the amount of professional time that will be spent and the level of expenses that will be incurred on behalf of the client. Unless this scope section is clear about what work will and will not be done during the assignment, disagreements over the completeness or thoroughness of the work can arise between client and consultant. These invariably revolve around whether there is sufficient budget remaining to perform the work to the client's satisfaction. Work that may be needed to satisfy the client may involve additional travel expenses as well as time. The consultant may see this as beyond the agreed scope of the work, while the client sees it as within that scope.

It is equally important to agree on what will *not* be done as it is on what *will* be done. Vague descriptive words such as "sufficient" or "adequate to demonstrate" and the like should raise red flags of warning that there may be a need to discuss the level of work proposed with the client and make sure that both parties are in agreement. The scope section provides the opportunity to clarify issues before work begins and before resources are committed.

Clients expect consultants to define the limits of the work they will perform, but some consultants seem timid in stating explicitly what they do *not* expect to do. Any consulting assignment is subject to surprises as discoveries are made in the course of the work. A carefully defined scope section can serve as a basis for agreement on additional work that may become justified as the consulting work progresses. Clients want to feel they are entering into a good business arrangement with their consultant, and a clearly defined project scope can give them confidence in this.

■ *Proposed Methodology*

The proposed methodology section describes in broad terms how the consultant expects to achieve the objectives of the assignment. This section comprises two elements:

- a basic description of approach; the key premises underlying the choice of technique to perform the work
- the methods to be used; the practicalities of applying the techniques selected in the real-world conditions of the client

Consultants are expected to be more than merely warm bodies available to perform technical tasks for clients. Increasingly, they are expected to provide clients with conceptual and theoretical insight into the operation of their enterprise and the environment within which it functions. Consultants who are selected on the basis of having done similar work in the past, or who are particularly knowledgeable about an industry or technology are expected to apply this special skill set to the client's specific situation. This means they must be able to select specialized knowledge from their previous work and develop principles to serve their current client.

At the same time, clients believe their situations are unique, and, to some extent, every situation is. Consultants should be able to help the client make the bridge between general theory and principles and the specific and unique practical requirements of the client's current needs. The proposed methodology section of the proposal provides consultants with the opportunity to demonstrate their abilities to do so.

In addition to understanding the general principles underlying the consultant's proposed approach, the client wants to know what the consultant plans to do in practical terms. For example, if this project is to be a survey, what kind (mail, phone, physical observation, personal interviews; structured or in-depth)? What observation methods are best for this assignment? What measurement techniques? The proposed methodology section addresses these questions and describes why a particular approach is proposed, and, perhaps also, why others have been rejected.

The proposed methodology section also provides an excellent opportunity for graphic displays. Conceptual diagrams depicting theoretical models and abstractions and premises developed as a result of similar work can provide effective tools to illustrate the consultant's in-depth understanding of the client's situation. Tables describing interactions between important external and internal factors help clients understand how the consultant sees the relationship between the client's operations and the environment within which it operates. Flow diagrams describing how consultant and client will collaborate can be introduced in this section, effectively using graphic communication.

Increasingly, clients want to learn about new concepts and techniques that affect their enterprise. They look to their consultants to instruct them and their staff, not just in techniques, but in basic principles as well. The proposed methodology section of a proposal is an excellent place for consultants to demonstrate their skill and sophisticated understanding, and the effective use of graphics can be a powerful tool for this. Clients appreciate that effective communication is an important key to a successful project; consultants that can demonstrate facility in both verbal and graphic

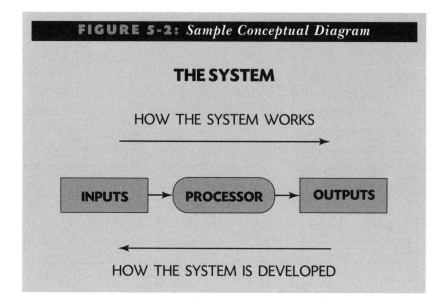

FIGURE 5-2: *Sample Conceptual Diagram*

THE SYSTEM

HOW THE SYSTEM WORKS

INPUTS → PROCESSOR → OUTPUTS

HOW THE SYSTEM IS DEVELOPED

communications reassure clients that they will be able to provide understandable results. Graphics can clarify, while excessive wording can bog down. Figure 5-2 provides an example of a conceptual diagram.

The conceptual diagram in Figure 5-2 depicts a generalized system model with input, processor and output. It further describes the two directions of flow that differentiate the way a system should be developed and the way in which it operates once developed. While systems are thought of as operating from input through a processor to accomplish an output, they should be developed in reverse order. The desired output should be specified first, then the enabling processor determined. Finally, the needed inputs can be specified.

The system concept can be applied to many situations and serves to illustrate the relationships between inputs (which may be resources, ideas, technologies, materials etc.), outputs (which may be any type of conversion of the inputs) and processors (which are anything that acts on the inputs to produce outputs).

The purpose of the conceptual diagram is to provide a basis of understanding between consultant and client. Consultants encounter similar situations in a number of environments and are able to develop these models to help focus clients on their situation more clearly. Models, such as the one illustrated above, when applied by a consultant to a specific client situation, can help clients understand their own situation better. Consultants and clients can discuss the issues clearly and appreciate together the dynamics of making improvements when they communicate on the same theoretical base. Increasingly, clients are requiring that their consultants not only examine their situation to make recommendations for improvement, but also want their consultants to increase their theoretical and substantive knowledge. Other examples of concept graphics can be found in Chapter 7, "Performing the Work."

■ *Proposed Work Program*

The sequence of steps involved in performing the work necessary to accomplish the objectives are described in this section. Each project is unique and therefore, to some extent, so is each work program. Nevertheless, there are some common patterns:

- The proposed work program should begin with some form of start-up step which signals to all parties that the assignment has begun. This should confirm key scheduled dates to mark progress, establish the client relationship structure (a steering committee, assigned client staff commitment etc.), and the administrative procedures for billing, among other things. This initial work step is discussed more fully in Chapter 7, "Performing the Work."
- The series of steps should be laid out in sufficient detail to let the client know what to expect in terms of demands on client staff, consultant on-site activities and the nature of the information to be developed in the course of the work. It is often advisable to break the proposed work program into steps and subordinate steps.
- Each work step, and sometimes each subordinate step, should have a defined purpose. Frequently, as the work is completed, specific elements will generate a deliverable of some type. That

may be a memo, an internal project-related note or document, a draft report or even a final report to the client. All items in this combination of working papers and reporting documents are the property of the client who is entitled to them. Exceptions, such as confidential interview notes and the like, should be specified. In describing the proposed work program, it is often helpful to the client to include a description of the expected deliverables that will result from the work steps that generate them.

• The more specific the information included in this section, the more likely the client will feel a sense of control over the project and the consultants performing it. Generally, the more confident clients feel in their relationship with their consultants, the less detail they require in the proposed work program. When a client and consultant have worked closely together, the client may dispense with the proposal altogether, preferring instead to trust the consultant to do what is needed. Clearly there are trade-offs: the level of detail consultants need to provide in describing the work planned will vary depending on the client's expressed wishes and the familiarity between client and consultant.

■ *Proposed Organization and Staffing*

In this section of proposals, consultants display their experience in assembling the right mix of skills and experience to achieve excellence in performing the work and in organizing the team to perform effectively. This section provides more opportunities to use graphics to present a project organization chart and a skills and experience matrix. Both should include provision for client staff participation, as well as summarize the fundamental attributes of the consultants who will be doing the work.

The designation of specific consultants should be regarded as a commitment. Substitution should be made only with client approval. There is often a time delay between the submission of the proposal and the notification of acceptance by the client. This leads to the situation where proposed staff are legitimately engaged elsewhere. In these cases, the client should be given the option of accepting a substitution of equal merit or postponing the project until the individuals originally proposed become available.

Project Organization Chart

Typical elements in a project organization chart are:

- The client representative is often a steering committee but frequently an individual manager or executive will be ultimately responsible for managing the consulting relationship.
- In most cases, the consultant in charge of the assignment is the project manager. In some complex assignments, however, there may be a project officer to whom the project manager is responsible. The project officer would have the responsibility for managing the relationship between consultant and client and accepting overall responsibility for the outcome of the project.
- Where a number of consultants are involved, they may be assigned to project teams or given specific roles that can be identified on the organization chart. The project teams will have team leaders who will be responsible for the team's performance.
- Frequently, additional experts on specific elements of the work will be included in the project organization. They can be identified as technical advisors, usually reporting to the project manager. Similarly, key individuals from the client's organization may be identified as supporting the project as client advisors, also reporting, for this purpose, to the project manager.

Figure 5-3 is a typical project organization chart for a fairly complex engagement. Simpler projects may involve as few as one person from the client, and one consultant. Where practical, however, even this simple relationship can benefit from a third person to ensure objectivity and quality.

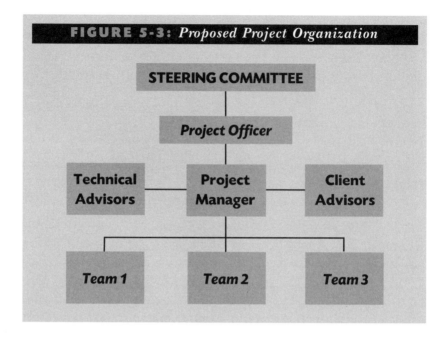

FIGURE 5-3: *Proposed Project Organization*

Skills and Experience Matrix

The skills and experience matrix provides an opportunity for consultants to display how well they understand the complex nature of clients' requirements. It also provides a means for the consultant to show how these needs have been satisfied by the proposed consulting team. These consultants may be augmented by client personnel assigned to the project, and they can be included in the matrix as well. Each case will have its own unique requirements for skills and experience. Figure 5-4 illustrates how a skills and experience matrix might look.

In addition to the matrix, brief outlines on the skills and experience of each of the assigned staff members should appear in this section. More detailed professional résumés can be appended to the proposal. These brief outlines should stress the relevance of the individuals and their suitability for the roles to which they will be assigned.

FIGURE 5-4: *Skills and Experience Matrix*

SKILLS AND EXPERIENCE REQUIRED

Assigned Staff	Specific Industry Knowledge	Industrial Marketing Research	Sales Force Organization and Management	Productivity Measurement Techniques	Inventory and Logistics Management	Cost Analysis
R. Johnston	Expert	Expert	Familiar	Basic Principles	Basic Principles	Basic Principles
B.J. Wylie	Familiar	Expert	Expert	Expert	Familiar	Basic Principles
R.W. Austin	Familiar	Familiar	Basic Principles	Expert	Expert	Expert
I. Offillitch	Basic Knowledge	Basic Principles	Basic Principles	Expert	Familiar	Expert
(Client Staff Assigned)	Expert	Basic Principles	Familiar	Basic Principles	Basic Principles	Familiar

■ *Timing and Costs*

Timing

Timing has two dimensions: the professional time involved and the elapsed time to complete the work. Some clients want to feel in control of the amount of professional time expended. They may request information on billing rates and how they are accumulated. This may occur particularly when the consultants are to play advisory roles, on call or on retainer. Some government clients require details about billing rates, how they are derived and how much time the various consultants will commit to the project, but most clients focus on overall cost.

Most consulting is in the form of projects with defined outcomes and completion dates. In these cases, clients are frequently concerned with the sequence of events and the timing of reporting sessions. Meetings need to be scheduled with the consultants to minimize the disruption of day-to-day activities that the project may cause. The proposal could include a chart illustrating how the work steps will be arranged and scheduled, and what the critical dates for formal meetings will be.

The project management and control technique to be used forms a key element in timing. Complex projects containing subordinate projects that can proceed independently, but that can affect the timing of other work steps, may require elaborate project management and control systems. When subcontracting arrangements are part of the project, and when key equipment purchases and/or technical design elements form a significant part of the cost and the work, these more elaborate control systems may be warranted. In these complex situations, project management may require administrative support resources that can add significantly to the total costs, but may be necessary to achieve on-time performance. Some consulting agreements include penalties to the consultant for late performance.

Yet, most consulting is not this complicated, and satisfactory control can be maintained through careful scheduling and monitoring of activities and deadlines. The Gantt chart which is frequently used in proposals is a common format for timing. It displays the various work elements, their sequence and timing, and the approximate elapsed time required to perform them. It is important to list the work steps exactly as they appear in the proposed work program. More detail may be required for actual project control purposes, but work steps headings are usually sufficient at the proposal stage to enable clients to assess consultants' commitment to effective control. A more detailed Gantt chart can be developed for project management as part of the start-up work step once the work begins. Figure 5-5 is an example of a Gantt chart illustrating the level of detail usually effective in proposals.

FIGURE 5-5: *Proposed Project Schedule (Gantt Chart)*

					Weeks From Start						
Work Steps	1	2	3	4	5	6	7	8	9	10	11
1. Start-up	▬										
2. Secondary Data Review	▬	▬									
3. Survey Setup and Training		▬									
4. Internal Interviews			▬	▬	▬						
5. Survey Execution			▬	▬	▬	▬	▬				
6. Analysis and Brainstorming							▬	▬			
7. Draft Presentation							▬	▬			
8. Present Results								▬			
9. Report Preparation									▬	▬	▬
Key Team Meetings	▬		▬			▬		▬		▬	
Formal Client Reporting	•		•						•		•

Costs

The discussion of costs in the proposal has several elements:

- The *principles* on which the fees are calculated and the expected *levels* of fees for the work described.
- How *expenses* incurred in the course of the work will be charged, and what type and level of expenses can be expected.
- How the *billing* process will be carried out.
- How the client's needs to *control* the fees of the engagement will be accommodated and *termination* of work.

PRINCIPLES AND LEVELS OF FEES AND COSTS

There are four basic principles on which fees are commonly based:

1. estimated

2. fixed or maximum

3. contingency

4. retainer

Each has its uses and limitations as clients seek to limit their fees and exposure to risk and at the same time, ensure they have the services of the consultants they want.

Estimated Fees

The traditional practice commonly used by the larger firms is to estimate the amount of professional time required to perform the work and calculate the estimated fees to reflect the total time of the professionals involved. Various professionals will likely warrant different billing rates, depending on their level of skill and experience.

Fixed or Maximum Fees

In recent years, clients have increasingly preferred a fixed or maximum fee quotation from professionals. This focuses the cost on output instead of effort. Not only does this limit clients' potential financial exposure, but many clients prefer the administrative simplicity this provides. They consider this arrangement as one of buying *results*.

Contingency Fees

Contingency fees have been common in consulting for many years, particularly for productivity improvement and recruiting projects. More recently, the related practices of benefits- or results-based billing have become more popular. There is potential for conflict of interest with this form of compensation, and there are questions concerning professional objectivity and ethics when compensation is based on achieving a certain defined result. Chapter 8, "Ethics and the Professional Consultant," addresses this and other issues more fully. As a practical matter, it is sometimes difficult to agree with the client after the fact about what results are directly attributable to the professional work and what would have occurred without the consultant's involvement.

Several large consulting firms have developed successful and lucrative practices based on contingency fees, and in the current business environment of downsizing and outsourcing, short-term priorities predominate. This may eliminate some of the ethical and practical difficulties contingency fees present. A variation – finder's fees – has been a common practice in mergers and acquisitions, development project financing and prospecting among other relationships in which consultants receive nothing until something results from their efforts. Many consultants and some professional organizations have actively discouraged this basis for providing consulting services.

Retainer Fees

Retainers are also a common means of compensation. This fee option is often selected when clients want advisors available on an ongoing basis or when clients want a series of similar tasks performed when they arise. An example is a consultant in tariffs and trade who is retained by clients to examine tariff rulings and to try to obtain favourable treatment under existing regulations as goods are purchased and cross the borders. Specific projects may arise, but these can be proposed separately.

The retainer is a regular (often monthly) amount paid to consultants committed to clients to provide on-going services specified by the client (for example, environmental scanning, market performance tracking, public policy monitoring etc.). Consultants on retainer generally are expected to be available for their clients on short notice. The retainer is calculated to cover the normal consultant billing rate based on an expected level of effort. It is important to note that this arrangement usually precludes, or at least limits, the consultant accepting work from the client's competitors. Retainer levels are arrived at through negotiation. They should be reviewed periodically and adjusted, depending on how much the client is making use of the consultant and how restrictive it is to the consultant's practice.

The expected level of cost is usually included in the proposal, even when the fee is merely an estimate. This confirms that the client and consultant are agreed on the overall level of effort anticipated. In some cases, however, particularly where research is a major component and the amount of work is clearly dependent on findings that are largely unpredictable, cost-plus arrangements may be desirable. These are open-ended projects in which the client agrees to the work regardless of cost because it is investigatory or developmental in nature, and the outcomes are difficult to predict. Clients who participate in cost-plus arrangements, wish to provide their consultants with the flexibility to do what is needed to accomplish the project's goals. The value of these goals generally far exceeds the probable cost of the consultant. In these cases, project control is usually accomplished through regular interim assessments and budget checkpoints.

Expenses
Expenses are usually a relatively small portion of total consulting cost and should be dealt with as a matter of administrative routine. They normally include travel and living costs, when consultants are required to be away from home, long-distance calls and other out-of-pocket incidentals. Many clients and consultants use standard per diem schedules (often consistent with government allowances) to reduce the administrative work in sorting through receipts.

Some charge for photocopies, faxes, typing services and such. Others regard these costs as part of the consultant's overhead to be recovered as part of the professional billing rates. The decision to charge for these expenses is usually related to their relative importance in each individual case. For example, if a client wants a large number of copies of reports resulting from the work, the cost of these reports may be charged separately and in addition to overhead included in fees. The proposal should clarify the consultant's practice in this regard. Some situations call for pricing that includes expenses. In these cases the consultant bears the risks associated with unforseen expenses. Such arrangements are most common where expenses are expected to be minimal or are relatively predictable.

Billing

Establishing the billing process in the proposal can avoid problems later and allow the consultant to demonstrate flexibility to the client. Some clients prefer a fixed monthly payment schedule; others like to pay on a progress billing basis. Progress billing is based on progress; it reflects the actual professional time spent on the project since the previous billing. Some projects warrant an initial payment as a mobilization charge to carry the project through the start-up, to fund initial expenses incurred to convene the consultants on site, and to secure other required resources (project office, special equipment and the like). This protects the consultant from early cancellation of the project by the client, which in many cases they can do with little notice and without cause. Conversely, some clients require a performance holdback, an amount to be paid on satisfactory completion. This protects the client against unsatisfactory performance from the consultant. Conditions for the release of holdback payments should be clearly outlined in the proposal. They should provide for the payment to be made within a specified time period following completion of the work unless a specific objection has been documented.

Proposals should confirm agreement on the timing of billings, the amount of time clients have to pay, and a statement of any penalties for late payment. This can be critical because of the sensitivity of professional practices to fluctuations in revenue. Some professional firms, in specifying their terms of payment, provide for late payment charges such as two percent per month for overdue accounts. These can be difficult to enforce, however, and many consultants rely on their ability to maintain good relationships with their clients to ensure prompt payment of their invoices.

CONTROL AND TERMINATION

Many clients are concerned about losing control over the costs, so most consulting agreements allow clients to stop the project at any time. Should they exercise this power, in most cases clients are liable only for the time and costs incurred up to the point when the consultants were informed of the termination of work. Some projects have other costs associated with disengagement (relocation of personnel etc.), and these should be provided for in the proposal. Other issues can arise when the basis of payment is other than just fees and expenses. For example, some projects provide for compensation to consultants based on achieving certain results (e.g., cost reduction). In these cases, provision for disengagement may be more complex. In any case, the parties' rights and obligations in the event of early termination of the project should be made explicit in the proposal.

The proposal may also permit consultants to stop the project early. For example, if the work program requires that the client assign staff to the project team, and this is not done to everyone's satisfaction, the consultant may call for the work to be halted and deferred until the situation is remedied. It is common for consultants to recommend a stoppage or major change in direction of the work when information comes to light during the project that indicates that continuing with the original work plan will not serve the client's purposes. At that point, consultants should seek clarification and obtain a new mandate to continue or revise the work program accordingly. Provision for this can also be included in the proposal. It reassures the client that the consultants will be alert on the client's behalf to emerging conditions that might affect the relationship. This can add to the client's sense of control.

■ *Summary of Project Deliverables*

Most (but not all) consulting engagements result in some formal documentation in the form of reports and hard copy of presentations. In addition, consultant files contain working papers and backup to analyses which have been developed in the course of the project. In some cases, potentially valuable libraries of secondary information are collected in the course of the work.

Technologies (software, measuring devices etc.) used in the course of the undertaking, but developed or obtained by the consultant independently of the project are usually kept by the consultant. Software developed in the course of the engagement is not so clear-cut, however, and an explicit agreement between client and consultant should be included in the proposal. Legal property rights issues can arise and should be anticipated in the terms of agreement inherent in the proposal. The proposal should describe the expected project deliverables as comprehensively as possible because, in many cases, clients see them as the only tangible output from the expenditure on consulting. (Some techniques for developing effective deliverables are discussed in Chapter 6, "Effective Presentations.")

■ *Appendices*

Most proposals contain a set of appendices that are included to provide the client with more detail on information in the proposal. A good rule to follow is, if it is referred to in the text, it should be an exhibit; if not, it can be an appendix. Appendices may be identified in the text but if they are referred to at length they should become exhibits. The appendices should be separated from the body of the proposal so that the proposal will be complete without them.

Typically, appendices to proposals contain the following:

- a description of the consulting firm submitting the proposal, with corporate brochures, summary descriptions of previous similar projects and reference letters
- professional résumés for the professionals to be assigned, possibly including summaries of previous relevant projects

- any other documents which may bear on the relationships, such as proof of financial sufficiency, required bonding certificates, sample licensing agreements or portfolio material displaying specific competence or achievements relevant to performing the work in this proposal
- client references – usually only when requested by the client receiving the proposal

---

CHECKLIST 5-6: *What Effective Proposals Contain*

Proposals that get the contract contain the following:

✔ **Covering Letter** – Delivers the proposal

✔ **Letter of Transmittal** – Submits the proposal and identifies key parties

✔ **Introduction** – Why we are submitting this proposal

✔ **Background** – Why the client is doing this work and why now

✔ **Project Objectives and Scope** – What the project will achieve, what will be done and what won't

✔ **Methodology** – How the work will be done

✔ **Work Program** – What will be done, start-up, sequence and timing

✔ **Organization and Staffing** – Who will do it and who's responsible?

✔ **Timing and Costs** – When and how much?

✔ **Summary of Deliverables** – What the client gets for the money

✔ **Appendices** – Company literature, reference and professional résumés

This chapter has described the elements of a complex proposal. See Checklist 5-6 for a summary of successful proposals. Some proposals will have all of these elements in considerable detail and result in a lengthy volume with substantial supporting material. In certain cases, particularly in competitive bidding situations in the public sector, two volumes are required: one for the proposal with all the sections except for costs, and a second financial proposal to be submitted under separate cover in which billing rates and cost projections are described in detail.

Fortunately, not all proposals are this elaborate. The vast majority of consulting projects are based on simple agreements between a client and a consultant that can be confirmed by a simple letter of one or two pages. Regardless, the material in this chapter provides a checklist to review. The relationship between client and consultant is contractual and both parties should be clear on all the implications. Not all elements of the agreement need be spelled out, but ambiguity should be minimized at the outset. Vagueness is the contract's worst enemy and can result in spoiling an otherwise productive relationship.

Effective Proposals

The main distinguishing feature between mediocre and effective proposals is that effective proposals are successful ones. Proposals should be a seamless part of the overall process of securing an engagement and an integral part of the total selling process. Ideally, the client should view the proposal as a confirmation of matters already discussed and agreed upon. It should contain few surprises and should anticipate the next step – that of getting started.

Yet, there may not be the opportunity for sufficient discussion beforehand to achieve this ideal. This is particularly true in tightly controlled competitions such as those in public sector bids where the proposal must bear a disproportionate responsibility for successful selling. Within this context, some proposals are better than others. Some of the distinguishing criteria are as follows:

- Content
- Style
- Appearance
- Attention to Detail

■ *Content*

The bulk of this chapter has focused on the issue of content and effective proposals demonstrate the discipline of addressing all these issues. The relative importance placed on the different content elements must reflect the concerns of the client. What to address in depth and what to combine with other things or eliminate from the proposal are matters of judgment on the part of the consultant. Consultants want winning proposals. Short, cryptic ones may win some, and elaborate and complete ones may win others; but it is a matter of providing clients with what they need. The background section of the proposal provides the consultant with the opportunity to demonstrate an understanding of these priorities, and the proposal content should reflect this knowledge throughout.

■ *Style*

Style refers to the language and tone of the proposal. The document establishes the parameters of the work to be done, provides a plan of action, establishes the relationship between client and consultant and forms the basis of a legal contract. It defines a business relationship in which mutual trust and cooperation are essential, and it reveals the nature and philosophy of the consultant. To be successful, the proposal must also be a "selling" document. See the section, "Putting Sell in Your Proposal" later in this chapter.

Policy and attitude issues need to be considered when deciding on style parameters. Policy concerns often surface because proposals make contractual commitments and promises of results. Legal language can be adversarial, almost combative in tone; yet, the proposal needs to reassure clients of the consultants' commitment to building a relationship of trust with them and helping them achieve positive results. Contract language can be complex and formal, and, in most cases, the same things can be said in simpler, more friendly terms that support the relationship-building process. An ability to use language with precision is often the key to developing a proposal style that can help build that relationship while satisfying contractual requirements. Clear, unambiguous writing with a positive tone, indicating an eagerness to work with this client on this project, takes effective writing skills and practice. A good proposal provides the client with the means of making adjustments to the project and demonstrates that the consultant is on the client's side in achieving a successful outcome from the project.

Some consultants prefer a less formal, more conversational, almost journalistic, style. Others opt for more formal, somewhat distant, language which they feel reflects their sense of objectivity and professionalism. The selection of tone is a matter of consultant sensitivity toward client decision makers. On the one hand, the more casual the tone, the more likely it is that the words dealing with the technical and contractual aspects of the proposal will lose precision. The less precise the words, the more chance of ambiguity. On the other hand, the more formal the tone, the greater the risk of depersonalizing the proposal and reducing its effectiveness as a "selling" document. Effective proposals communicate easily and completely with as few polysyllabic words as possible. The art of writing technical content in everyday language can be a communication powerhouse. All consultants should attempt to develop this skill. Above all, effective proposals use the style of communication that reflects the *client's* preferred level of formality in business relationships.

Whenever possible, major documents like proposals and reports should be read by a second person before submitting them. Many firms have "four eyes" policies mandating that all formal documents must be read by at least two people before they leave the office. Sole practitioners can usually develop relationships with trusted colleagues who can work with confidential material in this way. Some have family members who can read critically, and even if the technical content is high, can comment on the logical flow of the material.

■ *Appearance*

It has been said often that we live in a visual age. More and more, our communication reflects the fact that the majority of messages

INSIDER'S VIEW

Notice the current presumed importance of "power dressing" and recreational garments with designer labels. Do "clothes make the person?"

are passed among people who have grown up with television and computers with sophisticated graphics software. The instant transmission of visual material has become an integral part of our communication. Plain, typed documents that fail to take advantage of visual displays to enhance their messages are seen as boring and out-of-date. These attributes are transferred to the authors of the documents. Consultants who fail to respond to the visual requirements of modern communications are seen as boring and out-of-date.

Appearance is important in proposals in three main ways:

1. graphic support for content

2. exterior presentation

3. general firm image

Graphic Support for Content

Proposals offer many opportunities for graphic communication. Consultants should continually develop their skills in constructing conceptual diagrams to illustrate principles of effective performance. The search for new and better methods of displaying skill and experience, which reinforce the client's confidence that the consultant has captured the essence of the situation and the issues, is never-ending. Colour for interior and cover use is becoming increasingly common because its cost is now relatively low.

Where the selling process permits an audiovisual presentation, the proposal offers additional opportunities to demonstrate strong conceptual skill and clarity in communication. More complete discussions of presentation principles and techniques are found in Chapter 6, "Effective Presentations."

Exterior Presentation

Proposals should look professional. They can be standardized in appearance, or they can be customized for each client. Some professional firms have established cover formats that portray an image they wish to communicate and they use them for all proposals. Proposals, however, do not have to always look alike. Many effective proposals use the cover to present graphics that relate specifically to proposed clients and their particular situation. Customized, highly relevant covers for proposals can demonstrate that the consultant views each client as unique, with unique concerns. Some consultants use client logos on the covers of proposals, but this is risky and can backfire. Client logos on reports, once the work has been commissioned, are generally more acceptable and reflect the consultant and client jointly working on the project. Judgment as to what an individual client will appreciate is necessary in deciding on the external appearance of the proposals. Demonstration of good judgment can help differentiate and therefore sell the proposal.

General Firm Image

The set of standard company material, sometimes referred to as "boilerplate," is usually presented in the appendices. As outlined earlier in this chapter, it describes the firm, its credentials and the qualifications of the professionals being proposed. Although boilerplate material rarely sells the proposal, it needs to look professional. Its graphics and content can portray a consulting firm or practice that exemplifies any of a variety of images – modern, conservative, stable, trustworthy, aggressive, competitive, friendly, hard-working, successful, specialized, small, creative, substantial etc. Poorly done boilerplate or its absence can cause a proposal to fail.

■ *Attention to Detail*

Consultants must strive for excellence in communicating, including correct and effective document preparation. It has been said that at least two-thirds of most consulting time is devoted to communicating with clients or on their behalf. Experienced clients regard communications skills as essential in selecting consultants. Consequently, clients are more critical of sloppy writing practices and have been known to discharge otherwise competent professionals because of their lack of attention to the details in regard to documentation and writing habits. When a consultant presents a document that is error-free and professionally prepared, clients see this as a reflection of the thinking and general work habits of the consultant. Conversely, any failure in these details is often taken to indicate sloppy and careless thinking, slipshod work habits and even incompetence. There is no substitute for excellence, and today's clients demand nothing less.

No one expects consultants to be hair-splitting grammarians, but some errors are fairly common and can easily be avoided. The following are some typical examples of incorrect or inappropriate writing found in a recent sample of consulting proposals:

Structural Inconsistencies or Weaknesses

- The table of contents had five levels of structure. One section was labelled III.2.1.a(1).
- In several cases, there was only one paragraph in a subcategory (e.g., III.2.1 without a III.2.2). This raises the question of whether the second item was omitted, or why this paragraph was set apart rather than incorporating it into the main section.
- In several cases, the language changed within a listing, thereby destroying parallel structure. For example:
  – Start the Project
  – Conduct the Survey
  – Report Writing

The first two are imperative verb phrases in the active voice. The last one, "Report Writing," is a noun phrase.

Interchangeable Terms

The use of virtually interchangeable terms provides distinctions without differences and adds terms unnecessarily. For example:

The work program comprises several elements as follows: ... [A listing follows] ... The last point marks the conclusion.

The term "point" is introduced as interchangeable with "element" and is an unnecessary complication. Furthermore, it may add ambiguity and confusion as the reader looks for more "points."

Grammatical Errors

Avoid common grammatical errors, including improper sentence construction (e.g., incomplete sentences), ambiguous and logically incorrect sentence structure, dangling participles and propositions, split infinitives, incorrect tenses, incorrect words (e.g., "irregardless") and spelling errors. Most text software (Word, WordPerfect) features a spell check and grammar check feature. All documents should be scanned for these errors before release.

Inconsistency

Avoid the lack of internal consistency. The proposal is a single, complex document. The various parts must be carefully orchestrated so that each supports the other. When the wording of the proposed work steps is different from the listing of work steps that appears in a graphic, the client sees evidence of internal inconsistency. Similarly, when the proposed staffing is not related to the positions described in the proposed project organization chart, internal consistency suffers.

Effective proposals are remarkable in their consistent attention to these and other details. Use Checklist 5-7 to be sure your proposal is as effective as possible.

Putting "Sell" into Your Proposal

In Chapter 4, "Selling Your Services," attitude was described as central to the selling process. Similarly,

> **INSIDER'S VIEW**
>
> "William Tell shot an arrow through an apple standing on his son's head" is ambiguous because of the dangling participle "standing."

CHECKLIST 5-7: *Effective Proposals*

✔ **Content** – reflects what the client wants done and why the client wants it done now

✔ **Style** – reflects relationship protocol between client and consultant

✔ **Appearance** – proposal document looks professional
  – clear and effective graphics support the content
  – exterior presentation is unique, yet tasteful
  – general firm image is supported

✔ **Attention to Detail** – avoids common errors
  – structural inconsistencies
  – interchangeable Terms
  – grammatical errors
  – internal inconsistencies

the proposal should reflect the client-centred attitude throughout. This is particularly important in the background section where the consultant can demonstrate an understanding of the client's real concern and a genuine wish to help. By developing and proposing a work program that reflects this understanding, consultants can differentiate themselves as more committed to the client's true goals. Meaningful and consistent graphics demonstrate an attitude that communicates to the client that this consultant is prepared to put the effort into the proposal and believes that the opportunity to work for this client justifies that effort.

Consultants often regard themselves as problem solvers and see their clients as presenting problems for them to solve. The terminology associated with problem solving is familiar to consultants, and its use does not imply any positive or negative condition. Problems are neutral to them. However the very word "problem" does have a negative connotation in its nontechnical usage. The unnecessary use of problem-solving language can give a proposal a negative tone.

It has become a cliché to stress that good salespeople avoid using the word "problem" entirely and substitute it with "challenge" or "opportunity" instead. As with any generalization of this type, it is sometimes oversimplified to the point of mindlessness. Nevertheless, as with

> ## INSIDER'S VIEW
> The client knows there are problems; what the client wants to learn about are solutions.

most clichés, there is some validity to its underlying philosophy, and it can be a useful guide in adding sell to the proposal. Wherever possible, adjust word choice to emphasize the positive. Positive phraseology – using words like opportunity and challenge – tends to shift the attitude from the pejorative to the constructive. Focusing on what can be done is more positive than focusing on what is wrong. This positive attitude encourages the client and demonstrates that the consultant is optimistic about making a real contribution.

By cultivating the appropriate attitude, professionals see the issues and challenges from the client's perspective. The following are some of the attitudes that can lead to constructing effective selling proposals:

CONFIDENCE is demonstrated by the clear, direct and logical thinking patterns used in writing the document. This reveals the consultant's willingness to make commitments to performance.

EXPERIENCE is revealed by demonstrating that the client's needs are legitimate and that the use of consultants is justified and appropriate.

SUPPORT for the client's good judgment in performing this work at this time, and recognition that its cost is justified, are both indicated in the content of the proposal.

ENTHUSIASM is demonstrated by the positive words chosen by the consultant in describing a desire to help. Proposals that use the positive "will" instead of the conditional "would" in describing what activities the consultant considers appropriate and those that focus on benefits and opportunities for the client demonstrate enthusiasm.

Building the appropriate attitudes into the fibre and wording of the proposal can play an important role in the selling process. A good proposal is a successful one – successful because it makes a strong contribution to the selling process. The appendix at the end of the book contains a sample proposal and proposal letter. These are two extremes in that the proposal included is extensive and detailed – more than is often needed but nevertheless what is sometimes required. The proposal letter is typical of many agreements between client and consultant and demonstrates the same business relationship, but probably a closer personal relationship. It expresses this effectively in a few pages.

Marketing programs, selling skills and proposal preparation are three of the four keys to developing a consulting business. The fourth is presentation – how consultants communicate with clients, potential clients and the world in general. The next chapter focuses on presentations.

SIX

Effective Presentations

Consultants make presentations. To some observers, that is what consultants do; they may do other things as well, but they always make presentations. As a result, the ability to develop and make professional quality presentations is an essential characteristic of effective consulting. Effective consultants are effective communicators, and most find that presentation techniques are a critical part of their professional capabilities. There are many how-to books and articles that cover the basics of communication in presentations, and this chapter does not intend to duplicate these. It focuses on aspects of presentations often not covered in the standard books, the tricks of the trade and practical tips based on experiences and observations in the field.

Presentation Opportunities

Presentation technology has improved dramatically in recent years, and now consultants may be called upon to use the full range of tools, ranging from low-tech flip charts and white boards to high-tech multi-media computer-assisted graphics and projection. The range of visual options available for building and delivering presentations is staggering. The audience can be dazzled with full-motion, full-colour graphics including sound, sophisticated fading and transitions, etc. But along with this potential comes the danger that an inexperienced presenter will focus on form rather than substance. Clients are looking for content. They want professional communication that clearly and concisely illustrates key points.

The more sophisticated features of common presentation packages, like Power Point or Corel Presentations, can make presentations more interesting and effective, but in the hands of unskilled users, they can be counterproductive. Some results can be likened to home videos in terms of their lack of effective composition and content and the cacophony of poorly integrated images and special effects.

Consultants need to understand these technologies, because they are important tools, but they must be used judiciously. Their entertainment value can be useful at times, but stock graphics and formats have now become familiar enough to clients that they may in fact detract from the presentation, rather than help it. The standardized formats provided in the popular presentations software packages are convenient and can be used effectively for presentations designed as input to working sessions or for other informal presentations which justify little investment of time.

When sophisticated material and conceptual diagrams are required in the presentation, the presentation is probably better built without the constraining defaults of a standardized system. Standardized presentation software is the minimum level below which consultants' presentations should not go, and consultants should view them as such when developing presentations for clients or gatherings which include potential clients. Larger consulting firms may wish to have their employees observe a similar style and format for presentations in order to present a consistent firm image. They can accomplish this with macros embedded in the presentation commands. For the independent, however, differentiation from competitors and direct and customized focus on every individual client's situation is more important.

The following sections of this chapter discuss the full range of presentation options, their key strengths and limitations. It focuses on content and delivery because these two variables are affected by the various technologies the consultant may be called on to use. While the media may be the message to McLuhanites, to consultants, the message is the message, and the medium is merely the means of getting it across.

Consultants are called on to make presentations for various occasions. At times, the goal is to inform a broad public group of the consultant's experiences and knowledge of a particular or set of concepts and principles or information about some industry trends and patterns. At other times, the goal is to present specific material to a client or prospective client to inform and possibly stimulate discussion. At yet other times, the goal is simply to build an audience's awareness of consultants' capabilities. Each of these occasions calls for modifications to the presentation to suit the specific goals consultants hope to achieve. The following describes some of the common occasions for which consultants need to be prepared to make presentations.

Promotion

Consultants develop opportunities to present their credentials to audiences made up of potential clients and to that part of the general business public to whom they wish to be known. Every member of that public is a potential decision influencer and may suggest your services to other possible clients. In the present world of rapid organizational change and career shifting, today's non-client or competitor may be tomorrow's client. In modern careers with rapid ups and downs for everyone, those you meet on the way up are often the same people you meet on the way down. The promotion target group is therefore generally larger than the specific target market.

Presenting Credentials

Frequently, clients invite prospective consultants to present their credentials before asking them to present specific proposals for a project; this provides the client with the opportunity to screen a large number of prospective consultants without getting each to undertake the considerable effort required in preparing a full proposal. This screening enables the potential client to reduce the number of consultants submitting proposals and thereby makes the selection process more efficient for all concerned.

■ *Presenting Proposals*

Prospective clients frequently invite a short list of prequalified consultants to present a formal proposal to the client decision makers. This is the real selling opportunity that confident consultants welcome. A good presentation will frequently mean the difference between getting the assignment and coming in second.

■ *During an Assignment*

Presentations are often called for at several points during an assignment. At the outset of a project, the consultant or consulting team will want to address the client or the client's steering committee to lay the groundwork for project commitments. This meeting describes the relationship to be developed with the client and establishes specific schedules and responsibilities. Other presentations are made at progress meetings in the course of an assignment to keep the client informed and involved, and to present issues to be resolved. Special meetings with the client are frequently needed to discuss altering the course of the assignment and to set new goals in the light of new information or changed circumstances. At the conclusion of an assignment, a presentation is used to sum up the project experience, present final results and suggest additional work that the client might wish to consider.

■ *On Behalf of a Client*

Sometimes, a client wants other groups interested in the project to receive information related to a given assignment. Frequently, the client asks the consultant to play an important part. Since the consultant is often more experienced in developing and making presentations, the client may ask the consultant to develop one on behalf of the client and coach client staff in communicating effectively.

■ *Speaking Engagements*

Part of a consultant's marketing program involves making speeches, often with the use of visual aids. Many consultants prefer to use audiovisual techniques rather than make traditional speeches.

Know Your Audience

Every course on public speaking begins with the rule: know your audience. It is surprising, nevertheless, how often it is given only lip service. It is difficult to understand how one can set realistic and specific objectives for a presentation if one has not reflected on the specific makeup of the audience and considered the following:

IDENTITY Who will be there? What is their demographic, educational and experience profile? Are they all from within the same organizational unit? Which leaders and decision makers will attend?

SPECIFIC INTERESTS What is the occasion and why are they coming? What roles do the leaders and others play in the group? To what are they likely to respond?

PREDISPOSITION What are their basic beliefs? What will they want to do? How will this presentation support or challenge these beliefs and wishes?

EMPOWERMENT What are they able to do as a group or as individuals? Are the presentation goals relevant and realistic for them?

FEARS What concerns do they have about the consultant, the meeting and the subject to be presented? What will turn them against you?

These and similar considerations are particularly critical when presenting consulting findings and conclusions to client personnel. They are also important even when the situation is more benign, as in speeches – merely to provide information at a conference or to entertain after dinner. All presentations should strive for a level

> ## INSIDER'S VIEW
>
> If it's worth doing at all, it's worth doing with excellence so that it reflects the excellence with which you conduct all your work.

of excellence, and that requires a deliberate effort to structure the presentation with the specific audience foremost in your mind.

A particular set of factors is added when the presentation is to a foreign audience. Translators may be required. In this case, learn the timing in working with translators. It is more effective to give translators a whole paragraph and wait while they translate it rather than to give them sentences or part sentences – a process that results in a jerky translation and has the audience constantly shifting focus from presenter to translator and back again. If possible, give the translator a prepared text in advance. Also, humour rarely translates, so eliminate slang expressions, jokes and other culturally defined elements from your talk.

Set Specific Objectives

The basic purpose of a presentation is, of course, to communicate. The technically best presentation, effectively designed and constructed and flawlessly delivered, is only as valuable as its success in communicating the desired message to the target audience. Any successful presentation, therefore, is first and foremost focused on a communication objective. The communicator needs to have a clear understanding of what that objective is. Vague objectives, such as "to tell the client what we have done," or "to report our findings," are insufficient to define communication objectives.

The communication objectives should include the desired audience reaction – what you hope to achieve by this particular presentation. Statements such as "to help the client understand why what we have found is important," "to encourage the client to take certain actions," "to obtain support for a particular point of view" or "to stimulate a certain audience behaviour" are examples of specific communication objectives. They address the question, "What do we want to have happen as a result of the presentation?" By specifying these, you will be able to focus your presentation on the issues and priorities most likely to achieve your objectives. In addition, after the presentation has been made, you will be able to assess the degree to which the presentation achieved the objectives you have set. Some of these observable action goals might be:

- You receive a number of requests for copies of your talk.
- The client decides to act on your specific recommendations.
- The prospective client agrees to have another discussion with you.
- The prospective client asks for a formal proposal from you.
- The client accepts your proposal and schedules a start date.

Communication objectives stated in precise action terms such as these are the first steps in developing effective presentations.

Build Your Presentation

Once you have defined the presentation objectives and assessed the audience, you should be in a position to build the presentation. Presentations need to be constructed; they need a foundation – a structure on which to attach material – as well as material of substance to present. The following are some important considerations in building a presentation:

Foundation

What are you trying to say? This is clearly the most critical part of the presentation, yet it is often the most difficult to define. In order for the presentation to have a secure foundation, it needs a simple, unambiguous statement of what you want to say. The challenge lies in the dual requirement for simplicity and unambiguity. The foundation must support your presentation objective and reflect what you know about the audience. If you need more than one or two sentences to state what you are trying to say, you need to work on it more to refine it and focus your thinking.

■ *Structure*

This is the outline of your presentation. The venerated "tell 'em, tell 'em, tell 'em" principle is still the most reliable for most presentations. It starts with a clear statement that tells the audience what to expect, provides the information and arguments that are the subject of the presentation and ends with a summary of the key elements of the message presented. It begins and ends with the foundation and focuses attention on the material of interest. This principle can also apply to segments of the presentation in which it is appropriate to provide additional structure to help the audience/participants follow the more complex parts of the material.

■ *Material*

This is the message – this is where you accomplish your objective or not. It is where you succeed or fail in reaching your audience and in eliciting the response you want. A sound foundation and a rational and strong structure will get help keep your audience's attention; what you do with that attention depends on how you develop your material.

> **INSIDER'S VIEW**
>
> Inductive logic takes the form, "Specific and difficult goals are more effective. Here is the evidence: workers with specific and difficult goals improved productivity 90 percent, compared with the rest of the workers."

Consulting presentations usually seek to inform and to persuade. They usually contain findings, conclusions and recommendations that bear on the specific objective of the presentation. The style or form used can influence its credibility and acceptance. The logical format can take two forms: inductive or deductive. Some presentations, particularly research-based material, use the academic inductive approach which sets out to present information which supports or fails to support a particular hypothesis.

Consulting presentations often follow the deductive approach in which a series of findings are presented to establish a base of knowledge and conclusions drawn from them. Either can be effective, but it is important to make the choice consciously in order to present material concisely, consistently and clearly.

Select the Best Communication Method

Methods range from informal discussions to formal presentations

> **INSIDER'S VIEW**
>
> Deductive logic takes the form, "Workers with specific and difficult goals improved productivity 90 percent, compared with the rest of the workers. Therefore, we can conclude that specific and difficult goal assignment improves productivity."

using high-tech computer-based equipment. The presenter is often free to choose the type of presentation method to use, within practical limits of facilities and costs. Historically, the more elaborate the presentation in terms of audiovisual techniques, the more expensive the preparation and the more rigid the format. Consequently, the more formal and elaborate approaches were usually reserved for relatively large audiences. Today, modern computers and printers, standard equipment in any consultant's office, can produce sophisticated colour presentations for overhead or computer projected presentations at a practical cost. Cost is no longer the main determinant of presentation method. Other factors, such as the formality of the presentation, the facilities available, and the flexibility needed while presenting are more important. The use of flip charts and whiteboards provide the most flexible and informal interaction with the audience. Chalkboards have been largely replaced by whiteboards in industrialized countries, but be prepared for them in the developing countries. And remember, don't wear dark clothes when you are using chalk.

Overhead transparencies are still one of the most popular presentation methods, and they provide a workable compromise between structure and informality. There is ample room for flexibility and interaction between presenter and audience. Overhead projectors can be used with large audiences as well, under the right conditions. Overhead transparencies are probably the most popular presentation choice of consultants because of the versatility they provide, while still offering most of the visual effectiveness of more sophisticated equipment. Computer projectors add minor refinements to presentations such as various transitions and insert features, but this technology is still evolving and problems of file compatibility and equipment malfunction persist. Many consultants choose to bring a back-up set of overhead in case of computer projection difficulties. Effective consultants are usually highly accomplished in the use of transparencies in their presentations. Figure 6-1 summarizes the principal criteria for selecting from among various presentation methods.

Selecting the presentation method is usually the easy part. Preparing for the actual presentation so that the best use is made of the chosen method is more challenging. Each method has its special features, and there are many things that can go wrong with any method. The difference between an ordinary presentation and a professional one can be seen in two ways: the skill with which presenters use the chosen presentation method's special features, and the degree to which they anticipate and avoid problems. This skill and anticipation is born of practice and experience peculiar to each presentation option.

It is important to prepare for the special needs of the chosen method. Each method has special characteristics which should be understood. There are two types: those related to presentation content and delivery, and those related to the way in which equipment is incorporated into the presentation. We will now look at the various presentation methods and some key issues associated with them.

Speeches

Most consultants will be called on to make speeches from time to time. There is a distinction between speeches and presentations:

Presentation Method	Flexibility for Audience Involvement	Audience Size	Production Cost	Availability of Equipment	Comments
FIGURE 6-1: *Summary of Presentation Methods*					
Speech only	High – can be formal or informal	Unlimited	Lowest	High	Can be tailored to any occasion
Flip Charts, white- and and chalkboards	High – can be developed or modified on the spot	Small to medium	Low	Easily provided	Informal, often used in workshop format
Overhead transparencies	High – can be modified on the spot	Small to large	Low to medium	Easily provided	Most versatile – excellent graphics capability
Videocassette or 35mm slides	Lowest – cannot be modified	Medium to large	High	Limited – must be obtained	Formal – best suited to often repeated presentation
Computer-aided and operated	Limited – can be complex to modify	Unlimited	Low	Moderate – growing with technology	Evolving technology – reliability issues
Multimedia	Moderate – some elements have flexibility	Medium to large	High	Limited – must be assembled	Extensive preparation commitment

speeches are delivered without visual aids, and presentations call for visual aids in addition to oral content. This section will not duplicate the many books written on how to prepare good speeches and develop good speaking techniques. Rather, it will focus on a few items that can help consultants make effective speeches when they are called on to do so. After establishing the parameters of the speaking occasion, identifying the audience and defining the objectives, the consultant should be prepared for the following:

■ *Formality*

Speeches can run a wide range of formality. At one extreme is the formal speech at a special event and at the other, a near-conversational delivery of information to a group of individuals known to the speaker. At the formal extreme, the words should be carefully chosen and rehearsed, with printed texts available for distribution afterward. As the speaking occasion moves toward the informal, there is less concern about specific wording and the availability of printed text, and more concern that the tone is conversational.

■ *Facilities and Equipment*

Speeches can take place in any location. Because they usually do not involve visual material, facilities considerations for speeches are less constraining than they are for presentations. The key variable for speeches is sound. It is not always necessary for the audience to see speakers, but they must hear them. Sometimes a microphone is needed and possibly a lectern, which may or may not have sufficient light for the speaker to see notes or prepared text. Here are some reminders:

INSIDER'S VIEW

Do not be lulled by informality into public *faux pas* that may appear in the press and be ascribed to you, possibly out of context.

BE FAMILIAR WITH THE EQUIPMENT. This includes seemingly simple things such as how to adjust the height of the microphone and how to turn it on or off. There are many types of microphones from clip-ons to booms and pedestals. The type of sound equipment used may affect the freedom the speaker has to move around and gesture during the delivery. Clip-on mikes may affect the speaker's dress because of the need for lapels or something else to fasten the mike onto.

NOTE WHERE THE SOUND SPEAKERS ARE. Adjust the microphone position in order to avoid the feedback screech that results from the microphone pointing at a sound speaker.

PRODUCE SPEAKING NOTES IN LARGE TYPE. Make them bold, double- or triple-spaced to provide easy reference.

VISIT THE VENUE WELL BEFORE THE PRESENTATION. Test and become familiar with sound equipment, lighting and its controls. Determine what, if any, impediments may be presented by the seating format.

■ *Delivery*

Some speakers are comfortable speaking from notes; others prefer the security of written text. If public quotation is expected, a preapproved text may be mandatory. Many audiences find that the apparent spontaneity of presenters who speak from crib notes is more interesting and facilitates personal contact; however, formally written material need not be boring just because it is read. The more written text is used, the more the speaker must rely on the effectiveness of the word power contained in it. Similarly, a written text speech needs deliberate support from effective voice inflections, gestures, pauses and eye contact to compensate for a lower level of spontaneous animation. Speeches should always be rehearsed where possible in front of a friendly critic.

One important part of oral presentation is managing the audience. The speaker has significant influence over how the audience behaves and reacts over and above their interest in the content of the speech. The following are some of the special elements of good oral presentations:

RELAX AND PREPARE YOURSELF MENTALLY. Most people express horror at the prospect of having to get up in front of a group and speak. Reflect on the fact that almost everyone in the audience is happy to be there and that it is you, not them, who is making the speech. They are on your side and want you to succeed.

TAKE CONTROL AT THE START. As soon as you are ready to begin, pause and look over the audience. Most will immediately turn their attention to you and stop talking. If the audience is particularly noisy, wait longer before challenging them by raising your hand or beginning your opening remarks. Usually, merely standing up at the front and waiting for the hubbub to subside is sufficient to take control of a session, but sometimes it may be necessary to dim the room lights to force the focus on the speaker.

USE EFFECTIVE EYE CONTACT. Good speakers and presenters do not scan their audience. They look at individuals and pause a second or two to establish contact before moving on to another. They avoid fastening on any one listener and cover the whole audience evenly. Watch for the window effect. Some speakers favour the portion of the audience away from windows and need to a make special effort to include those listeners seated near the windows.

GESTURES SHOULD BE MEANINGFUL. Most individuals have nervous habits which often accompany their public speaking. Most of these bear no relationship to the subject of their talk but are more related to their efforts to speak. Rubbing your nose as if it itched might appear as if you don't know what you are talking about. This type of gesture is distracting and should be controlled. Other gestures that relate directly to what the speaker is saying are helpful and should be used deliberately for that purpose. Otherwise, the hands should be kept still.

INSIDER'S VIEW

One of the most difficult things is to keep your hands still. Try standing with your arms at your sides, hands relaxed and slightly curled, while you carry on a conversation. It is difficult, but with practice, it becomes natural.

Be careful with gestures when presenting internationally. Finger pointing may be all right in North America, but it is offensive and rude in other parts of the world, especially in parts of Asia and Africa. There, it may be better to close the hand and point with the thumb, but not in the Middle East, where the thumbs-up gesture is a rude insult.

SPEAKING TAKES PRACTICE. The celebrated British actor, Sir Ralph Richardson was quoted as saying, "The most precious things in speech are pauses." Most inexperienced speakers talk too fast and are unable to tolerate small moments of silence. They tend to fill these moments with "ums" and "ahs" that telegraph their nervousness to the audience. Experienced speakers and presenters use pauses for emphasis and to gather their thoughts, thereby reassuring the audience that they are comfortable and in control. Rehearsing a speech can reduce anxiety and help make the delivery calmer.

■ *Documentation*

Sometimes the need to provide printed text in support of a speech is obvious, such as when presenting a paper at a conference. On other occasions, printed texts are not required. For the consultant, however, it is usually a good idea to prepare a synopsis, if not a complete text, because very frequently, there will be a request for a copy of the speech after it has been made. In addition, many speaking occasions offer opportunities for desirable publicity if text can be made available. Even in confidential client presentations, copies of the remarks are usually appreciated so that client personnel can review them later.

All the principles of delivering effective speeches apply also to presentations. See Checklist 6-2 for a review of effective speeches. The only difference is that presentations (as defined for the purpose of this book) involve the use of various audiovisual aids. As a result, the presenter may be moving about more during the presentation and will certainly be seen as well as heard. The following sections of this chapter focus on how to make presentations using various audiovisual techniques.

CHECKLIST 6-2: *Effective Speeches*

✔ **Formality:** Full range from casual and entertaining to formally written

✔ **Facilities and Equipment:** Adjust lectern, lights and sound system, and locate speakers

✔ **Delivery:** Mental preparation, eye contact, gestures, enunciation and flow

✔ **Documentation:** Printed copies for distribution following speech

---

Flip Charts, Whiteboards and Chalkboards

All these presentation aids are used in much the same way. They can be prepared in advance, on the spot, during the presentation or in some combination. Their use generally implies a level of informality and spontaneous interchange with the audience for which the presenter needs to be prepared.

During a speech, the speaker is generally standing at the front of the room. Presenters often have more flexibility as to where they stand, how the room is laid out and how they move. They are automatically in control of what happens, and they have the ultimate responsibility for keeping discussions going where they want, directing that discussion and managing the agenda. The presenter should make effective use of movement – toward participants raising important points and back to the flip chart or board when it is time to conceptualize or summarize and relieve pressure on the audience. Pages of flip charts can be torn off and fastened to a wall for on-going reference as the presentation proceeds. Using the same four groupings as in the previous section on speeches, the following provides some specific comments regarding the effective use of these writing devices in presentations.

■ *Formality*

Although prepared flip charts are not uncommon during sales presentations, most consultants use flip charts in less formal situations and use them *actively* during presentations. Flip charts and boards are common in workshops and brainstorming sessions in which vigorous participation by the audience is desired and encouraged. Consultants often assume the role of facilitator as well as presenter. Achieving the presentation's objective is often dependent on the consultant's ability to read and use the dynamics of the group, as well as to contribute to collecting, ordering and summarizing the information being developed in the presentation. A balance between spontaneity and control needs to be established and maintained, and the level of informality should be balanced with the professional distance needed to assure credibility and impartiality.

■ *Facilities and Equipment*

Flip charts, whiteboards and chalkboards are inherently simple and for that reason, inexperienced presenters are tempted to underestimate the physical problems they can present. As with any presentation method, success is in preplanning and practice. The following are some of the most common issues to resolve when using flip charts and other writing devices.

> **MAKE SURE YOU HAVE GOOD EQUIPMENT.** Many stands are flimsy and prone to collapse during use. Too often the charts or boards do not fit securely on the stands.

> **ARRANGE THE ROOM.** The face of flip charts should be well lit, and the presenter should anticipate lighting. Avoid locating flip charts and boards in front of bright windows in the daytime unless drapes can be drawn. Lighting is of particular concern when using whiteboards, which are often prone to problems of glare.

> **ARRANGE SEATING.** The seating should be focused on the area where the flip charts and writing boards will be located, and ample room should be provided for the presenter to move about. The arrangement of seats also has an important effect on the dynamics of the group. A popular seating arrangement is the shape of a D or U. The D configuration implies a table, projector, screen and probably flip charts at one end of the room; the U configuration implies a wall-mounted chalkboard at one end. As the names suggest, these similar configurations place the audience/participants around the perimeter of the room, with the presenter(s) free to move about within the D or U and approach individuals to speak with them directly, as well as to stand back and address the group as a whole. Arranging in a D or U

stimulates discussion; classroom style may inhibit it unless wide aisles are available for the presenter to move about and involve all the audience.

The number of participants that can be accommodated in a D is limited, and more than 30 people is usually difficult to fit comfortably in a room using this configuration without affecting the ease of discussion. Classroom style can accommodate a larger number in the rows of seats. Sometimes a series of slanted rows with aisles is an effective compromise.

MAKE SURE YOU HAVE THE RIGHT MARKERS. There are at least four different kinds of markers, and each is designed for a specific use. Using the wrong kind can spell disaster in a presentation. Washable and dry-wipable markers designed for whiteboard use are clearly labeled and should be the only ones used on whiteboards. Other markers contain permanent ink, are not erasable from whiteboards and can damage the surface. Permanent markers are better suited for flip chart use because whiteboard markers bleed through most flip chart paper and mark several pages at once. Other markers designed for use on overhead transparencies or on writing paper do not erase from whiteboards and are generally too fine for effective flip chart use.

USE THE EQUIPMENT CORRECTLY. Chalkboard erasers should not be used on whiteboards and vice versa. Also, if you are using chalkboards, make sure there is a sufficient supply of chalk, preferably more than one colour.

MAKE SURE THERE ARE SMALL TABLES NEARBY. You will need these for your

INSIDER'S VIEW

It is a good idea to carry a container of window cleaner and some paper toweling in case someone makes the mistake of using the wrong marker on the wrong device.

notes and to put the markers down during the presentation. One of the most common and distracting nervous activities of presenters is fiddling with objects in the hands – markers, pointers and clicking ballpoint pens are the most frequent offenders. If you are not using it at the moment, put it down! Besides, things break when they are fiddled with excessively.

CHECK THE WALLS. If you are likely to use the walls to hang pages from the flip chart, make sure they are suitable. Some walls are papered or have paint that comes off with the tape used to hang flip chart pages. Always ask permission before using the walls.

CHECK SECURITY. Many workshops extend over a full day or more. The room may be vacated for lunch or overnight. Check whether it can be locked or whether it must be cleared at night, and inform participants accordingly. Sometimes the workshop is sufficiently confidential that more measures need to be taken. Check to make sure the competition is not meeting next door! In that case, a complete change of venue may be needed.

■ *Delivery*

As in all other aspects of presentations, using charts and/or boards should have specific objectives and planned agendas. These are often presented explicitly at the beginning to establish the tone and expectations and help focus participants on the topic at hand. Invariably, there is some time required at the beginning during which the audience/participants are being seated and other discussions are taking place in preparation for the presentation. Many presenters prefer to begin the prepared material on the second page of the flip chart, leaving the front page blank or merely providing a title. This allows them to control the timing by concealing the first set of material until the participants are ready to begin. As in any form of presentation, there is a discipline. Some of the elements of effective flip chart/chalkboard presentations are the following:

PRESENT YOURSELF EFFECTIVELY. The use of markers or chalk can be messy, so choose your clothing with this in mind. Chalk on a dark suit or a permanent colour mark on a white silk shirt or blouse can be distracting. It is often wise to empty pockets of bulky wallets and noisy keys and change before the presentation begins. You will not need these things during the presentation, and removing them will enhance appearance as well as reduce the tendency for distracting fidgeting. Another reason to empty your pockets before the presentation is that hands are irresistibly drawn to them when we are anxious, and we are always anxious when making important presentations.

LEARN TO USE TIMING. In presentations, as in comedy, timing is everything. One of the most useful tools the presenter has is timing. As facilitator and leader, you have control over the pace and rhythm of events as well as the sequence. Silence can be powerful, and experienced presenters are not afraid of letting time pass without intervening when they want to put pressure on the audience to participate.

PRACTICE WITH THE EQUIPMENT. The equipment should be a smooth extension of the presenter. Distractions caused by fumbling and clumsy adjusting of equipment scream inexperience and a lack of professionalism. This can be avoided by practicing with the equipment beforehand to understand how it works and is adjusted. For example, the apparently simple act of changing pages on a flip chart can cause the presenter difficulty if it is not handled correctly. The correct technique is to lift the page by a corner of its bottom edge, pull it out slightly from the pad, and lift it up and over the stand in one smooth motion. This allows the page to ride on a cushion of air as it curves to the back. Similarly, when tacking sheets from the pad onto walls, fasten them with four- to six-inch pieces of masking tape to each of the top two corners, angled slightly away from the middle of the page. Carry the page to the wall by the tapes, and press them into place. A little practice can make a lot of difference and impress the audience.

■ *Documentation*

Documentation of presentations involving flip charts and boards can pose special problems. Unlike prepared speeches, the specific content often develops during the presentation. Further, because much of the material was the subject of active discussion, the pages will be a jumble of points, conceptual statements and markings made in the course of discussion that may be difficult to reconstruct after the meeting. Flip chart pages can be collected at the end of proceedings, but they are often cumbersome and difficult to transcribe later. Reconstructing discussions that used boards can be even more difficult, especially after they have been erased.

Nevertheless, documentation is important to ensure that key parts of the presentation can be recorded for subsequent reference and action. Some advanced-technology whiteboards have the capability of producing copies of the material recorded on them automatically, but these are expensive and not generally available. One useful approach is to have someone record the presentation. This can be a junior colleague or a member of the client organization's support staff who is not otherwise required as a partic-

INSIDER'S VIEW

Reviewing the output of a flip chart presentation can be a humbling experience. Over time, you will learn to improve your handwriting and drawing skills after wrestling with some of the more creative, but undecipherable, collections of conceptual diagrams spectacularly overlaid with sets of arrows, circled items, underlines and general scribbles.

ipant. Try having the secretary or executive assistant to the most senior participant involved in the planning and organizing of the workshop from the earliest point. This person is invited to attend and accept responsibility for taking notes and recording important observations of the process to serve as the basis for documentation. This way, the documentation can be available to each participant very soon after the presentation. More importantly, this person frequently makes a valuable contribution to the substance of the meeting and brings to the gathering a sometimes unexpected point of view.

Checklist 6-3 provides a review of presentations making use of equipment discussed.

CHECKLIST 6-3:
Presenting with Flip Charts, Whiteboards and Chalkboards

✔ **Formality**
- – Moderate to informal
- – Encourages participation

✔ **Facilities and equipment**
- – Ensure acceptable quality
- – Arrange room
- – Arrange seating
- – Have the right markers, erasers, etc.
- – Have small tables
- – Check walls
- – Check security

✔ **Delivery**
- – Dress appropriately
- – Use timing, movement
- – Use the equipment smoothly

✔ **Documentation**
- – Complex, assign recording responsibility

Overhead Transparencies

Notwithstanding the growing use of computer-based projectors, overhead transparencies are still by far the most common type of audiovisual aid used in consultants' presentations. They have the advantages of simplicity, reliability, and familiarity. Overheads can contain all manner of content – from a photocopied page and handwritten notes to elaborate and multilayered coloured graphics. They can contain anything a computer can produce – with or without using Power Point or Corel Presentations Software. They can be altered during presentation and provide hard copy for easy documentation and distribution. In spite of their significant potential, and perhaps because of their ubiquity, their misuse and the resulting poor quality presentations seem to be common enough to be the norm. For the experienced presenter, however, the effective use of overheads provides the most practical and professional communications method in many situations. This versatility also means that there are many aspects of using overheads to be considered; they differentiate the professional from the casual communicator.

■ *Formality*

The fact that equipment must be set up and prepared when overheads are used automatically lends an element of formality to any overhead presentation. Nevertheless, the situation is sufficiently familiar to most people to permit a casual atmosphere if that is desired. Overhead presentations can be carried out in formal or informal settings, and the presenter can set the level of formality by the style of presentation used. They can be used for essentially one-way presentation of information to a group, or they can be used interactively, much like flip charts and chalkboards, to focus discussion. They can be the central focus of a presentation, or they can be used as a supplement to presentations and discussions that rely more on other methods. In short, overheads provide the full range of formality/informality options, allowing the presenter and the situation to set the tone.

■ *Facilities and Equipment*

There are many considerations with respect to facilities and equipment. The general rule of visiting the venue prior to the presentation is even more important when using overheads. Some of the

FIGURE 6-4: *Uses of Overheads and Slides in Presentations*					
Equipment Group	**Facilities and Other Operational Factors**				
	Size	**Lighting**	**Seating**	**Type**	**Critical Supplies**
Projector	Some cannot provide a large image to fill a large screen	Sufficiently subdued lighting; absence of glare on screen; convenient controls	Presenter and projector may block some seats	Bulb-in-base (nonportables) better suited for transparencies with overlays	Extension cord, spare bulb, extra table for overheads, notes
Screen	Dependent on room size and ceiling height	Walls or whiteboards provide poor results – inappropriate reflective characteristics	Large groups need high ceiling, screen raised and canted forward to reduce key-stoning[1]	Reflective screens	None
Overheads and computer slides	Avoid fine detail, small print for medium or large group presentation	Sufficiently subdued to permit viewing detail, but sufficiently lit to encourage participation	Classroom format discourages discussion, D or box format limits numbers	Some overhead production choices provide better definition and color capabilities	Frames for overheads, tape, pointer, overhead marker pens, cloth for cleaning overheads and projector lens

[1]Keystoning refers to the lack of squareness of the projected image caused by the projector not being on the same plane as the screen. It can occur horizontally as well as vertically if the projector is pointing somewhat sideways or up to a vertical screen. The result is that a portion of the overhead image is out of focus. The solution is usually to adjust or reposition the screen, but sometimes moving the projector is required, which is often a more complicated alternative because of the effect on seating.

long list of factors that can be observed and handled in advance include: the limiting factors such as ceiling height, seating and blind spots caused by the position of the presenter and the projector; lighting systems and how to alter the settings: turn lights on, off or down (particularly ceiling spotlights which can cause screen glare); location of electrical outlets; quality and size of the screen; and availability of side tables. Figure 6-4 summarizes some of the more common issues associated with the use of overheads and slides in a presentation.

Equipment for presenting slides (other than the 35mm slides discussed briefly later) is of two types: the traditional overhead projector, and the emerging computer-based projectors. Some of the latter still require an overhead projector but use computer-based inputs, and others are independent projectors connected to computers, usually laptops. The material to be presented is essentially the same in that a computer can print transparencies or transmit the same material to the computer-based projector. The more sophisticated computer-based systems offer the benefits of photos, full-action video, and sound. This may be particularly useful when demonstrating focus group results or documenting physical, environmental and site situations. In addition, computer projectors can provide some visual options for transition from slide to slide.

Regardless of the equipment selected, presentation is impossible if the equipment does not work correctly. The following describes some of the equipment-based issues which presenters face.

TRADITIONAL OVERHEAD PROJECTORS In the case of traditional overhead projectors, because this is an old technology, many clients have old projectors, and many of these are not in good repair. With any projection device lenses can become scratched and parts become loose or wobbly, making clean, stable and level images difficult to achieve. Spare light bulbs are often a problem. Machines that purport to contain self-stored spares rarely do, and changing bulbs can be difficult and even dangerous when

handling unfamiliar equipment. It is the presenter's responsibility to be sure the equipment works and to understand
the equipment better than most. Although it is inconve-
nient, it is a good idea to bring a backup projector, which
has a spare bulb, as well as an extra extension cord. You
will rarely need it, but when you do, you'll be a hero.

There are two basic types of overhead projectors, and it
is important to be familiar with each. The most common
is a type in which the source of light is in the base, which
is three to six inches thick. Some modern facilities include
a table top that has an overhead built into it and is flush
with the surface. This is a variation of the bulb-in-base overhead. The light shines up through the transparency to an
overhead prism lens that redirects the image to the screen.
This type of projector comes in several models, some of
which fold and are portable. Some have a spare bulb in the
base that can be shifted into place in the event of a bulb
failure. However, they have cooling fans that can be quite
noisy and can cause difficulties as they blow across the
tabletop, causing papers to rustle and fly if the presenter
is not duly prepared. This brings to mind a personal story.

A number of years ago many of our large multinational
clients preferred to have meetings in Toronto, where the
US-based executives could enjoy Cuban cigars. We recon-
vened on one such occasion in a client boardroom after
lunch, and the client executives were all indulging their
smoking passion over cups of coffee. As my boss switched
the projector on, I saw that the client president's cigar was
developing a long ash, and it looked precarious; he was
seated across from me, at the end of the table nearest to
the projector. Being young and eager to demonstrate my
awareness and sensitivity, I quickly pushed the partially
full ashtray across the table to the client, totally forgetting
about the fan in the base of the projector. In a moment
everyone in the room had cigar ashes in their coffee.

The second type of overhead projector is a slim portable that folds up to the size of a thin briefcase. The light source is overhead, shining down through the transparency, reflecting back up from a mirror lens that forms the base and transmitting to the screen through the overhead prism lens. In both types, focusing is achieved by raising or lowering the prism lens on its support rod. The size of the image is regulated by the distance to the screen. These slim-line portables look modern and have the advantage of being smaller and lighter than the bulb-in-base models. From the presenter's point of view, however, the slim-line model has the disadvantage of producing double images when overhead transparencies are framed or have overlays because the light passes through them twice.

COMPUTER-BASED PROJECTORS Computer-based projectors come in three basic types: fixed in place (found in classrooms and some large client presentation rooms), overhead projector mounted, and desktop projectors which need no overhead projector. The first is rare, the second may be a transition technology as the desktop system becomes more refined and trouble-free, and the third, which is its own projector, is still prone to operator and technical problems. Technology is evolving rapidly, and many of the difficulties experienced by presenters today will undoubtedly diminish as equipment shortcomings are overcome and presenters gain experience. However, today horror stories still abound, of malfunctioning equipment, lost files, and incompatibility problems.

Many of these are the result of inexperience on the part of presenters and support operators. The message for presenters is, take time to become experienced and proficient with the equipment before using it in a presentation. Although much of today's computer technology is very user-friendly, the options and settings of any new device require practice to gain the skill to use it effectively. A client presentation is not a suitable place to practice.

Checklist 6-10 at the end of this section summarizes key considerations in using traditional overheads. To this, one can add the following caveats, with respect to overhead and computer-generated presentations:

- Understand and practice with pointer options provided in the software; the simple manual pointer which can be placed on the overhead may not be available.
- Be careful of the high temperature generated by some equipment. It is recommended that bulbs be switched frequently to reduce burn-out. In addition, some computers and overhead machines can generate enough heat to make small boardrooms uncomfortable if there is insufficient ventilation or air conditioning.
- Have oversized notes on hand in case projection problems make viewing the presentation difficult on screen.
- If you are planning to use a computer, have a set of back-up overheads and/or printed copies of the material with you and a projector in case of computer system or equipment failure. Pretest all overheads before hand.

■ *Delivery*

Effective presentations using slides takes practice and confidence. All presentations should be rehearsed, preferably in front of a friendly critic. The content and the language to be used in presenting should be clear in the minds of the presenters and the visual characteristics of the slides familiar. Notwithstanding the usual rules of public speaking (discussed earlier under speeches) which still apply, the following special aspects of presentations should be observed:

INSIDER'S VIEW

The same transparency may not look identical with the two systems, so it is more important than ever to view the full presentation with the intended projector before making a presentation.

FACE THE AUDIENCE. Many presenters would really rather be part of the audience. Resist the temptation to look at the screen. Take advantage of the opportunity to move about, make eye contact and read the feedback signals. You already know what is on the slide, and you can refer to it in its location on the projector. Keep the occasions you turn away from the audience and face the screen to a minimum.

USE A POINTER. Most presenters look silly using exaggerated gestures in silhouette against a screen beside which they appear small. Avoid going up to the screen to draw attention to content. Use a sharp pencil, pen or other pointer, laid on top of, or lightly touching the transparency on the projector – not on the screen. Arrow-shaped swizzle sticks make excellent pointers. Computer software provides pointer devices which can be used effectively with a little practice. Gesturing with pen in hand can spell disaster when it touches and leaves a long and permanent arc on the client's boardroom screen. Also, it remains for the balance of the presentation. Laser pointers can be used for large groups where the presenter has an associate to operate the overhead projector, but these may be distracting if they cannot be held steady. If the presenter is near the projector, as is usually the case, a pointer on the slide is the most effective approach.

USE COLOURS, SHADING AND OTHER GRAPHIC DEVICES TO SUPPORT THE MESSAGE. Colours impart relative emphasis to the presentation, and some colours appear more commanding on some slides. Usually, black is neutral and may be weaker than a dark blue or green; red is customarily emphatic and draws the viewer's attention. Remember that some people, particularly males, are colour-blind, and may not be able to distinguish between red, green and brown. However, the use of italics and varying types and sizes of fonts provide other opportunities to express emphasis as well. Bear in mind that too many changes and variations are distracting. A mistake many presenters make is to use all capitals in the type: most viewers are not accustomed to reading all capitals and find the style distracting, even irritating.

Modern software provides a wide range of art options as well as convenient presentation formats. If you are an artist, you will know how to enhance your presentation with the judicious and probably subtle use of complex colours and graphic devices. You will also know how unappealing poor artwork can be. As a general rule, consultants should avoid the use of fancy borders, background fill and superficial or non-contributing clip art; these devices usually add little and can greatly weaken the presentation or irritate some clients.

The most common fault in presentation design is too many words and not enough meaningful visual material. In many instances, a good conceptual depiction can replace several typed slides. These are time consuming to develop, but the thought process demonstrated in designing a clear visual that depicts the relationships among variables is an analytical skill valued by most clients.

KEEP IT SIMPLE. Too many points on a given slide can lose an audience. The presentation will move more smoothly when each slide has a simple message to contribute to the whole. Good messages can usually be communicated with three or four points under each heading, one heading per overlay and no more than four overlays per slide. When there is a list of many items, each item should be kept to as few words as possible, and the list should be broken into groups of three or four, each on a separate overlay. Remember, this is a presentation, and the material is there to *support* the message, not carry the whole burden. Stick to brief, agenda-like points, and discuss each in turn. Avoid long sentences. Complex drawings, cartoons or printed pages are frequently too cluttered to be useful. They should be seen on a screen before they are included in a presentation to ensure they can be seen, read, understood and provide the desired effect. Frequently, they can be simplified to focus on just what is needed. One slide of a page from a book is one too many. If there is a table, chart or graph on a page that you want to use in your presentation, photocopy the page, cut out the table or chart you want, enlarge it and then make the slide.

KNOW HOW LONG YOU HAVE. A presentation which is too long for the time allotted has two outcomes, neither of which is good. It can run too long, in which case it may offend the client or conference organizers (to say nothing of the next presenters if this is but one presentation of several). Or the presenters will try to shorten and edit it on the spot, resulting in a rushed presentation. Either consequence is unprofessional and unnecessary. A fairly reliable rule of thumb is that most presentations use slides for about three minutes each. That time factor will provide a good estimate of the amount of time and allow the consultant to estimate the number of slides needed.

PAY ATTENTION TO YOUR HANDS. As indicated earlier, hands are a problem for most speakers. There is a particular concern when making a presentation because the presenter is moving, using a pointer and communicating in a very direct way with the audience. Make deliberate and meaningful gestures in support of what you are saying, but otherwise, keep your hands at your sides. Gestures and other aspects of body language are more obvious and therefore more influential when making presentations. Effective use of gestures strongly support a presentation, but unplanned body movements are distracting to the audience and indicate insecurity on the part of the presenter. When you are not moving the pointer, leave it at rest either on the slide in its last reference position or on the table beside the projector. If it is a manual pointer, do not keep it in your hands, or you will soon find yourself fidgeting with it.

USE THE LIGHTING.

Lighting sets the mood and locates the control in the room. When the presentation is to be fairly formal and most of the communication is expected to be one way from the presenter(s) to the audience, lowering

> ## INSIDER'S VIEW
> Watch some silent movies to see the dramatic usage of gestures, and feel their effectiveness.

the room lights focuses attention on the screen. Lowering only the back lights in a large room can add to the feeling of inclusiveness of the audience group. Normal lighting in most halls is bright, and leaving the lighting up signals to the group that they can participate at any time. Varying the light in the course of a presentation can tell the audience when to talk and when to listen. The presenter should be aware of the effect of the lighting and be prepared to adjust it if it is too subdued to encourage discussion. Turning the meeting room lights back to normal at the end of the presentation signals the end of the formal proceedings, and this may be used to start informal workshops and discussions.

PLAN FOR TALK TIME. Slide presentations focus attention on the presenter. Sometimes, the purpose of the presentation is to engage in discussion as well as to share information. During these discussion periods, the current slide may not be particularly relevant, and the presenter may wish to let the discussion flow. One option to allow for this talk time is to turn the projector off. This sends an important message to the audience – that this is a time for unrestricted discussion, and the presentation is, for the moment, of secondary importance. Leaving the projector on tells the audience that the presentation will resume in a moment and discussion should be restricted. If the projector is left on, it should have a slide on it to avoid a bright blank screen which is distracting and irritating to some. The cover or title slide or a previously used one referring to the current part of the presentation can be on the projector during the discussion. A common error is to put the next slide up in anticipation of continuing the presentation. Not only is this distracting, but it sends a strong signal that discussion is merely being tolerated and should be concluded as soon as possible. It may also preempt the presenter's upcoming remarks.

SUPPORT THE LEAD PRESENTER. Group presentations pose the problem of what those not currently presenting should do. The staging often has the group seated like a panel facing the audience. The non-presenters become a distraction, and their every motion draws attention. If they look into the audience, they make distracting and unproductive eye contact; if they look at their notes, they seem to be ignoring the speaker; if they interact with one another or fidget, they are even more distracting. The solution is for the nonpresenters to become part of the audience, look at the speaker and remain motionless. Notice how supporting cast members in a play or on television avoid stealing the scene by freezing and remaining completely motionless when their presence is temporarily not relevant.

USE CONSISTENT WORDING. When reading a statement from the overhead, the presenter should use the same words as those written. Viewers are reading along and become confused when they hear one set of words and read another, even when they are close. Similarly it is an important corollary to ensure that the graphics illustrate the point you are making accurately and do not provide conflicting or confusing information.

▪ *Documentation*

Slide presentations provide their own documentation in the form of hard copy counterparts of the slides. Computers can print both transparencies and hard copy of presentations, and, provided a colour printer is available, the printed output can be virtually identical to the slides in all respects. Some accommodation must be made where motion and sound were featured, of course. Service bureaus serving small businesses and home offices are becoming common in many cities and can produce professional quality coloured copies from compatible computer files at a modest cost.

Hard copy is the most common form of documentation for slide presentations. It is usually distributed at the conclusion of the presentation, but it may also be distributed at the beginning so that the audience can make notations on their individual copies. Most audiences will respond appropriately when asked to refrain from reading ahead of the presentation, but they need to be asked.

Hard copy should be bound like any other formal document, complete with cover page and table of contents (agenda), but it is incomplete in that it does not automatically contain the narrative portion of the presentation. Its value can be increased by adding written commentary to the hard copy. Key points in the presentation can be included on the page facing each slide copy or otherwise inserted in the document. Written documents live long lives. Any document should clearly state what it is and when it was provided because it may surface years later and need explanation. Hard copy of slide presentations are written documents, and they must also be labeled to avoid confusion with other later documents. The hard copy document should be clearly marked as the hard copy of a slide presentation so that it will not be confused with a formal report.

Using Overlays

When a given overhead contains a complex diagram or concept, or when it contains a number of points, it may be advisable to control the pace at which the audience receives the information. A common method used with overheads to restrict the material is to cover a portion of the overhead with a sheet of paper and gradually reveal the contents by sliding it down the transparency. This is sometimes distracting, and the audience frequently becomes more curious about what is about to be revealed than in what is being presented at the moment. Overlays are easily produced and will provide a more effective way of revealing the transparency in stages. Figure 6-5 is an example of a base transparency of a complex overhead that will require several overlays.

The same effect can be provided by the sequencing of material in computer-projected presentations. Material can be added to a base slide from the side or elsewhere, as desired. In most cases, one style should be maintained throughout to avoid distraction.

FIGURE 6-5: *Base Transparency*

THE BUSINESS SYSTEM

Input	Processor	Output

The base slide provides the presenter with the opportunity to describe the concept in general and enables the audience to prepare for the information to follow. In Figure 6-5, the slide presents a business system diagram, illustrating its three components: input, processor and output. The audience is then prepared to accept the next information within that frame of reference. Base slides can also be used to set out the axes of a graph, headings in a table or chart or the title to a list of points along with the first few to be covered. If it will be used as an overhead, the base transparency should be taped securely to a cardboard transparency frame. The first overlay is then produced as shown in Figure 6-6.

FIGURE 6-6: *First Overlay*

THE BUSINESS SYSTEM

Input	Processor	Output
Resources		
• Human		
• Information		
• Physical		
• Technology		
• Financial		

This focuses the audience on that part of the slide the presenter is addressing at the moment. In Figure 6-6, the presenter wishes to draw attention to the first set of material in the model. The overlay material or transparency contains only the relevant content, and if an overhead, it is fastened to the cardboard frame to which the base overhead is secured by a strip of tape that allows it to be hinged from one edge, usually the top. Similarly, the second and third overlays in Figures 6-7 and 6-8 focus on the sequence of material the presenter wishes to display.

Finally, with the fourth and concluding overlay, the presenter emphasizes the point or purpose of the slide. In Figure 6-9, the presenter has developed the principle that a system, comprising a set of inputs, a set of processes and a set of outputs, operates in one direction (left to right) but is designed and renewed in the reverse direction (right to left).

FIGURE 6-7: *Second Overlay*

THE BUSINESS SYSTEM

Input	Processor	Output
Resources	**Management Processes**	
• Human	• Structuring	
• Information	• Decision-making	
• Physical	• Communicating	
• Technology	• Leading	
• Financial	• Controlling	

FIGURE 6-8: *Third Overlay*

THE BUSINESS SYSTEM

Input	Processor	Output
Resources	**Management Processes**	**Results**
• Human	• Structuring	• Financial
• Information	• Decision-making	• Quality of products and services
• Physical	• Communicating	• Quantity of products and services
• Technology	• Leading	
• Financial	• Controlling	

FIGURE 6-9: *Fourth Overlay*

THE BUSINESS SYSTEM

Input	Processor	Output
Resources	**Management Processes**	**Results**
• Human	• Structuring	• Financial
• Information	• Decision-making	• Quality of products and services
• Physical	• Communicating	• Quantity of products and services
• Technology	• Leading	
• Financial	• Controlling	

FULFILLING THE MISSION

RENEWING THE RESOURCES

Each overhead overlay contains only the information being added and is taped to the same edge of the mounting frame so that they appear in layers or sequences, each contributing to the total overhead. As a set, they provide a continuous progressive display that can be integrated with the presenter's verbal material smoothly and essentially seamlessly. The speed of the presentation is under the presenter's control, and each overlay can be withheld until the preceding ones are clearly understood.

For a quick review on the use of overhead transparencies during presentations see Checklist 6-10.

35mm Slides

This option offers high-quality visuals, and the equipment, while still expensive, is becoming more available as technologies

CHECKLIST 6-10: *Using Slides or Overheads*

✔ **Formality**
  – Full range
  – Slides or overheads can be central or ancillary

✔ **Facilities – many issues (see Figure 6-4)**
  – Projector type, computer compatibility
  – Screen
  – Room layout
  – Lighting controls

✔ **Delivery**
  – Face audience, move about
  – Watch your hands, use pointer
  – Colours and overlays
  – Simple clear slides or overheads
  – Watch timing, plan talk time
  – Support speaker in group presentations

✔ **Documentation**
  – Hard copy of overheads or slides
  – Could have narrative on facing page
  – May be colour
  – Bound, clearly labeled as hard copy only

continue to evolve. The use of 35mm slides, because of their cost of preparation, are restricted in their use to large groups and/or presentations designed for repeated use. They are particularly well-suited for large group presentations in which the sequence of material to be covered can be fixed. These slides, familiar through their widespread consumer use, provide the opportunity to include good quality photographs in the presentation, sometimes a critical part of the project observations.

Similarly, high-quality graphics and photographs can be incorporated into 35mm presentations when needed. Most computer presentation systems also provide the opportunity to use markers and pointers when presenting, whereas 35mm slides require a laser pointer or an assistant with a hand pointer at the screen or operating the projector. Laser pointers can be distracting when they are poorly handled. They are extremely susceptible to jiggling and wandering, they require practice, should be shut off when not specifically pointing to something and should never be used the day after a party! The use of an assistant is desirable with slide projectors, even when the presenter is using remote carousel controls. The more complex the presentation equipment, the more the likelihood of malfunction.

Consultants frequently use several presentation methods simultaneously. It is not uncommon for a presentation to involve a computer or 35mm slide-based display of information, supplemented by an overhead presentation during which the audience interacts with the presenters, who also use flip charts and a whiteboard to explore ideas and to diagram principles. Experienced presenters move easily among these technologies, using each to its best advantage and managing the communication seamlessly and effectively. In this way, the technologies themselves become essentially invisible and irrelevant to the presentation.

Presentations can be an exciting and fulfilling part of the consulting process. When performed effectively, they provide an opportunity to communicate meaningfully with and influence clients and prospective clients. Good presentations demonstrate a professional level of concern for form, substance and commitment to detail. Clients and potential clients then understand that the consultant considers the audience to be important enough to justify the effort required to make a proper presentation. Every practical opportunity should be taken to reinforce this understanding and maintain the strong relationship needed for consultant and client to work together. Consultants should be familiar with all presentation methods, because they are tools. They should also be up-to-date on the latest technology for presenting and be able to evaluate which method is best suited for which occasion. Keeping abreast of new and changing technologies, particularly the use of computers and the Internet, is part of effective consulting. Improvements will continue to arrive at a rapid rate. As technology continues to provide more presentation options less expensively and more conveniently, consultants will incorporate them into their presentations, selecting them pragmatically to enhance their communication effectiveness.

Now that we have covered the question of marketing and selling your expertise and the importance of proposals and presentations, let us move on to see how it all comes together when you begin to actually do the consulting work.

SEVEN

Performing the Work

The moment of truth arrives with combined feelings of anticipation and anxiety. Now you must deliver on the promises in your proposal. You are confident that you can perform the work, but you must provide the advice for which you have been retained on time and backed up with facts. Furthermore, you need to work the new project into your overall set of activities and other time commitments. You need a structured approach – a blueprint to follow that will render the project doable.

There are essentially three dimensions to consider:

THE PRACTICE. How have you decided to operate your consulting practice as a professional?

THE PROJECT. How will you perform the specific project you are about to begin?

THE CLIENT. How will you work with individuals whose experience with consultants may be limited?

Each of these dimensions should be considered at the outset of every new project. This chapter addresses these three dimensions of performing the work.

The Practice

Each assignment is a business agreement with a client. It has all the elements of a contract: there is agreement on what you will provide, the benefits your client will receive and the basis on which you will be paid. In other words, there will be an exchange of value between two parties – you and your client. At times, there may be more than two parties, such as projects performed for a group of clients and projects for which consultants form joint ventures or syndicated relationships for the purposes of carrying out a specific project. These are unusual, but the same principles apply as in the simpler, two-party contract.

It is important to acknowledge this formal relationship because, regardless of how informal your relationship with an individual client is, there are important business and legal aspects to any assignment. When making a legal agreement, imagine that immediately following signing, the other party gets hit by a truck and is replaced by a complete stranger. Agreements often develop a life of their own.

In addition to business and legal considerations associated with specific projects, you are likely to be involved in many other activities at the same time. Whether you are part of a firm of professional consultants or provide consulting as a part-time activity, you need to manage your business. Building and maintaining a consulting practice requires an on-going program of business development. As your practice develops, you are likely to be involved in more than one project at the same time. Providing all your clients with the superior service to which they are entitled means operating the practice in an organized way and placing each new project in context with your practice and the policies you establish for it. There are three major elements of practice management: defining the practice, building the business and managing the business.

▪ *Defining the Practice*

Defining the practice is the process of developing your consulting practice to reflect your personal values. If you are employed by a consulting firm, developing your practice within that environment requires that you support the procedures, policies and values of your professional colleagues in that practice. Similarly, if you have established a practice in collaboration with others, you have obligations to ensure that your operating practices and policies fit with the group's requirements. Even if you choose to operate a small part-time practice, you need to define it in order to keep it focused and vital. Many consultants find themselves in practice more by accident than by design, but to remain professionals, they need to define the practice in order to build and manage it. The following are some of the elements of defining a practice:

STRUCTURE. Part of a large practice, independent, working alone or networking with others, part-time and so forth

SPECIALTY. Central technology, industry focus, special knowledge, training and/or experience

SCOPE. Market reach, use of teams, networking capabilities, international dimension

SIZE. Large, multifunctional projects, small part-time engagements

STYLE. Research, intervention, seminars and workshops, teaming with client personnel, advisory, counseling, facilitation, mediation and so forth

International Opportunities

An important consideration in defining your practice is the extent to which it will be international. Increasingly, individual Canadians and small firms are faced with foreign consulting opportunities, often brought to their attention by government agencies such as CIDA and the IFIs, clients with international requirements, academic institutions engaged in international initiatives or through the normal process of networking with colleagues. A decision to work internationally involves special preparations. For example, an up-to-date passport may not take much time to obtain, but it may be needed on short notice. Your doctor should be consulted regarding special shots and other precautions before traveling to some parts of the world.

INSIDER'S VIEW

Preplanning is a must. Some diseases such as malaria, rare in Canada, require vaccines that need to be administered months in advance of exposure.

A small supply of US currency should be kept on hand, not just for unplanned visits to the US. Although Canadian currency is easily convertible in many countries, it is not as universally acceptable as American. Also, not all foreign currency is freely convertible into Canadian or other hard currencies. You may need to require that you be paid in Canadian, US or some other convertible currency, and you may need to ensure that the amount quoted for your work will be converted at some agreed rate to protect yourself against devaluation of the client foreign currency.

You should understand the need for special clauses in your consulting agreements. For example, you may want to insert a clause to provide that the client will be responsible for all local taxes, such as withholding taxes that might reduce your net proceeds from the work. While most international taxes can be deducted from Canadian taxes, you should seek professional advice regarding witholdings and cases where taxes are in excess of Canadian rates or otherwise differ significantly in their application.

If international business is to be a significant focus, you may want to consider other corporate structures, perhaps domiciled in other countries, where international revenues can be held for further investment internationally as needed. This situation is true in Bermuda, for example, where domestic taxes are very low, and banking is secure.

Exchange and political risks enter into international decisions as well. The Canadian government has programs of instruction and videos to help Canadians traveling abroad and doing business internationally, but you are advised to build relationships with qualified accountants and lawyers. Different countries have different laws and different patterns of enforcement.

In short, international opportunities arise, and when they do, the practice should be prepared for them.

■ *Building the Business*

Building the business takes place in the context of your defined practice. In large firms, professionals have defined roles for their services. Individuals are encouraged to build the business and in some cases are assigned specific goals. Whether it is publishing articles, making speeches or developing clients through their technical expertise, each professional usually has some role to play in helping build the business. Invariably, the task of building the business competes for the time the consultant uses to work on client projects. With small firms in particular, the business development activities of article writing and speech making are often postponed while billable client work is given priority. This creates a "peak and valley" business that can lead to anxiety when cash flows follow the same pattern.

■ *Managing the Business*

Managing a consulting business is relatively straightforward. The day-to-day management takes place through the projects. The deployment and management of people, the assigning and monitoring of tasks and performance, the scheduling and carrying out of tasks associated with client requirements and the management of expenses are part of executing projects. Activities associated with building the business are scheduled and performed in much the same way as project tasks.

What remains is administration. That generally consists of accounting – essentially for corporate reporting and tax purposes – and control – to track the firm's overall performance. In large firms, these two streams of information are maintained through a set of regular routines, managed by an individual or group responsible for the firm's administration. The professional provides the needed information regularly (usually weekly) by filling in a form. In small firms, administration may be provided by an independent accountant or bookkeeper or maintained by the consultants themselves.

The accounting portion of the administration must be maintained in accordance with accepted accounting practice so that the firm, regardless of size, complies with legal and tax requirements. The second portion – control – is not required by law, but it is important to effective management of the practice. It consists of tracking measures of productivity in order to provide a comparison between what the practice is achieving and what was planned. This enables professionals to direct their activities where they seem to be doing the most good in terms of the development and profitability of the practice. Productivity comprises the relationship between time and money. The time information is captured from time records that allocate time spent among activities, defined as *chargeable* (billable) or *nonchargeable* (nonbillable). Chargeable time is that which clients pay for, and nonchargeable time is everything else, usually either business development or administration.

Consultants sell time; therefore, time is the most important single variable in managing a consulting enterprise. Administration focuses on time management and on expenses related to both the firm as a whole and to the individual assignments. Each assignment should have its own budget, the amount of professional time, the billing rate for that time and the amount of expenses that are expected to accrue to that assignment. It may be useful to set up more than one assignment at the same time for a client when there are several distinct tasks to be performed at once. Also, consultants can establish budgets for internal control purposes which are higher than the budget quoted to the client. This would indicate that the consultant plans to devote extra budgeted but nonchargeable time to that client's work for strategic reasons, such as anticipation of additional work later that will recover the invested time.

The basic management control then, is to record actual time spent and actual expenses incurred against the budget. Most of the time, hopefully, they will be about equal at the end of the assignment. Sometimes, however, changes occur in the assignment during the work. When this happens, consultants discuss them with the client, and, if possible, the budget is reviewed and adjusted accordingly. Sometimes consultants will accept small additions to the work content without adding to the budget. If the budget is too low, the work content has not been estimated accurately. In these cases, consultants usually absorb the extra work, writing the extra work off to experience or the normal business risk associated with submitting bids. Reviewing the relationship between budgets and actual time and expenses is important to the learning process as the consultant refines the ability to estimate. Experienced consultants frequently include an unallocated budget item for contingencies when a proposed project contains significant unknown factors. Usually this ranges from 10 to 25 percent, depending on the degree of uncertainty. It is easier to explain a contingency allowance at the outset of an assignment (and perhaps come in under budget) than to try to increase the budget after the work has begun.

When an assignment goes over budget (the professional time expended exceeds the amount of time budgeted and that can therefore be billed), overruns result. For proper control, the actual time spent should be recorded. Still, we are all human, and frequently overruns are understated because the consultant has chosen to take the hit and not report all the time spent in order to minimize the reported overrun. Consulting firms frequently reward employees on the basis of their utilization rate (percentage of total available time which is billed), and this can add to the incentive to underreport unbillable time. In a sole-person practice, such underreporting is merely self-deception and can mislead the consultant with respect to estimating time requirements in future projects. The comparison of actual versus budget needs to be accurate if the learning process with respect to time budgeting and management is to be maximized. A consistent pattern of overruns may mean consistent underbudgeting or inefficiency or both; situations which deserve attention.

Three important statistics are tracked in consulting practices for effective control:

> **UTILIZATION RATE.** As indicated above, this is the percentage of total available time that is billed to a client. Available time may be a standard work week of 35 or 40 hours or any number of hours the consultant plans to be available for professional work. A part-time consultant, for example, may plan to work on consulting an average of

10 hours per week or for two six-week periods scheduled into certain periods of the year. These hours become the available hours with which expected (budgeted) and actual chargeable hours can be compared to arrive at the budgeted and actual utilization rates.

REALIZATION RATE. This tracks the actual revenue received from clients per hour billed. The decision to bill a client for all the time spent is often separate from the decision to spend time on the client's work.

BILLING RATE VARIANCE. This is the ratio of realization rate to standard billing rate. Defined in Chapter 2, "Getting Started," the *standard* billing rate is the rate you hope to achieve for client work. It is the rate you use when estimating the fee in a proposal and establishing the budget. When the client actually pays for the work and the payment equals the consultants' standard billing rates times the hours that they charged for the work, the billing rate *variance* is zero. Variance occurs with overruns or when, for any other reason, clients have not paid the amount equal to the total chargeable time.

Comparisons of actual revenues and expenses to budgets (both at a project level and for the firm as a whole) highlight patterns, and regular reviews of these patterns help improve planning and

---

CHECKLIST 7-1: *Operating the Practice*

✔ **Defining the Practice** – select and focus on structure, specialty, scope (domestic/international), size, style

✔ **Building the Business** – develop and assign marketing activities, define goals, individual responsibilities

✔ **Managing the Business** – measure, track and learn from utilization rate, realization rate, billing rate variance, budget versus actual

identify current problems. Even if you are operating as an independent consultant, these simple measures should be tracked. This is a business venture, and there are tax as well as operating consequences of the activities of the business that need to be documented. See Checklist 7-1 for a summary of the steps needed when operating a practice.

The Project

Effective project performance can be grouped into three stages:

BEGINNING THE WORK. Starting with a review of the proposal, planning and scheduling the work, defining and assigning tasks to others involved, putting the administrative machinery in place and initiating data collection.

PERFORMING THE WORK. Applying the special expertise for which you have been engaged. This may be as straightforward as providing advice or conducting seminars, or it may involve complicated research and analytical activities as well as the supervision of others.

COMPLETING THE WORK. Preparing and delivering the interim and final outputs and deliverables of the project to provide the client with the benefits to be achieved by the project.

Every project is different, and not all of what follows may apply in every case. Nevertheless, the elements of good project performance described below can serve as a checklist to remind consultants of the discipline and thought processes that comprise professional consulting work.

■ *Beginning the Work*

Proposal Review

The first step is to review the proposal. Some time may have elapsed since you worked on it, and it is important to recapture the factors

INSIDER'S VIEW

As you reread your proposal, a sense of relief comes over you when you realize that the time and thought you invested in the proposal was thorough. It spells out what you must do and anticipates areas that call for research.

and conditions which led to preparing and submitting it. It may be a letter or a long proposal as described earlier, but nevertheless, it states what you have promised to do. The first rule of effective consulting is to deliver what you proposed – on time and within budget. If you are concerned that things have changed since the proposal was written, discuss it with the client now, not after you have started, and if the fees and timing need to be adjusted, do it now. The structure a good proposal provides can go a long way toward effective project performance. The process used to break the project into work steps and tasks when it was developed help construct project controls as well.

Start-Up Meeting

Depending on the type of project, your first task may be to plan for and schedule a start-up meeting with the client and/or the steering committee. The procedures you establish at the start-up meeting form the basis for later work. The dedication to professional discipline you demonstrate at the beginning of the project sends a message to all client personnel that you intend to perform the assignment according to plan and with rigor. It may be possible to relax some of the formal structure in the course of the work as you develop stronger relationships with client personnel and gain more knowledge of the client's situation. Conversely, it may be difficult to tighten the structure later. You will need to prepare several things for the start-up meeting: the agenda, a work plan, a schedule, an administrative subagenda, and data requests.

Agenda

Provide an agenda to the client a few days in advance of the start-up (or any future) meeting. The agenda may be a simple note such

FIGURE 7-2: *Sample Agenda*

MEETING AGENDA

Meeting Date: October 15, 1998

Purpose: To begin the project

Agenda Items:
- Review and confirm project work plan and task assignments
- Review and confirm project schedule
- Establish project administration procedures
- Discuss initial data requests
- General discussion
- Confirm next scheduled meeting

as shown in Figure 7-2, to be forwarded to each person scheduled to attend. The client may have a variety of reasons for including personnel in the process; therefore, it is not always appropriate for the consultant to provide the agenda directly to the client's staff. Often, assignments to consultant projects are seen as signals to the rest of the staff that an individual is being given special responsibilities and recognition, a process that the client may wish to control personally.

This agenda also serves as the outline for the minutes the consultant provides for each attendee following each meeting. The minutes should be limited to statements of agreed action and confirmation of project commitments, practice and timing. The combined agenda and minute statements then serve as documentation of decisions and progress as the project proceeds. This paper trail can prove helpful later to compare events and activities, as they take place, with recorded expectations and commitments.

Work Plan

Prepare a detailed work plan that is consistent with, and in greater detail than, the work plan that was included in the proposal. For example, your proposal may have specified the following as a work step:

3.1 – *Conduct a telephone survey of 30 active customers.*

For the work plan, this same work step might be described in detail as follows:

3.1.1 – *Compile a list of active customers.*

3.1.2 – *Randomize the order of the list and obtain telephone numbers.*

3.1.3 – *Review survey questionnaire and pretest by performing five initial test interviews.*

3.1.4 – *Review test results and modify questionnaire accordingly.*

3.1.5 – *Conduct survey of first 35 subjects on active client list according to agreed format.*

3.1.6 – *Summarize results of first 30 complete responses on form #3.1.6.1 as provided.*

By addressing the work steps at this level of detail, the full work content is clear and can be scheduled effectively. Everyone involved in the project can have their tasks defined in detail, and they should know all other tasks as well. Even when performing work alone, preplan the work in this detail. It keeps you on track and efficient in the face of other activities that might distract you.

Schedule

Prepare a specific schedule of events so you and your client can make detailed entries in your calendars for working sessions, meetings, presentations and due dates for documents, both draft and final. When meetings are scheduled well in advance, people can organize their work around them, and there can be few excuses for not being available to attend.

Administrative Subagenda

Present an administrative subagenda that clarifies issues regarding addressing and timing of invoices, expense practices and any other similar matters such as the process for clearing major expenses and the level of detail to be shown on invoices.

Data Requests

Present some initial data requests. These test the client's readiness to participate in the project and the quality of data available from client sources. Data requests, using forms that client staff can complete, can provide important basic information quickly and inexpensively. When contentious findings occur, it is often much easier to support conclusions drawn from client data than to defend the use of other data sources.

■ *Performing the Work*

Once the project has formally begun, the project plan becomes the guiding document as work is performed and supervised. Tasks will need to be assigned, research carried out, analytical tools applied and the work program managed. Some guidelines for performing the work follow.

Assigning Tasks

Assigning tasks becomes important when several consultants are working as a team and when client staff assigned to the project need direction. Each needs to know specifically what to do and how to coordinate with the others. In these cases, specific and unambiguous task assignments are essential to good project management. When client personnel are included on the consulting team, the need for effective leadership from the professional consultants is even greater, and successful work may depend on how well the tasks are specified and assigned. In complex projects, written assignment of work and a practice of distributing to everyone assigned to the project all memos and documents associated with task assignments may be essential. Even when the assignment involves only one consultant, it is often advisable to assign some work in writing to the client to ensure active involvement. Generally, the more clients and their staff can be involved in performing the work, the more committed they will be to implementing the result.

The detailed project plan presented at the start-up meeting may be in sufficient detail to assign specific elements, but more frequently, an additional level of detail is helpful. This is particularly true when assigning work to client staff who may not be accustomed to organizing their effort around defined tasks. Well-defined task assignments not only specify what needs to be accomplished and when, but also suggest how it is to be done and what project deliverable will result. For example, Figure 7-3 depicts a task assignment to conduct a set of telephone interviews.

Research

Research provides a basis of facts and are the consultant's best ally. An underpinning of facts is the foundation for the consultant's

---

FIGURE 7-3: *Sample Task Assignment*

TASK ASSIGNMENT

Date Assigned: October 15, 1998

Task Number: 2.3.3

Objective: To conduct 25 to 30 selected telephone interviews as per Step 2.3 in project work plan

Suggested approach:
- Develop list of potential respondents from company files and catalogs
- Obtain telephone numbers
- Review telephone interview guide as prepared in 2.3.2
- Complete telephone interviews, documenting respondent names
- Summarize results and submit summary to project manager

Responsibility: A. Brown

Budgeted Time: 2 person-days

Due: November 15, 1998

Deliverable: Listing of calls made and summary of responses on form 2.3.3.a (copy attached).

conclusions and recommendations. These conclusions and recommendations are an essential part of what most clients are seeking. Consequently, most consulting requires some research. Whether it involves only a few interviews or complex data gathering, it is designed to add information to the client's decision-making ability. Not all consulting work requires extensive research, but some does, so it is important that consultants be familiar with a wide array of research methodologies and tools. Among the most common research tools are the following:

SECONDARY DATA REVIEW

This comprises library research and Internet surfing to ensure that the project database contains the latest published material (properly identified as to source). Trade publications, special reports of government agencies and associations, research publications and periodical articles are among the most productive sources for many types of assignments.

CLIENT FILES

These often provide a great deal of raw data that can reveal much about patterns of operations. For example, a random sample of customer orders and invoices compared with shipping documents can often reveal much about customer service levels, back orders and delivery delays. Similarly, organization charts, along with selected personnel information can reveal a great deal about turnover and identify possible organizational trouble spots. Marketing and transaction information can identify patterns of behaviour of client customer groups.

CLIENT PERSONNEL INTERVIEWS

Interviews with managers and employees at all levels can provide valuable information about how operations are performed. Employees often reveal important deviations from policy that managers are unaware of. In one case, a branch manager refused to accept VISA because he didn't believe in credit. His superiors were unaware of this until it was revealed by an employee during a confidential interview. Many employees have files that contain special studies done in the past and other reports that may bear on the consulting task at hand.

IN-DEPTH INTERVIEWS
Interviews with industry and market leaders and other spokespersons are often part of consulting projects. Current voice-mail practices by many "knowledgeables" can make such research difficult because they effectively isolate possible respondents from independent consultants. Sometimes the client can assist in establishing some preliminary contacts from current active business contacts or other business acquaintances, and these can be further networked by the consultant to broaden the range of responses.

Respondents are usually more willing to grant interviews when they know for whom the research is being conducted. Many are concerned that the research is being conducted by organizations with which they deal on a day-to-day basis, and that the consultant will not treat the information in confidence. Some worry that the research has been commissioned by a competitor. Conversely, some clients are reluctant to be identified to respondents and wish for the research to be carried out in secret. Often this reluctance to be identified is based on a fear (usually unfounded) that customers or competitors might react negatively to the knowledge that they are using consultants. This reluctance can usually be overcome through discussion, and clients frequently see some possible benefit in being seen conducting the research.

SURVEYS
Surveys can take many forms. The most common are direct mail, telephone and personally administered ones. Each has its strengths and weaknesses. Standard attitude surveys carried out within organizations can be classed as personally administered because they are frequently handed out and self-administered, to be collected later.

Direct Mail
This takes time and usually results in low response rates. It is difficult to test for bias in the responses because the nonrespondents

are difficult to evaluate without secondary sampling. Direct mail can be expensive, with mailing costs and the cost of acquiring lists, but it may be cheaper than more labour-intensive alternatives for large-scale surveys.

Telephone Surveys

These have the advantage of fast turnaround from questionnaire development to response. Measures can be taken to reduce response bias and respondent selection, and response rates are high. The cost of interviewers is high, and the survey may be limited because the amount of time respondents will grant telephone interviewers is usually very short.

Personally Administered Surveys

Door-to-door and self-administered surveys can collect a substantial amount of data and can be controlled well for bias by selecting the respondents carefully, but this is the most expensive survey method.

Professional survey firms are well equipped to carry out this data collection, and the consultant can help the client engage a specialist firm rather than carrying out the research personally unless the consultant's own practice includes providing survey research services.

FOCUS GROUPS AND DELPHI

These are specialized research techniques, and they particularly useful when exploring less tangible topics such as conceptual understanding, developing consensus on future expectations and the like. They are not just discussion groups; they are research forums. They can be powerful tools when properly used, but they require highly experienced leadership and must focus on specific and somewhat limited subjects if they are to yield usable results. These two techniques are probably the most misused and abused of all. Frequently, clients try to carry them out themselves rather than employ professional researchers and moderators. The results are invariably disappointing, and clients then tend to discredit the methodology rather than admit that they were not done properly. As with any methodology, there are disciplines to observe if the results are to be meaningful. For example, with respect to focus groups:

- Participants should be selected with care.
- Groups should be facilitated by an independent skilled facilitator.
- The topic should be limited for focus to be maintained.
- Groups should always be done in pairs to limit the chance of individual group peculiarity obscuring group results.

Delphi research is used to develop consensus among a group of "knowledgeables" in the field being studied. The subject is broadly defined. For example, "What is Excellence in Management Consulting?" was the subject of Delphi research conducted recently by the Canadian Association of Management Consultants. In this method of research, a series of questions and statements is presented to the Delphi participants – the selected knowledgeables – concerning the question to be studied, and their opinions are received. The researcher reviews the responses and constructs a format that summarizes key elements of the responses and sends the results to the same participants for the second-round review and comment. This cycle may be repeated with a third summary and the results analyzed. Key considerations in using the Delphi research method are:

- Selection and commitment of panelists is critical.
- The framing of questions and the synthesizing of responses takes considerable skill, experience and knowledge about the subject under examination.
- Panelists' views should be sought at least twice, and probably three times, in order to derive a sense of agreement or consensus.
- The process requires considerable and skilled management in order to maintain the needed pace and the continued commitment and involvement of participants.

EXPERIMENTAL RESEARCH AND SIMULATIONS
These are techniques most likely to be used in academic and science-based consulting. A typical example is a goal-setting study

in which workers were divided into three groups and given different goal-related instructions. Their performance was tracked and
the results indicated the relative effectiveness of the three types of
instruction. These techniques require a good deal of involvement
by client management and often direct intervention by consultants
in the process being examined and for which experimental data is
being collected. Scientific research commonly uses experiments
and simulations. These approaches are expensive and are usually
used only in special research projects.

INTERNATIONAL RESEARCH

Further, if the project is international, researchers need to be familiar with translation-back-translation techniques to ensure that the
questions they are asking mean what they think when they are
converted cross-culturally. In addition, surveys may be illegal in
some countries, and special permission may be needed in others.
North Americans are accustomed to being surveyed and think little of it. The same survey in other countries may be sufficiently
unusual as to introduce respondent biases merely caused by the
process itself. Some cultures will resist answering in the negative
to certain questions for fear saying "no" will offend the questioner.
Respondents in other cultures may deliberately mislead the
researcher. Assumptions of literacy and numeracy levels and the
level of accuracy of official figures are other ways in which international research can prove troublesome and produce unreliable
results. Cross-cultural research may call for specialist involvement
to help consultants.

Consultants should be familiar with all types of research methodology in order to assist clients in selecting the best way to develop
the information base needed to support effective decision making.
They need not necessarily be proficient in conducting every kind
of research, but they should be able to understand the trade-offs
involved in choosing a particular method and in selecting a
research supplier if needed. This understanding of proper research

techniques is also important in helping clients understand the limits and validity of information that they encounter in the course of ordinary business activities. Above all, effective consulting calls for an orientation toward investigation and the development of objective information to assist in decision making. In other words, effective consultants appreciate the value of good research and encourage their clients accordingly.

Premises and Models

The consultant's communication skills are among the most important contributors to successful assignments. It is of little value for the consultant to solve the problem or get to the "right" answer if the information is not transferred to the client in a meaningful way. It has been said that the most intelligent person appears the same as the least intelligent if the person cannot communicate.

Frequently, consultants address issues that are familiar to them but not to the client, which is why the consultant was called in initially. Technical descriptions may be useful to and among the consultants but totally unintelligible to clients. Buzzwords like hackers, downsizing or outsourcing may now be in general use, but consultantese slang should be avoided, along with the growing number of acronyms that one hears. Clients don't know what you are talking about and find it confusing and even insulting.

Effective consultants can discuss complex issues in simple language. They often have a "tool kit" containing a variety of premises and models that can be adapted to a particular client situation. For example, a consultant may confuse a client by referring to "status incongruity" when referring to a particular organizational situation, but, when the image of a young rookie superstar trying to lead and change the way a team of veteran players performs is presented, the concept of status incongruity becomes meaningful.

PREMISES

Premises are assertions of hypotheses stating basic beliefs that can serve as the context for interpreting findings. For example, if one is looking at ways to motivate workers, a consultant can provide a context for the client to understand the results of an attitude survey by stating a premise connecting attitudes with motivation. The premise might state:

> *People tend to do what they like to do, and most people like to do things they do well. Further, most people want to do a good job. If we examine what employees like about their job, and if we can change their jobs to build on these likes, we should be able to help them improve their performance.*

The assertions about people's likes and their behaviour in the above statement are premises that interpret the results of an attitude survey. The client can separate the analysis of the survey data from the premises used to interpret it. If the client then has doubts regarding the conclusions, the premises can be questioned separately from the validity of the survey results. The use of premises helps client and consultant communicate more precisely, and therefore more effectively.

MODELS

Models are abstractions that describe the essential components and relationships in a situation. They are used like premises to help the client separate the logical foundation of a consultant's conclusions from the base of information used to reach those conclusions. As with premises, this helps the client and consultant communicate and address complex situations with clarity.

Some examples illustrating the use of models to help communicate are as follows:

- Throughout this book, the concept of a business system has been used in diagrams for various purposes. (See the overlay section in Chapter 6, "Effective Presentations.") It positions an enterprise so that any part of it can be discussed in a context understood by both consultant and client.
- The mock proposal in the Appendix contains a conceptual diagram of the balance between "push" and "pull" efforts in a marketing situation.

- A simple break-even chart, such as the one shown in Figure 7-4, is useful in discussing cost patterns and the effects of changing the ratio of fixed and variable costs on an enterprise's expected performance.

Some models, like the break-even chart, are traditional and established. Others are more whimsical. For example, the lily pond concept described below serves to alert clients to the need to understand the dynamics currently at work in their enterprise in order to forestall otherwise inevitable future events.

Models can be verbal or graphic, complex or simple and serious or humorous. As long as the model communicates to the client, it is a good model. If it fails this test of pragmatism, it is not helpful.

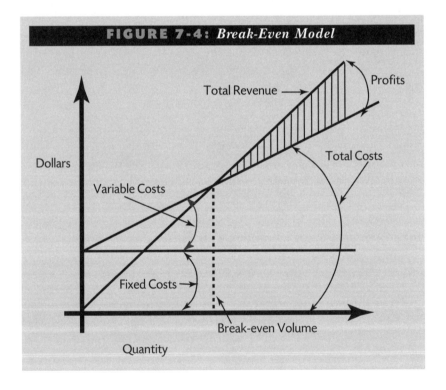

FIGURE 7-4: *Break-Even Model*

Project Management

The project must be managed to ensure that it is completed to the client's satisfaction – on time and within budget. Whether the

Another Perspective

THE LILY POND

Consider a lily pond of a specific size. In it grows a specific type of lily which doubles its numbers each day. You calculate that it will take 30 days for the pond to become completely covered with lilies, and you don't want that to happen. Now,

Q: When do you first notice that the pond is getting covered?
A: Probably when it is about half covered.
Q: And when is that?
A: On the *twenty ninth day*.

You knew all you needed to know about the process from day one. You wanted to intervene, yet you failed to take notice until the last minute, when it was likely too late to affect the outcome. The trick is to "cheat" on the previous 28 days and discover the lily ponds in your enterprise earlier by using what you already know.

project is a simple, one-person assignment or a complex team effort, the project management responsibility, assigned to the lead consultant, implies discipline and requires open and frank communication with the client. The project manager maintains a complete file that documents outcomes and work performed and compares them with what was promised. This ensures that all commitments are being met. The agendas and task assignment memos form a critical part of this file along with the summaries and data that result from performing the tasks.

The larger and more complicated the project, the more likely the client will require a formal and rigorous project management system. Conversely, the simpler the project, the more the project management requirements can be met with memos and meeting minutes. Many project management requirements can be met with simple scheduling, such as a Gantt chart,[1] which details the sequence and timing of the various elements the program provides.

---

[1] An example of a Gantt chart appears in Chapter 5, "The Proposal."

More sophisticated methods, such as CPM (Critical Path Method) are usually not needed unless there are significant purchases and subcontracts involved.

An important aspect of managing the project is recognizing the need to make changes as the assignment proceeds. Consulting involves discovery, and discovery may suggest that changes to the consulting assignment are appropriate. As new information surfaces, or if the client's circumstances change, it may be appropriate to make adjustments to the work plan. Of course, these need to be examined carefully before the consultant can confirm that previous commitments are no longer appropriate. In the course of the work, the client may appear to agree to changes in the project, but the consultant needs to be sure that this is, in fact, a change in the minimum requirements and not merely a set of suggestions or additions that the client interprets as within the current terms of the engagement.

The project manager must stay ahead of the team. When a team member, whether client personnel or colleague, is experiencing difficulty in performing the assigned work as specified and on time, the project manager needs to know as early as possible. Constant and open communication among team members is essential in order to anticipate difficulties and avoid problems. Nobody wants surprises during a consulting project. The project manager has the job of making sure the client can be confident that the work is proceeding as planned.

INTERNATIONAL PROJECT MANAGEMENT
Effective project management is particularly significant in international work. North Americans have a particular style of management with which they are familiar and to which they respond. Cross-cultural differences can cause difficulties if ignored. Even between Canadians and Americans – so similar in many ways – these differences occur, as illustrated in the following examples.

Managing in the international environment requires the consultant to be sensitive and aware of differences in values and protocols. Requests in some cultures need to be far more specific than

Another Perspective

TWO CANADIAN WAL-MART STORIES

Giant American retailer Wal-Mart has a very well publicized set of motivational exercises it asks its employees to participate in at the beginning of each day. Canadian workers went along with it until it came time to singing the national anthem. When this came up, the Canadians reportedly looked at one another with a "You've got to be kidding" expression. Nobody knew the words, and they weren't about to sing anyway. The national anthem in Canada has a completely different significance in everyday Canadian life than that of its American counterpart in the US.

Wal-Mart relies heavily on its Complaints Department for feedback in its stores in the US. Americans are quick to register complaints and make suggestions. In Canada, some stores were not performing as well as expected, but there were few complaints from the Canadian customers. A survey revealed that Canadians don't complain, they just don't come back.

in others, and the role and attitudes of the manager/supervisor need to be more structured in some than others. Delegation works in the US, but may not work in India where the subordinate may believe that it is his responsibility to do his job, and his boss' responsibility to do his own job. Informal, indeed friendly, behaviour is acceptable in some environments. In China, however, strict organizational protocol is important. Japanese decision-making systems and how they differ have been well-documented, and consultants working abroad have been alerted to the need for consensus and group harmony in Japanese organizations. Consultants working internationally may need to manage foreign associates and colleagues within foreign client environments. Although complicated and frustrating at times, it can be enjoyable and rewarding when the consultant is aware of the international dimension of professional behaviour.

DELIVERABLES

Clients frequently measure consultant performance in terms of deliverables; deliverables provide evidence that they are getting what they are paying for. Therefore, effective project managers focus on deliverables and as tasks are assigned and milestones reached, the question "What is the deliverable?" is frequently heard among consultants working together. In performing the work, consultants should be constantly aware of the next formal deliverable to be provided to the client. If possible, some consultants prepare outlines in advance of significant work steps to help them stay focused on deliverable requirements. Project deliverables, while rarely sufficient, are usually a necessary part of any consulting assignment and should always be a central focus in performing the various tasks comprising the assignment.

Review

During most assignments, the consultant and client get together to review progress and confirm the direction of the remaining work. These are sometimes occasions for presentations by the consulting team to a client steering committee. These presentations are critical points in the consulting process, and their effectiveness can have a major impact on its success. Presentations were discussed in depth in Chapter 6; however, some further comment with respect to the role of progress presentations and dry runs in managing the project is appropriate at this point.

PROGRESS PRESENTATIONS

Progress presentations are important milestones in the project. They provide an opportunity for the consultant to summarize information collected to date and build the conceptual framework within which it can be related to the client's goals. This provides assurance to the client that work is proceeding according to plan and that the expectations developed at the outset are still valid. In addition, progress presentations provide an opportunity to discuss changes in the direction of the assignment in the face of new information. It is wise to ensure that the client is informed of these desired changes before the formal presentation so that the presentation can take the form of confirming, rather than announcing, the changes.

DRY RUNS

Dry runs are important to ensure that presentations are relevant, logically consistent with the findings, polished and professional. They are perhaps the best mechanism to ensure this. It is not merely a rehearsal, but truly an integral part of the analysis and review process by the consulting team. They are occasions for creative thinking by consultants assimilating information gained to serve client goals. They should have the following characteristics:

- They should be built into the project plan. They should be scheduled at least four days before the scheduled presentation date so that the results can be incorporated into the presentation. This way, there is no excuse for last-minute postponement which might render the dry run useless and too late to affect the presentation itself.
- They should be scheduled on an open-ended basis. Effective dry runs are unpredictable as to the issues they will address and the time they will take, because they should focus on making the material as relevant and useful to the client as possible. These sessions are usually very productive and worth the time needed to complete them.
- Those who will be presenting should prepare overheads for the dry run as if the dry run were the actual presentation. Expensive final production of overheads can be avoided, but the level of detail should be sufficient to provide a critical review of the visual quality, as well as the content of all overheads.
- The dry run should be held using the overhead projector and any other visual aids that will be part of the presentation. A flip chart and/or chalkboard should be available during the dry run to help the discussion and exchange of ideas and concepts.
- Hard copy of the dry run overheads should be provided to all those attending the dry run for notation and comment.

- In the case of individual assignments or small groups, it often helps to invite a colleague who may not be involved in the assignment to attend and comment, provided client confidentiality is not compromised.

The focus on rigorous dry runs expressed in this chapter may seem excessive to some, but presentations are among the most important communication elements of assignments. Further, the dry run process is a critical part of the analytical review of findings, and the rigor of the consulting work is in direct relationship to the efforts put into the analysis. In addition, dry runs are critical in rehearsing and presenting effectively. Even the most apparently complete draft presentation usually undergoes substantial change as a result of critical review during the dry run. The advanced scheduling of the dry run ensures that there is sufficient time to revise the presentation and provide the client with a high quality and fruitful discussion.

Project Administration

Project administration takes care of the housekeeping aspects of performing effective consulting. As with most housekeeping, sloppiness and poor practice are noticed and cast a poor reflection on those responsible. Conversely, good project administration demonstrates the professionalism of the consultant and can differentiate the committed professional from the amateur. Project administration includes invoicing practices, level of details, time records and expense records.

INVOICING PRACTICES

Invoices should be rendered on time and contain all the relevant information. They should be appropriately addressed and referenced and contain the necessary tax and terms information. Some clients prefer to be invoiced on particular days of the month or other specific times to fit with their expected cash inflows. Consultants can modify their billing procedures to suit clients.

LEVEL OF DETAIL

Some clients require substantial detail in reporting on work performed and/or expenses incurred. Others wish to keep the details of the consulting work confidential and request only minimal information on invoices. The format, level of detail and requirements for supporting documentation are all matters that must be clarified at the beginning of an assignment.

TIME RECORDS

These are usually needed for internal use; however, on occasion, clients may request verification of time spent on their behalf. These records should be maintained on a weekly basis. Most consultants maintain detailed journals or diaries in order to manage their time, and many journals have forms for recording expenses and other administrative matters.

EXPENSE RECORDS

These are required for the consultant's operating records and tax purposes, as well as for reimbursement from clients. Experienced consultants are in the habit of requesting and retaining receipts ' for all expenditures, including incidental cash items such as taxi fares and parking. Most keep logs in their automobiles in which they record all business driving. In some consulting organizations, the expense report, submitted to the administrative personnel, is a key control device. The consultant does not get expenses reimbursed until all administrative responsibilities, including filing time records, are satisfied.

As indicated earlier, management of a professional practice actually takes place through the projects. The performance of the work, the management of the projects, serving the client and to some extent, the design and delivery of the services, all take place as part of projects. Project administration is a separate formal process that serves the business aspects of the assignment, but it is nevertheless part of the professional service. As well, motivating and training personnel and the management of subcontracted work is part of project management.

■ *Completing the Work*

Projects are completed when the terms of reference are fulfilled and the deliverables are turned over to the client. It is important that the client realizes that the consultant considers the work completed, and a specific meeting is usually provided in the work schedule for this purpose. Part of the consultants' responsibility is to keep the client aware of the agreed terms of reference and to confirm changes to the program and the budget as they occur. When consultants work closely with clients over a period of time, consultants can become accustomed to this informal relationship and fail to recognize when clients are requesting work in addition to that initially commissioned. A meeting at which all remaining deliverables, including final reports, are physically delivered punctuates the completion of scheduled work and reinforces the project nature of the relationship between client and consultant. The consultant had promised to perform certain agreed work, and the promise has been fulfilled.

Frequently, clients will have read the final report in draft form prior to this meeting. The revised and now final version is presented at this completion meeting. Draft versions should be clearly labeled as draft – not just on the cover, but also on every page – and clients should be advised to ensure all draft copies are either returned to the consultant for disposal or destroyed. Where possible, consultants should retrieve any draft copies still in the client's possession because pages of documents often get copied and resurface in a variety of contexts over time. It can be confusing if more than one version remains in client files, and both client and consultant can suffer as a result.

To review the broad steps in a project, see Checklist 7-5.

The Client

The essence of consulting is not merely the exercise of techniques and tools; it is providing clients with the means to address change.

CHECKLIST 7-5: *The Project*

✔ **Beginning the work – the Start-up meeting**
  – Agenda
  – Work plan
  – Schedule
  – Administration
  – Initial data requests

✔ **Performing the work**
  – Assign tasks
  – Develop and review premises and models
  – Manage the project
  – Complete the work program using dry runs to prepare for presentations, client meetings, reports
  – Administer the project – invoicing, time and expense recording

✔ **Complete the work**
  – Hand over deliverables
  – Replace draft reports with finals
  – Confirm completion with client

Whether a client wishes to develop and implement a new technique or technology, adopt a new strategy for the enterprise, examine a market opportunity or improve the motivation of employees, all clients have in common a concern with change. They want to change something, or they want to decide explicitly not to change something. There is something they are not satisfied with and believe can be improved, or there is something that they want to understand better in order to manage it. The consultant can help the client achieve the maximum benefit from the consulting experience by recognizing that the client is not as skilled as the consultant in working in a project environment. The consultant is responsible for helping the client maintain focus squarely on the goals the client hopes to achieve.

■ *Focusing on Client Goals*

There are some general principles for consultants to follow to improve their effectiveness in maintaining a client-focus:

Proposal Review

Review the proposal frequently. It is the basis for the client relationship. It contains the terms of reference for the work to be done and the reasons for it. Every report and recommended action should be in the context of the two key questions addressed in the proposal:

- Why is the client doing this project?
- Why is this project being done now?

The answers to these questions reveals clients' motivation and provides guidance regarding their expectations from this assignment. Focus conclusions and recommendations squarely on the clients' goals.

Vision

Help the client develop a vision of the future in which the desired changes have occurred. Compare it with the present situation to highlight the areas in which change must take place in order to progress to the desired future condition. Explore the issues involved in change.

Communication Format

Develop a format for communicating with the client that involves frank exchanges regarding the examination of options and the weighing of pros and cons. Identify areas where facts are lacking and arguments are based on unsupported assumptions and questionable premises. Provide relevant and focused facts.

Listening

Listen carefully to all client comments and discussions involving client personnel. Learn to identify signals that indicate potential resistance as well as potential support for change. Find the champions.

Feedback

Draw out comments and arguments from those resisting change or expressing doubt about the validity of information being presented. Help objectors articulate concerns, and find the information needed to obtain their support. Most resistance is based on strong beliefs, and these should be respected and addressed. If warranted, additional information should be provided. Unresolved issues can lead to disruptive behaviour from individuals who feel they have not had a fair hearing. Remove the obstacles to change.

Conflict

Conflict arises from many sources, but it can usually be detected when one or more parties perceive the situation as win-lose. When conflict grows, communication shuts down. Encourage communication within the client organization.

■ *Managing the Client*

One of a consultant's most important responsibilities is to help the client be a good client. Consultants usually have much more experience with the client/consultant relationship than most clients. Clients are more accustomed to maintaining and building the on-going process of their business. Projects are unusual and designed to change things, not maintain them. By recognizing this basic difference in orientation, consultants can take the initiative to act on a number of factors that can affect the working relationship:

Documentation

Written communication is one of the sets of skills the consultant is expected to bring to the consulting relationship. Clients appreciate the consultant's discipline and ability to provide good documentation. They rely on consultants to keep the assignment under control and often call upon them to provide written support for various tasks. Consultants often draft letters and memos for the client to approve, sign and send, as well as issue formal reports, agendas and minutes of meetings.

Reports should contain substance, and they should be professional in appearance and format. Each should build on the previous one to maintain consistency and a thread of logic that connects them to each other and to the central focus of the assignment. Modern computers can provide sophisticated graphics and other elements for a polished display, and visual consistency can be used to reinforce logical consistency. By providing the professional discipline, particularly in the written documentation – which forms a lasting part of the assignment – consultants help the client participate effectively without unnecessary diversion from day-to-day responsibilities. Written documents, unlike spoken communication, tend to live on after the assignment has been completed. They may emerge from someone's files years later, and their professional quality not only helps to identify them in appropriate context, but their appearance speaks of the professionalism of the author.

Deadlines

Time management is another of the skill sets in which consultants excel. Consultants sell time; therefore, they learn to manage time effectively. Clients have time commitments as well, and the consultant can help them manage the available time to enable effective participation as well as tend to regular business. The consultant should schedule meetings well in advance and resist rescheduling unless requested by the client. Conversely, the consultant should maintain flexibility to accommodate the client's schedule. Deliverables should be provided in appropriate draft or final form on schedule. Punctuality for appointments is important, and the consultant should keep meetings as short as practical and as productive as possible. Many clients appreciate the consultant reconfirming upcoming scheduled activities, including meetings and key events that require client attendance.

Client Education

Consulting assignments involve learning. New information, new concepts, new insights and new perspectives should be shared with the client. The consultant is responsible for helping the client stay in tune with project accomplishments as they occur. Scheduled progress meetings and presentations may not be sufficient; additional activities might be needed to help the client personnel participate in the learning opportunities the project provides. Sometimes it is wise to keep the senior client representatives well briefed to help them stay ahead of the rest of the staff and, in turn, advise the consultant regarding special sensitivities and priorities that may bear on the success of the project.

Administration

Consulting budgets and payments are rarely a routine part of client administrative systems, but consultants have considerable flexibility with respect to the form and timing of invoices and can accommodate client requirements. The consultant has a responsibility to help the client satisfy administrative needs as easily as possible.

Different types of consulting have their own distinctive character and level of client involvement. Much of the practice of effective consulting is common sense and is based on respect for clients and what they want to achieve. Above all, effective consulting means personal and professional integrity on the part of consultants. Clients need to trust their consultants and consultants need to earn and maintain that trust through rigorous application of the specialty for which they were retained. Furthermore, clients need to experience consultants as honest and objective in research, dependable and reliable in behaviour and committed to the highest ethical standards in relationships with clients. In short, clients are entitled to trust the consultants' values as expressed in the way they manage their practices, the projects and the clients. Use Checklist 7-6 to ensure the client and the consultant are focused.

CHECKLIST 7-6: *Client Orientation*

✔ **Stay focused on client goals**
- Review proposal, client's original intentions and expressed needs
- Help client articulate vision of the unfolding future
- Communicate frankly, precisely and completely with client
- Listen to what the client says
- Help facilitate change
- Manage conflict and encourage constructive discussion within client

✔ **Manage your client effectively**
- Help clients understand consultative process, project orientation
- Document effectively
- Observe deadlines
- Help your client build knowledge and understanding – teach your client
- Make administration easy

Managing projects constitutes the bulk of the day-to-day operating concern of consultants, but managing the consulting business has strategic level issues as well. In Chapter 2, the process of deciding what kind of consulting enterprise to start or become involved with was discussed. While Shakespeare's well-known observation that the "past is prologue to the future" may still apply, the seemingly ever-accelerating rate of change characteristic of our modern world has the effect of shortening the portion of the past that can be usefully projected to forecast the future. Understanding the dynamics at work in the present may be more helpful in building a consulting business that will have a better chance of weathering any "outrageous fortune" that rapid (some say discontinuous) change may produce.

EIGHT

Ethics and the Professional Consultant

Ethics defines professionalism. As consultancies of all kinds continue to grow with the shifting structure of enterprises and the accelerating pace of technologies and the changes they stimulate, ethical behaviour will become even more important for clients distinguishing among individuals and firms offering advisory help and related services. Because ethics is such a root variable in effective consulting, it warrants a chapter of its own.

The growing influence of ethics in consulting is demonstrated by the concern of consultants and the organizations that represent them for practical and up-to-date codes of ethics or codes of professional conduct. In 1997, the Institute of Certified Management Consultants of Canada (ICMCC), now the Canadian Association of Management Consultants (CAMC), completed a rigorous review of its code and published revisions with which all its members must comply. The following section summarizes this code.

The CAMC Code of Ethics

The CAMC Uniform Code of Professional Conduct (code of ethics) identifies four distinct stakeholder groups for which ethical responsibilities are detailed. These are: the public, the profession, other members and the client. Figure 8-1 describes the general code for each of these stakeholder groups.

FIGURE 8-1:
CAMC Uniform Code of Professional Conduct (Abridged)

RESPONSIBILITIES TO THE PUBLIC

Legal – Act in accordance with the laws.

Representation – Speak on behalf of members only when authorized.

Public Protection – Avoid behaviour unbecoming to the profession.

RESPONSIBILITIES TO OTHER MEMBERS

Review of a Member's Work – Should you be asked to review the work of a colleague, inform that person before starting the work.

RESPONSIBILITIES TO THE PROFESSION

Knowledge – Keep up-to-date on the Code of Professional Conduct and on your areas of special expertise.

Self Discipline – Report unbecoming professional conduct by another member.

Responsibilities for Others – Be sure that any consultants working with you abide by these rules.

Image – Protect the reputation of the profession; avoid activities that hurt the quality of your advice, and do not carry on business that detracts from your professional status.

RESPONSIBILITIES TO THE CLIENT

Due Care – Act in the best interests of the client; provide professional service with integrity, objectivity and independence; do not encourage unrealistic client expectations.

Business Development – Do not use methods which detract from the professional image of the institute or its members.

Competence – Take on only work you have the skills and competence to perform.

Informed Client – Reach mutual understanding with client on objectives, scope, work plan and costs before accepting work.

The International Labor Office (ILO) in Geneva identifies more than 60 countries that have similar associations and codes. Such a code is a necessary but not sufficient requirement of professionalism. The ILO states:[1]

> *Any consultant whose ambition is to become a real professional must clarify his or her own conception of ethics and the norms to be observed in working for clients. This applies equally to external and internal consultants, as well as to persons who intervene in a consulting capacity although they are not full-time consultants.*

The issue of ethics permeates every aspect of a professional relationship and the consultant is responsible for the impact of professional activities on a host of stakeholders, ranging from the client and other professionals to the community and society at large. Ethical considerations are part of the personal requirements of consulting and influence whether you should become a consultant and what work you will accept. Ethical issues also arise in marketing and selling your services as well as in performing work and managing your business.

Ethics Complicate Decisions

The norms expressed in the Codes of Professional Conduct of the various professional associations can be helpful, but they cannot hope to prescribe behaviour to suit all situations. Consider the following two examples:

- In 1984, in Bhopal, India, more than 2000 people were killed as a result of an accidental leak of methyl-isocyanate gas from a plant owned and operated by Union Carbide. The company had conformed to all local laws when it constructed the plant, although these laws were considerably less stringent with respect to safety than laws in the US. What were the ethical

---

[1] *Management Consulting – A Guide to the Profession*, 3rd (revised) edition, Milan Kubr (ed.) (Geneva: ILO, 1996), p. 121.

responsibilities of the professional who designed and built the plant and of the managers who operated and maintained it? They had adhered to the applicable codes, but the results were disastrous.

- A partner in a public accounting firm discovered that the management of a major Caribbean bank and audit client had approved some very large loans and if they failed to perform, the bank's liquidity position would fall below safe limits. The partner felt that normally, as the auditor, his firm could fulfill its disclosure responsibility to the shareholders by commenting on special transactions in the notes to the financial statements. This situation, however, posed another ethical dilemma. By alerting shareholders to the increased risk these loans represented, shareholders/depositors might react by removing their deposits, selling their shares or by taking other actions which could impair the bank's solvency. While the loans might prove to be considered unwise, they were nevertheless legal. What were the ethical responsibilities of the auditor to the shareholders and to the general public who had placed their confidence in the health and stability of the bank? In this case, the auditor decided to report on the loans, taking great care to describe them in the note using as objective and dispassionate language as possible, leaving any assessment of possible added risk to the shareholders.

These illustrations are large enough to have legal consequences as well as raise ethical questions. Union Carbide was sued in India for not adhering to the more rigorous US standards and was ordered by the Indian Supreme Court to pay nearly US$ 500 million in damages, even though the company maintained that the accident had been sabotage. In the second example, the loans failed to perform and were renegotiated. The bank was saved, but the management was fired. The audit partner and his firm would have likely faced a possible large stockholder suit had he withheld the information. What if the loans had performed? If his reporting on the information had caused the bank to suffer major damages due to loss of investor and customer confidence, the bank might equally have sued the audit firm for a large amount. To add to the drama, the audit firm, while insured, was a partnership nevertheless, and any award in excess of their coverage would have to have been paid out of the partners' personal resources.

Not all ethical dilemmas are this dramatic. Most are part of day-to-day activities and can be viewed as doing the "right" thing. Unfortunately, that is not always simple and clearcut. The right thing is a complicated mixture of individual values inculcated by family upbringing and community norms and further affected by broader societal, corporate, professional and other work-related values.

Figure 8-2 depicts the complex network of values that comprise or affect ethical behaviour:

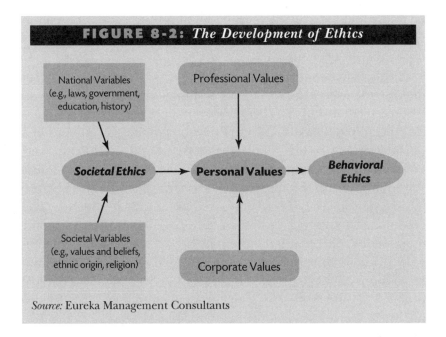

FIGURE 8-2: *The Development of Ethics*

National Variables (e.g., laws, government, education, history)

Professional Values

Societal Ethics → **Personal Values** → *Behavioral Ethics*

Societal Variables (e.g., values and beliefs, ethnic origin, religion)

Corporate Values

Source: Eureka Management Consultants

Since ethical issues are rarely clear-cut, professionals need to be prepared for questions which will present themselves at various points in the consulting process. The following section of this chapter examines each of the major elements of operating a consulting practice and identifies and discusses some of the ethical issues commonly encountered.

Ethics in Accepting Assignments

Ethical behaviour is the expression of morality and has its roots in the essential values of the individual. Professional integrity requires discipline and adherence to a strong set of principles and beliefs. Furthermore, like justice, ethical behaviour must not only be done, but it must be seen to be done as well. The appearance of possible unethical behaviour can be damaging even when no unethical behaviour is actually taking place. For this reason, some consultants with wide investment portfolios often put them in the hands of an independent trustee to avoid any appearance of a direct interest in the companies and organizations in which the consultant has an investment. In this way, decisions to invest or to disinvest are made by the trustee, not by the consultant, and thus, cannot be said to be related to any particular knowledge the consultant may obtain in the course of client work.

In carrying out some assignments, the appearance of a conflict of interest, even when the consultant is satisfied that there is none, can cost the relationship. If a client discovers a possible conflict of interest (recent past work for a competitor or supplier, investment in a product or service that might form a part of the consultant's recommendation etc.), the ethical basis for trust can be undermined. Without this trust, the consultant's work may be irrelevant because it will likely not be believed and acted upon with confidence. The consultant should be alert to these possible situations and clear any questions of conflict with the client before accepting an assignment.

Individuals who are not prepared to place their own personal reputations on the line to demonstrate integrity and independence probably should not become professional consultants. The following are some situations in which you should decline to provide professional service:

- If you are invited to perform work for a client with close ties to or serving the same markets as another client for whom you have recently worked, you should decline. You have been privy to the plans and beliefs of the past client and have been entrusted with knowledge and information that might be very helpful to the prospective client but to which that potential client is not entitled. Regardless of how much the new client work is desired, you should decline on the basis of a conflict of interest. Even though the work with the past client has been completed, the confidential information gained is still current and could have an effect on the prospective client's decisions and on the consultant's recommendations. Both the prospective client and the past one will appreciate your decision to decline the opportunity to serve the prospective client. Even if the past client and prospective client agree to you doing the work, it is probably best to decline.

- If you have a personal connection with a prospective client, through a relationship with a member of the client staff or an investment in the client or some organization which is important as a potential supplier or customer to that client, you should declare this conflict and be prepared to decline the assignment. You want to ensure objectivity and your ability to maintain the client's trust. Public accounting firms require employees to declare any interest in audit clients and may require them to divest if there is any question of compromising the firm's objectivity.

- If you have a personal bias or set of beliefs which may affect the objectivity of your work, or have expressed publicly a point of view which can draw your impartiality into question, you should decline. These beliefs or stated positions should disqualify you from participating in work that may be affected in fact, or in appearance, by your personal beliefs. Consultants, like many responsible citizens, sometimes become active in organizations that promote certain points of view (Pro-Choice, Sunday store openings, etc.).

An institutional corollary to this is the case when you are called on to conduct research that supports a particular point of view for a lobbying organization. You need to recognize that if you support the client's advocacy, you become linked with it, and that may disqualify you from work for clients whose position may differ.

Institutional Conflicts

These ethical principles apply to consulting firms as well as to the individual consultants they employ. In-house consulting divisions may have particular difficulty in achieving credibility, if not objectivity, when examining basic management issues that affect the organization as a whole. For example, it is probably impossible for an internal consultancy to assess policies that affect the role and place of the internal consulting division itself.

Some consultancies are associated with nonconsulting firms that market products and services. For example, IBM Consulting Group, Towers Perrin and Mercer Consulting Group are parts of larger organizations that offer other products and services. Special policies are needed in these situations to guarantee independence and objectivity on the part of their consultants on assignments that may involve client concerns regarding these other interests. Auditing firms maintain careful separation of their auditing from their consulting business. Auditors are responsible to shareholders; consultants typically work for management and sometimes these interests conflict. In addition, most accounting-based consultancies advise a consulting client's auditor when providing professional services.

Some firms provide "bundled" services in which they provide consulting assistance and implementation products, systems and other resources as one package. Technical projects such as systems design, the development of employee benefit packages and turnkey engineering projects often call for the consultant to make product and supplier selections as part of providing their service. When these products and services are provided by a parent or related company, consultants' objectivity is impaired. There is no inherent ethical breach in providing consultative services as part of tailoring and implementing solutions to client problems provided the bias toward a particular proprietary solution or product is known by the client/customer at the outset. Presenting the consulting portion of the work as totally objective and unbiased may be unethical, however, when in reality, the "solution" is known in advance by the consultant.

The Code of Professional Conduct of the European Federation of Management Consulting Associations (FEACO) deals with professional autonomy as follows:

> *Whenever a consulting company is legally or financially under control of a nonconsulting body, there should be a written undertaking to guarantee that no pressure will be exerted which may prejudice the opinion or the advice of the consultancy.*

As further protection, both for the consultant and the consultancy, FEACO guidelines state that:

> *A consultant who delivers advice must be able to do so with complete freedom and be protected by a* clause de conscience *from the management of the consultancy firm.*

This differentiates the professional consultant from the salesperson who is presented as a consultant but is really representing a specific drug company, telecommunications supplier or the like.

Ethics in Marketing Professional Services

Published codes and guidelines contain statements of principle that affect the way consultants market their services. For example, CAMC states, as a general principle that:

> *A member shall not adopt any method of obtaining business which detracts from the professional image of the institute or its members.*

The FEACO guidelines state:

> *It would be considered a breach of [the code of professional conduct] for a consultancy to issue promotional material including advertising which is likely to mislead or give the public a false impression of the consultancy's capabilities, or could be construed as claiming advantages from one member of a national association over its other members or contain remarks or implications which could be interpreted as being derogatory of any other member of the national association.*

The basic principle in marketing a professional service is honesty. Puffery may be acceptable in most marketing, but in the case of professional services, it is regarded as unethical if it is patently untrue, deliberately misleading or implies that competing colleagues are somehow less competent or ethical. Professionals should present their services and credentials honestly and, if required, verifiably. They should stress positive qualities (size, years in business, number of clients served, range and types of services, awards received etc.), and express their commitment to excellence and quality performance. They may also describe commitment to ethical practice and support for trade and professional organizations. While focusing on the positive, they should nevertheless avoid superlatives in their descriptions unless they can be proven.

Effective promotion should not require self-aggrandizement, but it should focus on what the consultant has done and the benefits clients have received. It should make no promises or guarantees of results over which a consultant has no control. It should seek to demonstrate competence and effectiveness. Client endorsements and referrals are becoming more widely used as the field of consulting expands. Articles and presentations that share important findings and concepts and demonstrate expertise in dealing with typical problems and issues are often the most efficient and effective way to promote professional services. These are particularly strong when done jointly with clients, or as part of client promotional activities such as press releases.

FEACO guidelines also state that it is unethical for a consultant:

> to accept an assignment, the scope of which is so limited that the consultant is aware that the client will receive either ineffective advice, or advice so incomplete as to require him to seek further advice, without being aware at the onset of the assignment that this will be the case.

Although the rule of *caveat emptor* (buyer takes the risk) is often cited as integral to the way business is done in many cultures, it has little place in marketing professional services. A relationship of openness and trust between buyer and seller cannot be founded on trickery. The practice of progressive selling is unethical if the consultant has no intention of delivering stand-alone benefits from an assignment but uses it to trap the client into a second, more lucrative assignment. This is also referred to as "camel" selling, after the notion that once you allow a camel to put its nose into your tent, before long, the whole camel is in.

That does not rule out phased approaches to consulting where the client knowingly embarks on a consulting plan that may involve additional work. The key difference is the full knowledge and awareness on the part of the client of what benefits to expect from the work and the cost and commitment that may be involved.

Ethics and the Selling Process

Selling to some is unethical by definition. In Chapter 4 the selling process is described as finding a way to help clients. Clearly, there is nothing inherently unethical in selling when a business relationship that benefits all parties is the objective. Perhaps selling has acquired its unethical reputation because some salespeople sometimes use unethical practices.

Ethical selling ensures that the buyer is not influenced by misleading promises or guarantees. Client expectations for the assignment match those of the consultant, and the consultant ensures that the client retains control over the consulting process. Professional consultants do not accept assignments for which they are not qualified, nor do they make false claims of qualifications and abilities.

From time to time, consultants may be offered commissions or other inducements by suppliers who want to use the consultant's relationship with the client to help sell their own products or services. In most cases, this is a form of bribery and is clearly unethical if not illegal. The CAMC International Code of Professional Conduct provides the following minimum guideline in relation to commissions and other financial interests:

> *A member will neither accept commissions, remuneration nor other benefits from a third party in connection with recommendations to a client without the client's knowledge and consent, nor fail to disclose any financial interest in goods and services which form part of such recommendations.*

It is also unethical for a consultant to pay a commission for an introduction to a client without informing the client. When commissions or finder's fees are involved, the consultant must disclose that fact to the client and can proceed only if the client does not object.

A consultant was retained by a large retail chain to evaluate and recommend an order for point-of-sale terminals (we used to call them cash registers) to be installed in all its branches. The assignment included managing the competitive bidding process, and the amount of money involved for the purchase was in the tens of millions of dollars. Some of the bidders offered lavish visits to their head office and production facilities (with his wife, if he chose). It was clear that these were inducements intended to influence his choice, so he declined.

Frequently, a consultant is in a position to exercise strong persuasive power over a client, particularly when the client is in trouble and has no clear understanding of the causes of the problems. Sometimes the client grants consultants powers to implement changes. For example, increasingly consultants are being empowered to carry out implementation steps following recommendations made and accepted by their clients. Some consultants provide outsourced services such as computer system support or human resource management. The consultant's power under these conditions is still under the control of the client and thus is not unethical. If this power is used to expand the consultant's mandate (sell more work), it can become self-serving and unethical. Consultants should provide clients with effective means of evaluating their performance.

Consulting remuneration is usually in the form of fees plus expenses. Fees may be time-based or a fixed amount agreed upon in advance. Usually, the client is given an estimate. In some cases, such as in the case of audit fees and special investigations, the setting of a fee estimate might be considered a means by which the work can be limited; in these cases, fee estimates are not provided. Generally, consultants provide estimates and regard them as maximums unless changes to the terms of reference are made and an adjustment in fees agreed to.

It is becoming increasingly common for clients to hold consultants accountable for the results of their work. One way of doing this is to base all or some portion of the fee on results. Contingency pricing is acceptable where it is normal practice such as in recruiting and staff selection, mergers and acquisition work and the search for licenses. It is unethical, however, when contingent fees can prejudice the independence of the consultant. For example, if the consultant is remunerated based on short-term results, but sees negative long-term consequences of decisions to achieve these short-term results and does not warn the client, that behaviour is unethical.

Consultants generally do not intervene directly in client operations. Clients make operating decisions, albeit influenced by consultants' recommendations. For this reason, the benefits of consultants' work are often difficult to calculate and attribute directly to the work. Contingency fees should be avoided when results cannot be attributable directly to the consultants' performance.

Fees are generally based on effort and time expended by consultants. In addition, consultants seek to recover costs incurred in performing the work. Expenses are normally billed at cost. This contrasts with expenses incurred in agency relationships where marking up expenses is normal practice. Advertising agencies, for example, frequently provide services such as research and counseling for a fee. They typically also provide ad production, media buying and design and artwork. It is typical for agencies to accumulate these costs on behalf of the client and mark them up by a set percentage. While the practice of marking up expenses is an accepted part of agency relationships, it is not in the consulting profession. Consulting clients pay for professional effort, and consultants consider any incentive to incur excess costs as a conflict of interest.

Similarly, it is considered unethical to incur unreasonable costs in the conduct of an assignment and charge them to the client. Consultants are expected to travel and live with normal business comfort when on assignment, but you should have a policy. Good judgment in this regard is usually consistent with good ethics.

INSIDER'S VIEW

If you want that $50 bottle of wine with your dinner, pay for it yourself; however, when the client takes you out to dinner and orders it, enjoy it as a perk of the assignment.

Stating a policy to a client may be as informal as a making a verbal assertion as to a principle or practice which you observe in all cases. These assertions form part of the relationship and should be discussed at the outset to indicate how the client can expect the consultant to behave in the course of the work. Many practitioners build a file of memos containing written statements of policy which eventually are incorporated into a policy manual and serve as documented guidelines for associates and subcontractors as well. This provides a basis for defining professional conduct which is fair and reasonable. Clients deserve to know that the consultant has considered these matters of ethics and acceptable practice and can discuss their appropriateness and purpose in context of specific client requirements.

Performing the Work Ethically

Ethical issues often arise during the work itself. The following are some examples:

■ *Secondary Proposal Opportunity*

Suppose the marketing manager of a transportation company senses he may be facing discipline for poor performance when a consultant is hired by the president to evaluate the firm's marketing program. The marketing manager decides to conduct a market study to provide information in his defense. He asks the consultant to put in a proposal to perform the marketing study. The marketing manager may need consulting help, but the consultant should probably decline this assignment, because it would compromise objectivity. The consultant has been engaged for other things and must maintain focus on the executive client (in this case, the president) and should bring such overtures to her attention for disposition. Invariably, the president will instruct the consultant to defer action on the supplementary assignment (market research) until the first one has been completed satisfactorily. If a similar request came from the president, the situation would be quite different.

Frequently, in the course of an assignment, the terms of reference for the assignment change and are expanded in the face of findings. When extensions of the work are incorporated as amendments to the original terms of reference, they are approved by the initial client representatives and do not constitute a conflict of interest. It is important, nevertheless, that major changes be documented and agreed to in writing by all parties. Verbal agreements can get lost in memories, but written documents live forever.

■ *Protecting Confidences*

Consultants are often privy to confidential client information. Care must be taken to recognize the confidential nature of this information and protect it assiduously. The safe policy is to regard all project and client information as confidential and available for disclosure only with the written permission of the client.

People in client organizations are also frequently asked to talk about their ideas, thoughts, experiences and opinions in confidence. Individual contributions are usually of little value to client management, but the collective views are of real value. Any information of this type gained in confidence must not be revealed without the express permission of the person who gave it. The same applies to information provided by customers, suppliers and others interviewed in the course of an assignment.

> **INSIDER'S VIEW**
>
> Beware of cocktail party chats! Even the client's identity should not be revealed.

■ *Intracorporate Secrecy*

Suppose a large division of a multidivisional retail-based company has commissioned a major review of its operations. The division vice-president requires secrecy from other divisions so that he can announce the results and planned changes at the appropriate time and under the appropriate circumstances. The consultants are instructed accordingly, and even if they are in contact with staff from other divisions, they are to remain silent about the existence of the project. The consulting team is satisfied that the vice-president is acting ethically within his mandate, and so the consultants have no ethical requirement to reveal their activities outside the division.

■ *Honesty in the Work Place*

The integrity of the work itself can be the subject of ethical questions as well. Unethical consultants have been known to fabricate information and falsify interviews, claiming to have accomplished work that was really not performed. Project managers need to ensure that assigned consultants are performing properly and that work reports and time records are accurate and can stand up to scrutiny. Checking back on interviews and spot verification of source material may be required. Consultants are legally responsible for the validity of professional recommendations, and flaws in their defense can be costly as well as professionally damaging.

■ *Attribution*

Consultants make use of secondary information such as trade literature, government statistics and special studies. This information is copyrighted, and permission for its use should be obtained when warranted. Sources should be identified and attributed when material is used in client reports and other documentation. This enables the client to verify data independently and ensures that there can be no question of plagarism.

■ *Recruiting*

When working closely with assigned client staff, overtures may be received from the staff regarding employment with the consulting firm. Recruiting from client personnel is unethical. If a client employee has announced her intention to leave, the situation can be discussed with the client and the ethical issue resolved. A recruitment advertisement in the press is not considered an invitation to a specific individual.

■ *Other Examples*

Ethics is an attitude which puts the client's interest above the consultant's and recognizes that the integrity of the profession as a whole is vital. It is relatively easy to discuss in the abstract but may not be as simple in practice. There are no easy answers to all ethical dilemmas. Each must be assessed individually and evaluated as to its moral dimensions in the judgment of the consultant. The key criteria are in terms of the interests of the various stakeholders – the client, past clients, colleagues, the profession, and the community, as well as the consultancy. The following is a sample of other ethical dilemmas commonly faced in consulting:

- The client requests that you deliver a gift to a key customer, and you suspect it may be a bribe.
- Your client wishes to sell a chemical product, which has been banned in most countries as harmful to the environment, to a country which has not yet banned the product.
- You have located a source of foreign supply for your client, and you know it is cheap because of that country's use of child and slave labour.
- You believe your client is knowingly applying racist policies in hiring and deploying personnel, but these practices have no connection with the work you are performing.
- Your client has just fired two individuals who you know have been active in attempting to recruit workers to join a union.

The professional consultant places a high value on integrity. Integrity in turn is based on individual values and morality. The practitioner must be alert to ethical conflicts and dilemmas and be prepared to confront them squarely and, where appropriate, discuss them with clients to determine how they can be resolved. Although Codes of Professional Conduct and policy manuals can provide some guidance, not all consultants will resolve ethical dilemmas the same way. In the end, professionals must choose to accept and perform work which is acceptable to their own consciences in order to maintain their integrity. While consulting is a business, it is also a profession conducted by people who are accountable to their own morality as well as the bottom line.

Research Versus Espionage

The key ethical issue that differentiates research from espionage is whether the individuals responding to a survey are being deceived by the consultant. Respondents who want to know for whom research is being conducted are entitled to a truthful reply from the consultant. That answer could be one of the following:

- My client has asked that I not reveal his identity, but I can assure you that my client is not a competitor of yours.
- My client is or may be a supplier to you or your industry.
- My client has given me permission to be identified to you, but I would like to delay telling you who my client is until we have completed the interview so as to not influence your responses.
- I'm not at liberty to divulge my client's identity, but I assure you that no individual responses will be revealed to my client.

If the respondent answers questions under these circumstances, the ethics of the interview are intact.

Not infrequently, clients, including foreign government agencies, approach consultants to conduct research in various industries. They wish to acquire data regarding competitors' plant size, machine configuration, types of skills employed and other cost and operations-related information. Consultants can accept these projects ethically on a best-efforts basis and collect all the information requested, provided ethical standards can be met. Consultants cannot ethically engage in deceit in order to obtain the information. The test for the consultant is whether the consultant has to lie or mislead the respondent as to the purpose of the research or the identity of the client.

Stopping the Project

The consultant should let the client know when an assignment is not going as planned. This may be because the client's staff have been unable (or unwilling) to provide the support to the project as agreed or because external events (legal developments; bankruptcies of major customers, creditors or suppliers; death or resignation of key executives; etc.) have intervened. Sometimes, early findings from the project research can cast serious doubt on the basic assumptions underpinning the assignment. The consultant should not incur more cost until the client confirms that the assignment should proceed in spite of the changed circumstances.

One client was passionately convinced of the value of a new medication that he believed had cured his son of asthma and hay fever. Research showed using the drug would be expensive and limit its market to only the most severe cases. The client's proposed venture to market and produce the product would be only marginal as a business at best. The consultants stopped the project to discuss the matter with the client. The client requested that they continue but significantly changed his venture plans.

Staff Selection and Subcontracting

Clients are entitled to know who will perform their work. The consultant who works with the client and develops the assignment has the responsibility to ensure that it is carried out effectively. Large consultancies may assign teams of specialists to perform work, but the original consultant who the client trusts nevertheless has responsibility to ensure that the client receives the benefits promised. Unfortunately, some high-profile consultants have developed a reputation for "bait and switch," a practice in which the client expects to be served by one consultant but instead finds that the work is being performed by another, more junior consultant. This is unethical and casts doubt on the integrity of the profession as a whole.

This also applies to subcontracting work. With the growth of small practices, it is common for consultants to form teams, which may consist of independent consultants or professionals drawn from more than a single firm. One consultant or consulting firm is usually the consultant of record, or lead, and the others are responsible to that consultant. They are, in fact, subcontracted or joint ventured for the purpose of the assignment. The client should be informed of all such relationships since they may affect the staffing of the assignment and the level of control the assigned project manager can exercise.

Deliverables and Property Rights

Deliverables belong to the client unless prior arrangement has been made to assign or share property rights. An ethical question can arise in determining whether a particular process, system or software, for example, is a deliverable or not. The basic rule is that if they were developed prior to the assignment and introduced as proprietary items, they remain the property of the consultant; if they were developed in the course of the work for the client, they are client property. Ethical issues arise when the product or system has marketable value. Basic systems may be altered substantially to satisfy a specific client's needs. Does this constitute the development of a deliverable product accruing to the client? Consultants should anticipate these situations and reach agreement with clients early in the project to determine how proprietary rights are to be determined and the proceeds of marketing them distributed.

Enforcing Codes of Ethics

Codes of professional conduct refer to many aspects of professional practice, and their enforcement is the responsibility of the profession itself. Where institutes and other professional accrediting bodies exist, they can discipline members for breaches of the code by suspending or rescinding membership. Many consultants, however, are not members of such institutes. Some professional bodies, such as the legal, engineering and accounting professions, have significant control over a member's ability to practice in that there are legal sanctions that apply when certain professional activities are performed by nonaccredited people. Most consulting, including management consulting has not achieved this status, and the field is open for anyone to enter, regardless of qualifications. One exception is the Certified Management Consultant (CMC) designation provided by various provincial institutes, but most consultants are not members of these.

Professionalism is generic, however, and membership in an institute is not a prerequisite to a professional attitude and behaviour. Professionalism requires that conduct is ethical and that work habits be disciplined and businesslike. Effective consultants develop and operate with a disciplined approach, maintain good records (both business operating records and client-related archives), perform according to agreed terms of reference and provide specific and workable recommendations on schedule and within agreed budget limits. In short, professional consultants do what they say they will do and do it to the best of their ability. Most client complaints come as a result of consultants not following their terms of reference, not delivering what was promised and not performing on time. Formal ethical concerns are less frequent, but to many clients, sloppy and unprofessional behaviour is unethical.

Ethics and International Consulting

International consulting poses a special ethical dilemma. What is legal and ethical in one country or culture is not always legal and ethical in another. When there is a difference, what is ethical practice for the consultant? When is it appropriate to follow the dictum, "When in Rome, do as the Romans do," and when is it unethical to behave in certain ways regardless of where one is? Philosophers have been arguing this dilemma for centuries. Cultural relativists support the view that ethics are based on values accepted by a culture and should be observed in that context. Alternatively, universalists hold that there are universal and objective ethical rules which apply to all human behaviour, regardless of culture. Bribery is often used as a core issue in discussing this dilemma. Universalists argue that virtually every country in the world has laws that prohibit bribery. On the other hand, cultural relativists believe that these laws differ as does enforcement, depending on the cultural values of the various countries.

Bribery may be a basic issue of ethics, but it is not the only one that consultants face when they practice internationally. For example, in selecting a team, consultants consider it unethical (and possibly illegal) to use religious affiliation, race or gender as determining factors. Some countries, however, feel differently. In some Moslem cultures, women would have difficulty because of local constraints regarding their role and place in society. They might be prohibited from driving or moving around freely in public. Similarly, a Jewish consultant in some Arabic states may face constraints. Assigned staff must provide the client with the best service possible, and if their movements and activities and access to people are limited, the client is probably not being served effectively. Consultants are also not well-served when assigned inappropriately. Firms have ethical concerns for the safety and well-being of their staff as well. In these cases factors such as religion, gender and even race might need to be considered.

Another example involves "informed consent" to ensure that participants in research or respondents to a survey are properly informed as to the purpose of the research and have an opportunity to decline to participate. Concern is for the respondent and to avoid the possibility that participants may be unknowingly harmed by the results (e.g. side effects from medical research, increased productivity targets, etc.). In China, permission to carry out survey research of any kind must be obtained; this is not automatic and may apparently be withheld arbitrarily. China is a tightly controlled totalitarian country and any kind of information gathering is closely monitored. Researchers and respondents, as well as any official who wrongly grants permission for research to take place, are liable for punishment, if all protocols are not carefully observed.

International Ethics and the Law

During the past several decades, a number of attempts have been made to resolve ethical issues associated with international business by agreeing on binding conventions which could criminalize certain activities. International agencies such as the Organization for Economic Cooperation and Development (OECD) and the UN have issued guidelines and recommendations to member countries.

Much of the emphasis has been on illegal payments. In 1977, the US passed the Foreign Corrupt Practices Act (FCPA) which essentially holds US citizens accountable to US laws, even when they are abroad. It does, however, recognize some of the practical realities of companies trying to do business in foreign cultures. Specifically, while it outlaws bribery, it permits "grease payments" – in essence, relatively small payments made to minor officials to encourage them to move proceedings along more quickly. Critics of the legislation point to the vague language in parts of the law and its failure to define how small is small and how low is low when describing permitted "lubrication or grease payments."

In March 1996, 21 of the 34 members of the Organization of American States (OAS) signed the Inter-American Convention Against Corruption (ICAC). The US signed this convention in June 1996, and Canada is expected to sign shortly. This signaled the growing belief that the bribing of public officials in the conduct of international business could be condemned generally and that countries were ready to take action to embody this ethic in statute.

On December 17, 1997, the 29-member nations of the OECD signed the Convention on Combating Bribery of Foreign Public Officials in International Business Transactions which extends many of the provisions of the FCPA to other countries, thereby "leveling the playing field" for Americans operating abroad. Nonmembers were urged to sign as well; Argentina, Brazil, Bulgaria, Chile and Slovakia signed in December of 1997. Although a number of definitions and corollaries will undoubtedly await tests in court, this establishes the principle of universality, at least with respect to recognizing some activities associated with public officials as corrupt throughout most of the world.

At the beginning of this chapter, Figure 8-2 illustrated that societal values are important determinants to behavioural ethics. To some extent, therefore, we are ethical products of the societies of which we are part. As consultants increasingly become involved in international projects the differences in societal values among and between cultures becomes apparent. While some basic human rights values are becoming adopted generally throughout the world, even these are not universally accepted by all societies. Clearly, local laws should be observed when working in another country, but ethical choices are not always that straightforward.

Consultants that operate internationally often find that ethics are increasingly becoming a matter of personal values and beliefs as to right and wrong. The famous French writer, Albert Camus, was quoted as saying, "Integrity needs no rules."[2] For a summary of the ethics and professionalism issues see Figure 8-3.

By its very nature, professional consulting relies on the individual consultant for ethical behaviour, and effective professionals protect their integrity above all else. Throughout this book, the emphasis was on professionalism. At the same time, the focus was on effective consulting as a commercial enterprise. There is no inherent conflict between professionalism and commercialism. All professionals charge for their services, but there can be issues of conflict of interest and professional competence that must be understood and incorporated in the practice of providing professional services.

---

[2]Jonathon Green, *The Pan Dictionary of Contemporary Quotations*, Pan Books Ltd. London, 1989.

FIGURE 8-3: *Ethics and Professionalism*

- Ethics defines professionalism

- ICMCC Code of Ethics centres on four stakeholder groups:
  - The public
  - Other members
  - The profession
  - The client

- Ethics complicate decisions with dilemmas and conflicting values, when:
  - accepting assignments
  - operating within institutions
  - marketing professional services
  - selling professional services
  - performing the work
  - distinguishing research from espionage

- Ethical concerns may require projects to be stopped

- Ethical behaviour extends to staffing and subcontracting

- Project deliverables can raise ethical issues

- International consulting increases ethical challenges – cultural relativism versus universalism

- International laws concerning ethics are emerging

Professionalism is a concept that defines providing a service for a fee. But it is also a privileged position in society that implies ethical behaviour.

NINE

Looking
Ahead

So you have finally completed your first assignment. You have set up your practice, marketed your professional services, closed the sale, completed your formal proposals, done your presentation and completed the assignment. While the first assignment is important, it does not a consulting practice make. Practices need to be sustained and effective procedures instituted if they are to succeed and survive over time. Whether the practice is to be a sole practitioner, a small firm or a part of a large firm, the principles are the same. It is a business and needs to make money. To make money, it needs to be managed, and the key to managing a professional practice effectively is to manage the projects and clients effectively. Effective management of each ensures that the prime determinant of success – delivering quality work – remains the focus of the consultancy. Quality work is more than merely providing promised deliverables and results on time and as agreed. It also means that the consultant has maintained a sharp focus on what the client is trying to accomplish. To do so the consultant and client must communicate constantly throughout the process – making changes when indicated – and forge a partnership in change which will have lasting effects after the project is completed.

It is no surprise that the largest single source of new business for successful consultants is past clients. The three key dimensions of a consulting practice – quality work, timeliness and reliability within all working relationships, and effective management of finances – are almost exclusively the province of effective project and client management. The administration of the business – managing receivables, payables and taxes and in some cases financial reporting and payroll – while required and therefore necessary, should not be confused with running the practice.

To Expand or Not

Success leads to more success for effective consultants. As good marketing and selling, along with excellence in performing the work, establish the business, its reputation grows and opportunities for consulting work begin to challenge the capacity of the professionals to do the projects and at the same time maintain the ongoing marketing efforts essential for long-term survival of the practice. Decisions are required on the future of the enterprise. Should the firm expand, and, if so, how?

For the independent working out of home or client offices, the signal is clear: the time committed to billable work is now limiting the time available for developing more business. The following four options should be considered:

- Continue at the present level of work, probably increasing the billing rate in response to the growing demand
- Negotiate a position with an existing firm or federation that can add administrative and marketing support in return for a share of the billings
- Add capacity, both for business development and for serving clients, by subcontracting work and using professional marketing services
- Plan and form a small firm which will employ other professionals and support staff

> **INSIDER'S VIEW**
>
> Consultants often augment their core capabilities by hiring contract workers. The emphasis on strong project management and network management has increased in importance as "virtual firms" of consulting teams emerge as units to compete for consulting projects not previously available to small consultancies.

Each of these is a valid strategy, and choosing among them involves both personal and business considerations. The following describes briefly each of these four expansion options:

■ *Continue Along Present Lines*

Individual specialists and recognized experts as well as part-time consultants, such as university professors, frequently select this option. A consulting practice can provide a comfortable, in some cases lucrative income and many successful consultants choose to remain individual independents. Often they are invited by other professionals and firms to collaborate as technical support subcontractors. The two main challenges they face are staying current in their field of expertise and balancing the longer term need for sustained business development with current client demands.

The first of these, staying current, requires continuous professional development, a concentrated effort to stay abreast of the literature in the field, seeking out colleagues for discussion and concept sharpening, and frequently attending conferences which might attract more competitors than clients. Change is constant and increasingly rapid in the face of emerging technology. Skills and knowledge lose their currency quickly under these conditions. Sustaining a professional practice requires service maintenance and enhancement, like most products. The current demand for consulting services may be substantial, but that is now; tomorrow's demands for the same services may be sparse.

The second challenge, supporting the longer term business development needs, is obviously critical to sustaining a practice. Sustaining a practice of this type over time requires that non-billable time to be regularly scheduled. There is always a delay between the time when specific business development activities are undertaken and the appearance of new business. Consultants who focus solely on client requirements and postpone business development activities until the client work is complete are guaranteed the excitement of a peak-and-valley business. During periods of intense business development activity, the business will experience a net cash outflow as expenditures on travel, telecommunication, mail and so on increase. During such a period, inflows from billings dwindle and may even stop. In time there is a race between the last funds available for promotion and the first new client billing. For most professionals, the level of anxiety this produces is unpleasant and stressful. Selling effectiveness and sufficiency of promotional resources and effort can suffer as a result, thereby further exacerbating the situation. This pattern is all too common among new independents.

The discipline of planned, scheduled and regularly executed business development efforts definitely pays off in the long term. Although in practice, non-billable time cannot have the same priority as chargeable client time, few practices achieve a degree of constant and steady flow of client work without continual effort at marketing their practice.

■ *Join a Firm*

Once independent consultants have demonstrated the ability to attract a clientele and provide clients with a definable quality service, usually over a two- to three-year minimum period, they become potentially valuable to firms, large and small. They can often negotiate a good employment or contractual arrangement that exchanges some of the billings they generate for the advantages the firm has to offer. These may include the benefits of the firm's reputation in a broader marketplace, and skilled professional colleagues who can help build breadth and depth to the individual's practice through involvement in more and varied assignments. In addition, of course, the firm provides administrative and marketing support and possibly greater stability through exposure to a wider market and more constant business inflows.

Arrangements with firms vary from full employment status to contract-by-contract fee sharing. Some agreements provide for consultants to remain independent and be available to the firm for a set number of days a week, and free to conduct their own for the remainder, provided there is no conflict of interest. (This can be successful when the specialty is clearly unique within the firm and client bases can be distinguished.)

There may be equity participation, and administrative requirements, such as weekly time sheets and expense reports. The financial elements of this choice, including tax implications, need to be considered. As indicated earlier, taxes for employees are materially different from those for independents running their own businesses. Income realized by the independent after joining a firm, in the form of a salary with benefits and some profit share or bonus, may be higher or lower after taxes.

Some consulting organizations are formed so that the consultants are federated independent practices instead of employees. In these federations consultants operate independently but share premises and administrative services and may collaborate as needed to serve clients. Some such groups attract the interest of Revenue Canada who may question whether they are in fact federations, or in reality a normal company with employees. It is not always clearcut, but many federations have argued successfully for their structure and consequent tax advantages for their professionals. One factor is the degree to which all professionals derive all their income from the federated firm. Independents should seek clarification of their position before joining a consulting firm structured as a federation. Joining a consulting firm as an employee is clearcut, however, and can be readily compared with the independent consultant's current position.

■ *Add Capacity*

A compromise between joining a firm or federation and continuing as at present is the use of contract associates, both for client work and for business development. Because consulting practices are essentially run through projects, independents can easily form productive collaborations with other professionals and technical experts. As a general rule, the consultant that initiates the work with the client performs most of the work and is, therefore, the prime contractor. All others are sub-contracted to that lead consultant. This is not always the case, however. In some cases clients specify a lead consultant who will exercise project management responsibilities and manage the subcontractors who perform the bulk of the work. In any case, the lead consultant has final responsibility to ensure that the client receives the highest quality service from the professionals, and that the work is completed on time and within budget. By bringing together the best international talent available, some independent consultants compete successfully with larger firms for large and complex projects. These consultants are able to satisfy the client's requirements for strong project and subcontract management and quality assurance.

Expansion of the business on a project-by-project basis in this way is complex and exciting, because it involves wider ranging and more diverse consulting with larger clients. It relies on professionals experienced in responding to effective project management and control, who can build and maintain a high level of trust and confidence in each other's ability and who are firmly committed to performing with excellence, on time, and within budget. In other words, there must be a spirit of teamwork. When these collaborative teams run into difficulty it is usually because one member fails to perform, or because there is a dispute over money. Effective project management can catch substandard performance early and arrange for changes in the work assignments or make other staffing decisions to ensure that the quality of the project is not compromised. Financial arrangements may need to be adjusted as well, and when this happens, the lead consultant may be called on to demonstrate effective negotiating skills and diplomacy.

In general, many disputes over money can be avoided by agreeing at the outset how the fees will be divided, how budget increases or reductions will be handled and how expenses will be budgeted, charged and recovered. In this way, the professionals are rewarded for results and share fairly in the risks or benefits of budget reductions or extensions. This is generally preferred over approaches which budget the time and pay the consultants on a billed time basis, because this compensates effort, rather than results and can lead to disagreement about performance. Once these issues are out of the way, work can proceed with full professional attention from all involved.

In the chapter on Marketing, the use of public relations professionals was discussed in some detail. This service is available to independent consultants and can greatly extend their business development efforts when used effectively. Expansion on a project-by-project basis, often referred to as "knowledge-working" tends to convert an independent's practice to fewer and larger projects. These larger and more complex projects usually require most of the independent's attention for significant periods of time. The use of contract marketing services is one way to maintain a constant level of business development effort while project work is performed.

■ *Building Your Own Firm*

Many new consulting firms are started by three to five professionals who have worked together for a larger firm or on a few projects and decide to try their own approach. They are usually experienced professionals with a track record of business development and effective performance, and they are familiar with the administrative framework of a professional firm. Like any entrepreneurial enterprise, the new firm should be well planned and appropriately financed. Among the first acquisitions will be office space and one or more support staff. Although most of the office requirements can be rented or leased, including the set of electronic and manual items which comprise a consultant's office, including copier, fax machine, computers, telecommunications system, files, furniture, etc., it always represents a commitment of resources at the start. Typically, these new firms begin with one or more immediate projects from clients who are aware of the competence of the consultants. These initial engagements fund the start-up and launch the new firm. Very quickly, however, marketing programs need to be brought to bear and a new clientele established.

Sometimes individual consultants succeed in building a substantial firm. This typically takes several years and may progress through several of the expansion options in sequence. For example, early success can be handled by increasing rates and adding part-time administrative help while operating from home offices and client premises. Expanding the practice with the help of subcontracts and adding professional PR support can maintain the growth and eventually lead to the critical mass of business on which to base a formal enterprise.

Personal reflection is important when addressing the option of starting and building a consulting firm. The consultant or consultants involved need to satisfy themselves that they are prepared to undertake the challenge of managing the enterprise, once established. As a manager, the consultant needs to envision the firm growing and developing according to plans, and possess the enthusiasm for grappling with the myriad of details that are part of running a company. This includes such things as reviewing financial performance, dealing with creditors, banks and government agencies, hiring and supervising support staff, overseeing administration and payroll, and the like.

Unlimited Opportunity for Consultants

Whether you decide to expand your firm or remain a sole practitioner, the opportunities for consulting are substantial and growing. Many have tried to measure the market for consulting, but by its very nature it defies measurement. As indicated earlier, few organizations have a budget specifically for consulting; therefore, studying corporate budgets for consulting will not identify how big the market is. The total amount billed by recognized consulting firms does provide a measure, but it is historic by definition and, in what is believed to be a fast-growing market, it understates the current reality. Furthermore, it does not take into account the myriad of small and part-time consultancies which represent a significant market segment.

One could argue that the market potential for consulting services is unlimited in that consultants frequently make their own markets. Many assignments develop as a result of consultants taking the initiative and approaching a potential client with a possible business opportunity. Effective, benefits-focused selling can often convert that perceived opportunity into a consulting assignment for an appreciative client. To the extent this happens, consultants create their own markets. Consultants who watch and understand change are in the best position to create these markets.

Consulting is about change. When things are changing or need to change, consultants thrive. They flourish when change is driven by growth and prosperity, and many also serve clients undergoing changes due to retrenchment and downsizing. Intensified competition puts pressures on organizations to rethink their approaches and redirect resources. This creates change. Today's world is characterized as a world of constant and accelerating change. It is logical, therefore that consulting continues to attract many newcomers who contribute to and build profitable enterprises serving the needs of change. Consider the following forces for change:

■ *Technology*

Not only is technology continuing to evolve, but its very nature is causing structural changes to occur in all walks of life. Consider the changes caused by Internet marketing, which has introduced major new competitors to established business – the Internet marketing of automobiles and houses, for example, and the impact this has on car dealers and real estate agents. Or consider the intensified globalization of large organizations by custom designed Intranet systems capable of transmitting and disseminating vast amounts of data and information throughout the world and serving as venues for otherwise impractical virtual meetings. Imagine the as yet not fully understood impact of the mass distribution of information of all kinds throughout the world and its effect on institutional accountability.

■ *Globalization*

Fed by the changes in technology and information management, consider the impact on marketers and suppliers facing new and powerful competitors throughout the world anxious and ready to compete for their customers. Or the effect on enterprises and states, large and small, of integrated financial organizations capable of moving mass amounts of wealth in response to day-to-day shifts in supply and demand for money. The speed with which the "Asian crisis" has rippled throughout the world is an excellent example.

■ *Balkanization: Globalization's Mirror Image*

Many national boundaries date from times past when the world was delineated by adversarial superpowers. Pre-existing cultural pressures, unleashed by the collapse of the USSR and the ending of the Cold War, and supported by modern technology, are now enabling new countries and alliances to form around the world and others to divide or change size and shape. These too are forces of change and increase the need for consultants.

As the scope and rate of change continues to increase and competitive pressures intensify, organizations need to adapt to and anticipate changes in their current environment, and they need to enhance their abilities to change as well. Organizations are increasingly developing structures and options to help them address the pressures for change. Outsourcing permits organizations to reduce or eliminate whole segments of their enterprise. This can create financial flexibility and responsiveness so the organization can react to rapidly changing levels of activity. Consultants are one version of contract employees, who can assume some of the activities required in the enterprise, but remain independent businesspersons who, depending on the contract, can be released when the work is completed or no longer required.

It is safe to predict that the next millennium will see continuing rapid growth in the consulting field. As indicated at the beginning of this book, consulting is not new; what is new is the growing breadth and depth of consulting opportunities developing as the forces of change continue to stimulate greater participation of consultants in all kinds of enterprises and institutions.

It is also safe to predict that as more clients become more familiar with the practice of working with consultants, they will demand more of their consultants – more in terms of effort, more in terms of expertise, and more in terms of real value in their pursuit of desirable change. As the standards for excellence for consultants rise, so, too will the hurdle which separates the average from the good. Consultants will be called on as never before to show their professionalism in the quality of their work and most of all in the integrity which defines them as professional.

APPENDIX

Sample of Formal Proposal

It is usually good practice to regard all aspects of consulting as confidential unless the client advises otherwise – it is up to clients to make public what they wish.

This **Sample Proposal Cover Page** has the basic content required: title, date, the designation "proposal," and the identity of the two partners.

There is an opportunity to express some creativity in the design of the cover, but usually conservatism is appreciated when clients evaluate consultants, and the cover of the proposal is often the first tangible evidence clients have of a consultant's style.

Private and Confidential

Towards Improved Sales Force Effectiveness

a Proposal to

INTERNATIONAL FOODS DIVISION CAPITAL FOODS INC.

August 19, 1998

from

CANDO Management Consultants

423 Consultant Way, Somewhere, Earth
Phone/Fax (700) 738-4877

– (1) –

CANDO Management Consultants

423 Consultant Way, Somewhere, Earth
e-mail cando@cw.com • Phone/Fax (700) 738-4877

Mr. Arthur Mometer, President
International Foods Division
Capital Foods Inc.
2100 Ladel Street
Toronto, Canada M2T 4N1

August 19, 1998

PRIVATE AND CONFIDENTIAL

Dear Mr. Mometer:

Re: "Towards Improved Sales Force Effectiveness" proposal

It was a pleasure meeting with you and your Marketing Director, Bob Fairweather, last Thursday in your office. A strong and balanced marketing strategy has always been International Food's hallmark, and we agree with you that continued success requires constant reassessment of your position.

You have identified your key marketing issue at this time as finding the best balance between 'push' and 'pull' activities. All elements of the marketing mix are critical, but it is not always clear what each contributes to success. The activities most associated with the 'push' side of the equation (trade promotions, pricing programs, in-store activities) focus attention on the sales forces; 'pull' activities (positioning, product design, pricing, packaging, advertising, consumer research, etc.), focus on the consumer and, can reduce the need to offer discounts and other 'push' expenditures. This, in turn, might permit you to refine the activities of your field sales effort to focus on gaining faster acceptance of your new product items. It makes sense, then, to examine the current role and effectiveness of your sales efforts as one part of your 'push/pull' equation.

We are pleased to submit our proposal, "Towards Improved Sales Force Effectiveness," for your review in this regard. Our proposal incorporates the results of our preliminary analysis of the information you provided, our two discussions with you and with Bob, and some additional information we were able to locate from public sources and our files.

We are confident that we can help the International Foods Division strengthen its total marketing effectiveness and look forward to working with you and your staff as you address the significant opportunities for growth in the next five years. I will call you next week to set up our next meeting.

Yours very truly,

CANDO Management Consultants

Jean Bostick, CMC, Partner

JB/dw

This **Letter of Transmittal** is included in the proposal and is an integral part of it and of the overall selling process.

Salutation is formal, because the document is a formal part of the relationship.

The tone of the letter is personal, but retains the formal relationship between parties entering into a business relationship.

The letter summarizes the client's key concerns which give rise to the opportunity for the consultant to offer assistance.

Letter includes a conceptual element which introduces the key premise which provided context for this particular proposed approach.

The proposal is positioned as part of a larger and on-going interest in the client's success.

The proposer has done some 'homework' as further evidence of interest in this client and this challenge.

Consultant keeps control of the situation and indicates the next step.

This **Table of Contents** is necessary on long and complex proposals of the type demonstrated by this disguised model. Letter format may be sufficient for proposals covering more focused relationships and projects; however, the topics covered in this Table of Contents should be considered in any case. They each define a dimension of the relationship, and articulating them at the outset of the project can avoid difficulties later.

TABLE OF CONTENTS

CANDO Management Consultants

I

INTRODUCTION

International Foods Division (IFD) of Capital Foods Limited is undertaking a complete review of its Marketing program. A Change Committee of three senior managers has been named to assess the markets for special recipe canned soups in Canada and improve IFD's place in it. IFD has decided to obtain consulting assistance to help this committee accumulate the needed information and to provide objective expertise.

IFD has advised us that requests for qualifications were sent to 20 pre-selected consultants, and 15 have responded. CANDO Management Consultants is pleased to be one of three firms IFD asked to submit complete proposals, including specific qualifications statements.

This proposal, "Towards Improved Sales Force Effectiveness," presents our approach to helping you address the role of your sales force in marketing your special recipe for canned soups. We see this project as supporting the Change Committee's mandate, and we will work closely with its members to produce actionable results.

We understand that this is the Change Committee's first experience with consultants, and we accept the responsibility for helping the committee establish effective control over the project and monitor our performance. Effective and open communication is the key to a productive working relationship, and we will provide leadership in this regard.

This project promises to be an interesting one, and we at CANDO Management Consultants look forward to working with you, the Change Committee, and your staff in its accomplishment. We will be happy to meet with you for further discussion and clarification of this proposal on your request.

CANDO Management Consultants

This section deals with the emerging business relationship between client and consultant. It provides a brief background of how the two parties have come together to this point. In essence, this section of the proposal is directed towards client personnel who may not yet be involved in the project and provides archival statements about the initial intent of the relationship.

Throughout this proposal, the consultant reinforces the notion of client (rather than consultant) control. This is the client's project and it responds to their needs and priorities. This is not the consultant's project attempting to understand the client's needs. The client wants real help from their consultant.

The **Background** section sets the scene for the work itself. It provides an opportunity for the consultant to demonstrate experience and familiarity with the situation. The consultant can introduce key concepts and premises at this point to strengthen his/her position as knowledgeable.

Importantly, this is ➤ **not a rehash** of information the client has provided; it should add to the dialogue that has already taken place between client and consultant.

The focus at this point is on the merits of the project; the reason for the work to be done.

Here, the focus shifts to address the timeliness of the project; the reasons for the project to be conducted **now**. Both issues, the merits of performing the ➤ work and an understanding of why the client has chosen this time to perform it are essential to demonstrating to the client that the consultant truly identifies with this client's needs at this time.

II

BACKGROUND

Canada's food distribution is unique among developed countries in the degree to which it is concentrated. Almost 70% of all packaged goods sales are made through nine corporate chains and centrally-controlled groups.[1] In Ontario, the largest market, this concentration is even greater.

This concentration, coupled with the tight central control of each store by the retailer, creates a powerful lever with which retailers can demand trade concessions from food manufacturers. Buyers and merchandising managers can promise results for firms prepared to be generous with promotion allowances and the like. Conversely, lack of their support can seriously hurt a product's sales performance at retail. In short, a small group of powerful buying departments decide whether to stock, or not to stock a particular product and, once stocked, how much support to provide the product through competitive shelf positioning, special displays, in-store promotions and other merchandising activities. Merchandising support costs money, and that is what you consider when developing your 'push money' budget.

The main counterbalance a manufacturer has to this retailer leverage is the level of consumer demand, or the 'franchise' a product enjoys in the marketplace. Each year, when you negotiate your promotion plan with the retailers, the strength of your consumer franchise is brought into sharp focus. The orchestration of your marketing mix is reviewed and activities adjusted constantly to reflect changing consumer and competitive conditions to maintain and build this franchise. Advertising, couponing, promotional events, product enhancement, and presentation improvements all cost money as well; this is your 'pull money' budget.

IFD is addressing the classic dilemma of allocating marketing resources between 'push' and 'pull' programs. In March of 1996, market intelligence reports indicated that consumer franchises in several of the key products have strengthened significantly, and market share has risen to the point where the balance between the consumer draw and the in-store presentation may have changed. In July of 1996 IFD established a Change Committee comprising the top managers of the Marketing, Sales and Operations departments to review the balance between 'push' and 'pull' programs and establish budgets for the next five years.

---

[1]"Food Distribution in Canada," *Retail Views*, Canadian Retail Council for the Consumer, Toronto, Spring, 1996

CANDO Management Consultants

The Committee will assess the cost-effectiveness of each set of market-related activities rigorously and objectively and establish plans to which all departments can be committed. Three distinct areas of inquiry have been identified: namely, consumer program effectiveness, retail program effectiveness, and sales force effectiveness. We concur with this approach, and particularly endorse the separation of the sales force considerations from other activities because its role can change in response to changes in the other two areas of inquiry.

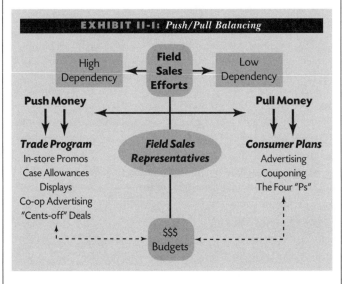

EXHIBIT II-1: *Push/Pull Balancing*

High Dependency ← **Field Sales Efforts** → Low Dependency

Push Money ←→ **Pull Money**

Trade Program
In-store Promos
Case Allowances
Displays
Co-op Advertising
"Cents-off" Deals

Field Sales Representatives

Consumer Plans
Advertising
Couponing
The Four "Ps"

$$$ Budgets

Exhibit II-1 depicts this relationship among the three areas. As the effectiveness (weight) of the 'pull money' increases, the dependency on field sales efforts is reduced; conversely, as the effectiveness of the 'push' activities increases, the need for greater retail sales effort is felt. A retail sales effort can be considered a balancing factor in the 'push/pull' trade-off.

IFD has recently appointed Mr. Bob Fairweather as Marketing Director. He brings a substantial level of field sales experience to this post. This change provided an opportunity to reassess the priorities associated with marketing strategy and particularly the role of field sales. The annual cost of putting a salesperson on the road has been estimated at between $450,000 and $800,000;[2] it is therefore both timely and appropriate for the committee to focus on sales force effectiveness. This proposal offers our assistance in this regard.

[2] "Sales Costs in Canada", *Retail Travellers' Association*, Montreal, January, 1996

CANDO Management Consultants

The use of conceptual diagrams can be a powerful illustration of the consultant's familiarity with the real issues at play. It also serves to provide the client with a measure of the consultant's conceptual strength and ability to communicate graphically. This can frequently be a strong differentiating factor among competitive proposals. Generally, any meaningful opportunity to use graphics in support of the textual content should be used.

This is a subtle reference to current organizational changes which further necessitate for this project to be undertaken now; new players signal a new game. The purpose of this sort of comment is to demonstrate that the consultant is sensitive to the 'politics' of the project, as well as its overall merit and timing imperatives.

The reference to economic costs provides an order of magnitude for the client to compare benefits with project costs which will be provided with the fee estimates later in the proposal.

Objectives should be described in blunt, unambiguous language. The consultant should avoid vague or general terms which may refer to non-specific benefits of general improvement and focus directly on the outcomes and goals against which the client will measure the project's success.

This is the **client's** objective.

These are **the Project's** objectives.

This reinforces the **"work with,"** rather than **"work for"** philosophy to which the consultant is committed.

III

PROJECT OBJECTIVES AND SCOPE

A. OBJECTIVES

The IFD Change Committee has divided its mandate into three areas of inquiry as follows:

- Consumer Program Effectiveness
- Retail Program Effectiveness
- Sales Force Effectiveness

This proposal addresses the last of these three: Sales Force Effectiveness. The Committee's challenge is to determine the role and performance required by the sales force needed to achieve cost-effectiveness, relative to budgeted activities in the other two areas of inquiry. IFD has asked for professional management consulting assistance in this regard; accordingly, the consulting objective can be defined as:

To determine the importance of field sales activities in supporting special recipe foods marketing, and assess IFD field sales efforts in this regard.

Specifically, the tasks to be performed in this study will accomplish the following:

- Determine the importance of field sales activities relative to other retail-directed activities in effective sales generation as described by retail buyers.
- Identify the criteria used by retail buyers to evaluate the effectiveness of field sales activities of food marketers.
- Determine the effectiveness of the IFD field sales force relative to competition as perceived by retail buyers.
- Identify and evaluate opportunities for IFD to improve the effectiveness of its field sales efforts.

This project is designed to contribute to the mandate of the Change Committee. The project team will work with the Committee to integrate the findings of this project with other information developed by the Committee.

CANDO Management Consultants

B. SCOPE

This project focuses on the activities and effectiveness of the IFD field sales force. The Project Team will collect and assess information from three sources:

- Interviews with retail buyers and other retail executives.
- Published information from public and trade sources in the US and Canada.
- Observations and discussions with IFD field sales representatives during the course of one-day field trips.

This is not a market survey. In the course of discussions with buyers, other market information useful to IFD will be collected, and it will be included in our reports. Nevertheless, the primary concern of the project team will be to accomplish the objectives as described.

We will restrict our assessment to those aspects of sales force management which bear on the Committee's objectives. It is not our intention to evaluate the size and make-up of territories, customer prioritizing policies, or sales compensation practices unless these and similar aspects emerge as important to assessing field sales performance.

Our interest is in aggregated information, not specific comments by specific people. All discussions with individual buyers and sales representatives will be in confidence; specific remarks will not be reported nor attributed to identifiable situations without prior agreement on the part of the individual to be quoted.

This describes not only what the project will include, but its **limits** as well; it includes what the consultants are committed to do, and what they **do not** plan to do.

These limitations should not be contentious and should not surprise the client. Any contentious items of scope should have been cleared through discussions with the client prior to this proposal submission; this should only provide clarification and confirmation.

It is important once again to avoid vague language which may mask unresolved differences between what the client expects to have done and what the consultant plans to do. This is a critical section of the proposal with respect to establishing client expectations.

CANDO Management Consultants

This section describes the overall concept of the consulting project and how it will be accomplished.

IV

PROPOSED METHODOLOGY

We are proposing a work program based on in-depth field interviews with key spokespersons from the food retailing industry. This will be augmented by secondary information available through sources external to IFD as well as internal information from IFD files. In addition, our professionals will accompany two field representatives for one day each as they perform their work. We have found this multi-source approach to be particularly effective in examining sales force effectiveness.

We considered the option of proposing a broad ranging survey of retailers, but believe this interview-based program more desirable for the following reasons:

The consultant acknowledges that there are alternative methodologies which may have some merit, but thoughtfully rejects them based on sound and experienced judgement. This may remove competition from further consideration.

- Questionnaires are too restricted with respect to the information they can obtain.
- Key IFD customers may be among the non-respondents.
- Key respondents can be identified easily, and CANDO has established relationships with the firms involved.
- Your Committee needs the type of specific first-hand observation and discussion-based information which can be developed only by experienced professional consultants.

In our judgement, although some cost savings could result from the use of surveys, the results would not prove useful to your Committee. The methodology we are proposing, by contrast, provides the benefits of in-depth confidential discussions with the people whose judgment counts most in assessing field sales performance – your key customers. Our professionals will become privy to advice and comments not available to your sales representatives. Conclusions and recommendations based on this type of information are generally more valuable because of the accuracy, frankness and objectivity the interviews provide.

CANDO Management Consultants

V

PROPOSED WORK PROGRAM

We propose a work program comprising the following six steps:

1. Project Start-up

2. Internal and Secondary Data Review

3. In-depth Interview Program
   a) Planning and Scheduling the Interviews
   b) Conducting the Interviews

4. Field Sales Trip

5. Analysis of the Results of Steps 2, 3 and 4

6. Presentation of Results
   a) Presenting the Draft Report
   b) Providing the Final Document

Exhibit V-1 presents a schematic view of our proposed approach. The remainder of this section describes each work step in detail.

A simple and straightforward listing of what is to follow.

CANDO Management Consultants

This illustration shows the work program at a glance.

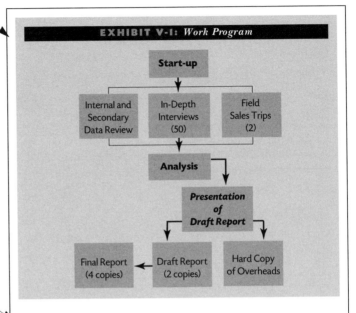

EXHIBIT V-I: *Work Program*

Start-up

Internal and Secondary Data Review

In-Depth Interviews (50)

Field Sales Trips (2)

Analysis

Presentation of Draft Report

Final Report (4 copies)

Draft Report (2 copies)

Hard Copy of Overheads

Brief statements highlight the purpose of each step and what is included.

Details of Work Steps

1. PROJECT START-UP

This step punctuates the beginning of our work with you and provides an opportunity to finalize commitments as to responsibilities and timing, and to ensure that everyone's expectations of results are the same. As the first formal meeting, it confirms the project organization and signals the commitment of specific IFD and CANDO personnel to the Project Team. This work step involves a meeting, conducted by our Project Manager, of approximately a half day in duration. At this time the CANDO team will discuss our detailed plan and schedule progress meetings. We will agree on the make-up of the Steering Committee, the characteristics of the key deliverables, and the process of announcing the project within IFD. Any outstanding administrative issues will be resolved at this time as well.

2. INTERNAL AND SECONDARY DATA REVIEW

The Project Team will require a base of information to relate the characteristics of the food industry and your firm to the results of the in-depth interviews. Historical and market trends, sales patterns, sales territory assessments, past promotion history and analyses, other consultant and research reports, and competitive reviews will be among the internal items we will examine with the

CANDO Management Consultants

assistance of your assigned staff members. Clarifying interviews with a few of your senior executives may be required as well, as we seek to understand and interpret this material.

In addition, trade statistics and published information regarding trends and patterns affecting canned specialty products such as yours will be collected from government and library sources as well as our own files. We will conduct internet searches of all major North American sources to ensure we have exhausted all practical avenues. Additional published and unpublished information from trade associations and professional sales organizations will be collected during Step 3 in the work program.

3. IN-DEPTH INTERVIEW PROGRAM

a) Planning and Scheduling the Interviews

The consulting team (the CANDO professional members of the Project Team) will establish contact and schedule interviews with senior executives and managers engaged in the following activities:

- Merchandise planning and buying for corporate chains;
- Merchandise planning and buying for independent groups;
- Managing trade associations;
- Managing stores and store districts;
- Editing food industry publications.

We will develop an interview guide which we will discuss with you prior to conducting these interviews. This guide will indicate the topics to be covered and illustrate how the responses will help us construct some key deliverables.

b) Conducting the Interviews

On the one hand, the community of corporate retail food chain buyers in Canada is small due to industry concentration. On the other, there are still many important independent food retailing organizations and voluntary groups. Earlier studies we have conducted in your industry have indicated that there is a wide variation in the level of central control over store policy even within organization type. This variation may have important significance to the role and effectiveness of field sales efforts. We estimate that we will require a minimum of 30 in-depth interviews with a variety of senior spokespersons in order to establish generalizations with confidence. These interviews typically last for between one and two hours and cover a wide range of relevant topics. We will focus particularly on the following in this project:

- What is happening to the market for canned specialty foods, and how are the patterns changing?

CANDO Management Consultants

- What makes some firms more successful than others in this market; what are the key success factors, and how do they rate in relative importance?
- What are the strengths and limitations of various firms?
- How can a firm improve its performance in the short run?
- What role does the sales representative play, and how important are sales representatives?
- What makes a good sales representative in this market, and why are some better than others?
- How do the sales representatives from IFD and its main competitors rate with respect to the factors which make good sales representatives?

We can perform this work step effectively without revealing who our client is, should you consider this necessary. We strongly suggest, however, that you permit us to reveal your identity at the end of each interview. We have found this to have several advantages:

- Access is made easier;
- Respondents are more forthcoming when they know that the client will be identified to them;
- Specific comments received after revealing your identity can be particularly helpful, but the objectivity of the earlier discussion will not have been compromised.

Most of your customers will be flattered to be asked to help one of their suppliers improve performance and will be impressed that you consider improving your ability to understand their needs sufficiently important to retain independent consulting help to examine it. Often it makes competitors nervous as well we are told.

4. FIELD SALES TRIP

> Explains the sequence of this step, as well as the work planned.

After starting Step 3, but before all in-depth interviewing has been completed, we will arrange to spend two days in the field with each of two of your sales representatives. They will naturally schedule a varied and busy day to impress us, and we welcome this effort. We will not regard these as 'typical' days in the field, but rather displays of the kinds of activities in which your field representatives are involved. The purpose of these two field days is to provide your consultants with a first hand understanding of the practical realities of field operation, both through observation and through the informal discussions with the sales representatives. This helps to ensure that any recommendations we make with respect to field operations are realistic and practical.

CANDO Management Consultants

5. ANALYSIS OF RESULTS OF STEPS 2, 3 AND 4

Our analysis begins with the early information collected during Step 2 and continues until the final report is issued. Our basic premise is that the main challenge a marketer faces in succeeding in the food market in Canada is differentiation. How can IFD stand out among its competitors as better, in ways that count in the marketplace? Our analysis will centre on this theme.

We will identify and explore the factors which affect the trade support you and your competitors receive. We expect such factors as promotion plan, historical relationship, brand power, pricing policy, as well as field sales support to be among the key factors. For each factor your perceived performance, and that of your chief competitors, will be recorded and compared, and means of improving your performance described. We will develop and use appropriate ranking and scoring systems to provide precision and clarity of results. Trend analyses of IFD's recent history and market share attainment will help the Project Team confirm your performance relative to comparable industry characteristics.

6. PRESENTATION OF RESULTS

a) Draft Report

The full and complete communication and understanding of your results is essential to any successful professional engagement. Your consulting team will develop a complete report describing all findings, conclusions and recommendations, and prepare an in-depth presentation for your review. We expect this review to take the best part of a day to complete. Portions of the presentation may be made by your own staff who have participated as part of the Project Team. At the conclusion of this presentation and the discussion it generates, we will provide you with two copies of a written draft report and hard copies of any overhead transparencies used in the presentation.

b) The Final Report

Approximately a week after the presentation of the Draft Report, we will meet with you and discuss any modifications you would like to see in the final report to ensure clarity and precision. Substantive information and conclusions cannot be altered, but ambiguities, vagueness, and other sources of confusion need to be removed, and clarification provided where it is needed. We will replace your copies of the Draft Report with four copies of the Final Report within a week of discussing your suggestions.

Note the practice of collecting drafts to ensure they are removed from circulation.

CANDO Management Consultants

VI

PROJECT ORGANIZATION AND STAFFING

A. PROJECT ORGANIZATION

Exhibit VI-1 presents a schematic of the organization structure which we suggest for this project. We believe this project team should report to a Steering Committee comprising yourself and, by your invitation, the members of the Marketing Planning Committee. Others whom you feel should participate will be welcome, of course.

Some organization structures can be complex, but this schematic should be kept as simple as possible.

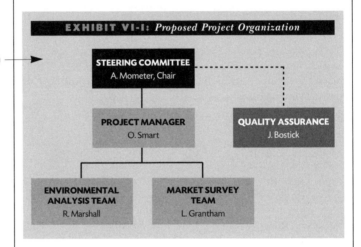

EXHIBIT VI-1: *Proposed Project Organization*

Brief statement of role and purpose of position as well as identifying incumbent selected.

The Project Team will be led by Mr. Orville Smart, CMC. As Project Manager, Mr. Smart will be responsible for ensuring that the project is completed on time and within budget. He will personally perform a substantial portion of the work as well as directing the efforts of the rest of the Project Team. He will be responsible to the Steering Committee to ensure that the work program is executed as agreed.

Note the commitment of senior professionals to the client for quality assurance.

Mr. Smart will also bear the responsibility for ensuring that the work is of top professional quality and to this end, he will be jointly accountable to the Steering Committee and to me, as a partner of CANDO Management Consultants. I will assume ultimate responsibility for quality assurance and client relationships in this professional engagement.

CANDO Management Consultants

The Project Manager will have two two-person teams reporting to him, the Market Survey Team and the Environmental Analysis Team. The Market Survey Team will include Ms Lois Grantham, P.Eng., Senior Consultant working with your staff assignee. The Environmental Analysis Team will be led by Mr. Bob Marshall, Senior Consultant, working with your staff assignee.

Mr. Smart will participate in scheduling and conducting the Market Survey Team interviews. Ms Grantham is fluently bilingual and will conduct interviews in French where appropriate. I will accompany Mr. Smart and Ms Grantham on a few of their interviews to gain a first-hand perspective. Ms Grantham will conduct one of the two Field Sales Trips; Mr. Smart will conduct the other. The Environmental Analysis Team will focus on the secondary data review and the development of trends and other analyses relating to IFD and its environment.

> Note commitment to senior level involvement in the actual work being done.

It is important that your staff assignees be drawn from positions with IFD that will enable them to play leading roles in the subsequent implementation of recommended changes. They will be intimately involved in the various steps of the work plan and will become important members of your consulting team. Much of the information gathering and analysis will be performed by them under our supervision, and they will likely participate in the presentation of results. They will be as thoroughly knowledgeable of all aspects of the work as any of our assigned professionals, and committed to the results. Their stature within your organization also transmits to the rest of the organization your commitment to addressing the marketing issues with the serious intent to improve performance.

B. PROJECT STAFFING

Exhibit VI-2 is a Skills Matrix. It lists the key areas of skill and experience which we believe are critical to the success of this project, and it indicates how the Project Team includes these requirements. It is clear that all areas are well covered by the team we propose, and that the two IFD staff members you assign will provide strength in terms of their practical knowledge and experience in the food industry in Canada.

CANDO Management Consultants

EXHIBIT VI-2: *Skills Matrix*					
STAFF SKILLS AND EXPERIENCE REQUIRED **ASSIGNED:**	O. Smart, CMC	L. Grantham, P. Eng.	R. Marshall	IFD Staff member #1	IFD Staff member #2
Consumer Products Marketing	■	■	■	■	■
Food Distribution in Canada	■	■			■
Sales Force Evaluation	■	■			
Secondary Data Research and Analysis	■	■	■		
Economic and Financial Analysis	■		■	■	
Project Management and Client Relationships	■				

Orville Smart, CMC, Project Manager

Mr. Smart is a Principal with CANDO Management Consultants, and has senior responsibility within our firm for Marketing and Strategic Planning projects. He is particularly well qualified for your project for the following reasons:

- During his six years with CANDO he has exercised project management responsibilities on more than 35 assignments, many of which involved complex multi-functional teams. He has a proven record of successful project completion, on time and within budget.
- He has directed a marketing project for a leading confectionary manufacturer concerned with the launch strategy for a new line of soft toffee products. Trade relations as well as market mix considerations were of prime importance to this client. The launch proceeded, taking into account the information and recommendations emanating from the consulting team, and early indications are that it is meeting strategic objectives.

Although full résumés are in the proposal's appendix, key relevant experience can be highlighted here – probably no more than five or six items.

CANDO Management Consultants

- He led a survey of senior executives in the Canadian pharmaceuticals industry for the Association of Canadian Pharmaceuticals Manufacturers to establish industry wide practices to validate the expenditure of cooperative advertising funds by the retail trade. The results were incorporated into a brief to the Federal Government commission concerned with retail practices.
- He conducted a set of four surveys and analyses for the Royal Commission on Food Pricing to detail the structure of the retail and wholesale interface systems in the food industry in Canada, and to determine the impact of their activities on food prices. His successful completion of this work required the full cooperation of the chains and independent retailers and the trade associations which represent them. Mr. Smart was called on to address annual meetings of the associations discussing the results of this work.
- Prior to joining CANDO Management Consultants, Mr. Smart was Operations Manager for a major Canadian dairy products manufacturer, a position he held for three years.

Pre-consulting history is often impressive to a client.

(Similar abstracts from the professional qualifications of the other named professionals would be provided here as well, with comments which make their qualifications clearly relevant to this proposal.)

CANDO Management Consultants

VII
TIMING AND COSTS

A. TIMING

Assuming your staff can be made available within two weeks, we can schedule the start-up step immediately. The elapsed time to complete can be affected by a number of factors outside of our control, such as important respondents being away, important industry events, and so on; however, based on our experience with projects of this type, we suggest you plan for a four month long project from start to presentation of our Draft Report. Exhibit VII-1 presents a Gantt chart illustrating our proposed project schedule. The chart also indicates the proposed timing of informal and formal meetings. Informal meetings are internal to the Project Team; formal meetings involve the Steering Committee.

EXHIBIT VII-1: *Proposed Project Schedule*

PROJECT WORK STEPS	ELAPSED TIME FROM START:	1	2	3	4	5	6	7	8	9	10	11	12	13	14	15	16
													WEEKS				
1. Project Start-up		■															
2. Internal and Secondary Data Review			■	■	■	■											
3a. In-depth Interviews – Planning and Scheduling			■	■	■												
3b. In-depth Interviews – Conducting					■	■	■	■	■	■							
Field Sales Trips							■	■	■	■							
Analysis of Results of Steps 2, 3 and 4							■	■	■	■	■	■	■				
Draft Report and Presentation													■	■	■	■	
Final Revisions																■	■
Project Checkpoints Informal		❑				❑							❑		❑		
Formal		○					○							○			

Note: This is the same listing as in Proposed Work Program.

B. COSTS

Our fees are based on the professional time and level of skill required to perform the work to our mutual satisfaction. We estimate that the fee for this project will be between $120,000 and $150,000. If you wish, we can arrange a fixed billing schedule to suit your requirements. Expenses such as travel, living, ◀—Note flexibility in long distance telephone charges and other incidentals are extra billing arrangements. and will be billed to you at cost, as incurred on your behalf.

You may stop the project at any time for any reason should you deem it necessary. Should this occur, you are liable only for the fees and expenses incurred to the date of your notice to stop the work, plus, any additional costs specifically related to the disengagement of our personnel, such as cancellation charges for travel, and relocation of our staff.

As a measure of comparison, this cost is about equal to the ◀—This helps put cost of a typical sales representative on the road for about three project costs in months. The potential benefits of refining your total marketing perspective of and selling budgets to reflect current needs of the market are a regular costs of the multiple of this number. This project is well justified financially. business.

CANDO **Management Consultants**

This section is last (after cost and timing details) to end the proposal document on a positive note – emphasizing the tangible outputs the client will receive.

VIII

SUMMARY OF PROJECT DELIVERABLES

The verbal communication that takes place during the process of working with a client on a project of this kind provides many of the real benefits of the work. As information is developed, some of it can be used immediately, without waiting for formal reporting sessions. Informal discussions among client-consultant teams often contribute to the analytical process, and synergy within the team accounts for much of the success of the project.

Notwithstanding the above, the written documentation of the project, the deliverables, provide the formal record for repeated reference over time. This record can be the base against which future reviews are compared to track improvements and other changes. Copies of reports can be distributed and studied to form the basis for policy formulation and discussion. In most cases, the deliverables are the only tangible results of the expenditure on professional services. It is important, therefore, that your expectations and ours with respect to deliverables are the same at the outset of this professional engagement.

This project will result in the following deliverables:

- Two copies of the Draft Report "Towards Improved Sales Force Effectiveness";
- One copy for each member of the Steering Committee of the hard copy of the overheads used in support of presentation of results;
- Four copies of the Final Report "Towards Improved Sales Force Effectiveness";
- A library consisting of the secondary documents and publications collected during the project;
- Working papers, including blank interview guides, project administration documents and memos, but not including completed interviews and notes containing protected individual comments of respondents.

We consider all project documents to be available to our client, with the exception of items protected by prior agreement. Additional reports and documentation will be provided on request, at additional cost.

Final benefits statement and wish to be selected.

We believe this project will provide substantial short and long term benefits to IFD in the form of new insights and fresh input to key policy issues. CANDO Management Consultants is eager to help IFD in discovering new opportunities for profits as we explore together the role and effectiveness of your field sales force.

CANDO Management Consultants

APPENDICES

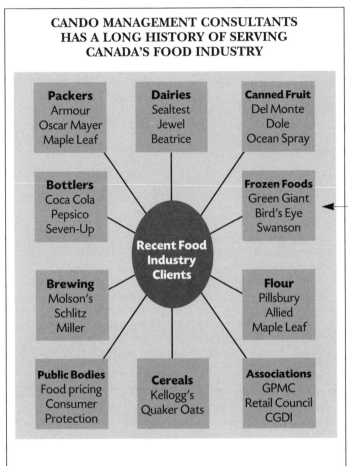

CANDO MANAGEMENT CONSULTANTS HAS A LONG HISTORY OF SERVING CANADA'S FOOD INDUSTRY

Packers
Armour
Oscar Mayer
Maple Leaf

Dairies
Sealtest
Jewel
Beatrice

Canned Fruit
Del Monte
Dole
Ocean Spray

Bottlers
Coca Cola
Pepsico
Seven-Up

Frozen Foods
Green Giant
Bird's Eye
Swanson

Recent Food Industry Clients

Brewing
Molson's
Schlitz
Miller

Flour
Pillsbury
Allied
Maple Leaf

Public Bodies
Food pricing
Consumer
Protection

Cereals
Kellogg's
Quaker Oats

Associations
GPMC
Retail Council
CGDI

CANDO Management Consultants

This diagram would appear as part of the appendix to the proposal accompanying a statement of general qualification for CANDO.

Illustrates and focuses specific CANDO qualifications to do this work.

Detailed professional résumés of assigned CANDO staff are also included as part of the proposal appendix.

Sample of Informal Proposal

This **Sample Proposal Letter** is used when the relationship is more informal. It covers the same subject matter as a formal proposal, but with less supporting detail. Essentially, it confirms conversations which have taken place and serves to construct the relationship into a formal agreement.

Note the informal salutation

Objective

Background rationale – why do it?

Why now?

Work plan

Project organization and staffing

Note assurance of personal responsibility for quality and client satisfaction

---

CANDO Management Consultants

423 Consultant Way, Somewhere, Earth
e-mail cando@cw.com • Phone/Fax (700) 738-4877

August 19, 1998

Mr. Arthur Mometer, President
International Foods Division
Capital Foods Inc.
2100 Ladel Street
Toronto, Canada M2T 4N1

PRIVATE AND CONFIDENTIAL

Dear Arthur,

It was good to see you last week and get caught up on our current activities. You have quite a challenge at International, and, as we discussed, we may be able to help.

This letter will confirm our understanding whereby we will work with your staff to determine the importance of field sales activities in supporting special recipe food marketing, and assess your field sales efforts. Clearly, it is always a good idea to review how well your field sales program fits with your consumer franchise and optimize your push and pull budgets. It is particularly timely to do so now with Bob Fairweather taking charge. We look forward to working with him in this.

We will focus our activities on three areas: the trade and your competitive position with retailers, the market trends as indicated in your files and our sources, and your sales representatives and how they are currently experiencing the market place. By combining what you already know with what we can find out, we should be able to develop the optimum field sales program.

Orville Smart will manage the project, and along with Lois Grantham will conduct a minimum of 30 in-depth interviews with key representatives from the retail trade. I will participate in some in order to get my own first-hand understanding. Orville and Lois will also spend two days each in the field with two of your sales reps to develop a keen understanding of what they are experiencing. Bob Marshall will work with your people to collect and examine the latest market information from library and Internet sources and combine it with what you already have on file. This will be analyzed and provided as input to the results of the trade survey and field experiences.

– (1) –

– (2) –

We will report progress regularly to the Steering Committee that you and Bob Fairweather will establish and I will make sure Bob is fully aware of developments as they occur throughout the process. At the conclusion, we will present the results with our recommendations to the Steering Committee and provide hard copies of the presentation at that time. We will then provide you with a draft report to review before we finalize it and give you the four copies you requested. — Deliverables

In addition to the formal deliverables, we will have amassed a valuable library which we will organize and turn over to you, along with any working papers you feel you need.

The project should be complete in four months. Our fee will be between $120,000 and $150,000 and we will bill you in three monthly amounts of $30,000, plus a fourth invoice reconciling the actual amount incurred. Expenses are extra and will be billed at cost as incurred. As a matter of comparison, this is — Timing and costs only slightly more than the cost of putting a sales rep on the road for three months.

As you plan for the introduction of the new products you spoke of, a well-balanced effort between field sales and marketing is important. Not only will you benefit from successful and cost-efficient initial introduction efforts, but the on-going — Benefits to end on expenditures to support the products once launched will be well a positive subject managed, too. As you know, we at CANDO are highly experienced and knowledgeable in the food industry in Canada. I am con- — Credentials fident we can help International Foods improve profitability and market effectiveness significantly with this effort.

I appreciate this opportunity to work with you. I will call you — Keeping in control in a few days to set up our next meeting. Perhaps you and Bob of the selling would like to come to our offices and meet our professional process team.

Best regards,

J. Bostick, CMC,
Partner

JB/dw

INDEX

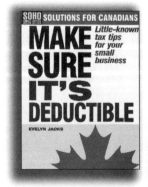

Proven Solutions for Canadian Small Business

WHAT TO SAY WHEN YOUR CUSTOMERS WON'T PAY

Every business has to deal with accounts receivable. But collections doesn't have to rely on intimidation tactics and threats. Learn the most effective ways to get your due—and keep your customers too.

$18.99 (paperback) • 0-07-560411-6

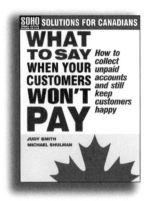

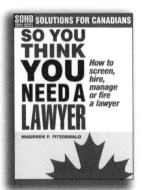

SO YOU THINK YOU NEED A LAWYER

Almost every small business owner needs a lawyer at some point. Gain the knowledge and confidence necessary for getting first-rate legal advice when you need it.

$18.99 (paperback) • 0-07-560226-1

WHERE TO GO WHEN THE BANK SAYS NO

Finding the right sources of financing can be an ongoing struggle for SOHO owners. This is a road map to the many alternate methods for financing your business.

$22.99 (paperback) • 0-07-560225-3

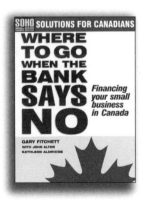

SO YOU WANT TO BUY A FRANCHISE

How can you be sure you are buying into a successful venture and not pouring your money down the drain? Get all the information you need before signing on the dotted line.

$22.99 (paperback) • 0-07-560419-1

Available at bookstores across Canada